INDIANA JONES AND PHILOSOPHY

The Blackwell Philosophy and Pop Culture Series
Series editor: William Irwin

A spoonful of sugar helps the medicine go down, and a healthy helping of popular culture clears the cobwebs from Kant. Philosophy has had a public relations problem for a few centuries now. This series aims to change that, showing that philosophy is relevant to your life—and not just for answering the big questions like "To be or not to be?" but for answering the little questions: "To watch or not to watch *South Park?*" Thinking deeply about TV, movies, and music doesn't make you a "complete idiot." In fact, it might make you a philosopher, someone who believes the unexamined life is not worth living and the unexamined cartoon is not worth watching.

Already published in the series:

Alien and Philosophy: I Infest, Therefore I Am
Edited by Jeffery A. Ewing and Kevin S. Decker

Avatar: The Last Airbender and Philosophy
Edited by Helen De Cruz and Johan De Smedt

Batman and Philosophy: The Dark Knight of the Soul
Edited by Mark D. White and Robert Arp

The Big Bang Theory and Philosophy: Rock, Paper, Scissors, Aristotle, Locke
Edited by Dean A. Kowalski

BioShock and Philosophy: Irrational Game, Rational Book
Edited by Luke Cuddy

Black Mirror and Philosophy
Edited by David Kyle Johnson

Black Panther and Philosophy
Edited by Edwardo Pérez and Timothy Brown

Disney and Philosophy: Truth, Trust, and a Little Bit of Pixie Dust
Edited by Richard B. Davis

Dune and Philosophy
Edited by Kevin S. Decker

Dungeons and Dragons and Philosophy: Read and Gain Advantage on All Wisdom Checks
Edited by Christopher Robichaud

Game of Thrones and Philosophy: Logic Cuts Deeper Than Swords
Edited by Henry Jacoby

The Good Place and Philosophy: Everything is Fine!
Edited by Kimberly S. Engels

Star Wars and Philosophy Strikes Back
Edited by Jason T. Eberl and Kevin S. Decker

The Ultimate Harry Potter and Philosophy: Hogwarts for Muggles
Edited by Gregory Bassham

The Hobbit and Philosophy: For When You've Lost Your Dwarves, Your Wizard, and Your Way
Edited by Gregory Bassham and Eric Bronson

Inception and Philosophy: Because It's Never Just a Dream
Edited by David Kyle Johnson

LEGO and Philosophy: Constructing Reality Brick By Brick
Edited by Roy T. Cook and Sondra Bacharach

Metallica and Philosophy: A Crash Course in Brain Surgery
Edited by William Irwin

The Ultimate South Park and Philosophy: Respect My Philosophah!
Edited by Robert Arp and Kevin S. Decker

The Ultimate Star Trek and Philosophy: The Search for Socrates
Edited by Jason T. Eberl and Kevin S. Decker

The Ultimate Star Wars and Philosophy: You Must Unlearn What You Have Learned
Edited by Jason T. Eberl and Kevin S. Decker

Terminator and Philosophy: I'll Be Back, Therefore I Am
Edited by Richard Brown and Kevin S. Decker

Watchmen and Philosophy: A Rorschach Test
Edited by Mark D. White

Westworld and Philosophy: If You Go Looking for the Truth, Get the Whole Thing
Edited by James B. South and Kimberly S. Engels

Forthcoming

Joker and Philosophy
Edited by Massimiliano L. Cappuccio, George A. Dunn, and Jason T. Eberl

Mad Max and Philosophy
Edited by Matthew P. Meyer and David Koepsell

Ted Lasso and Philosophy
Edited by David Baggett and Mary Baggett

The Witcher and Philosophy
Edited by Matthew Brake and Kevin S. Decker

For the full list of titles in the series see www.andphilosophy.com

INDIANA JONES AND PHILOSOPHY

WHY DID IT HAVE TO BE SOCRATES?

Edited by

Dean A. Kowalski

WILEY Blackwell

This edition first published 2023

Registered Office
John Wiley & Sons, Inc., 111 River Street, Hoboken, NJ 07030, USA

For details of our global editorial offices, customer services, and more information about Wiley products visit us at www.wiley.com.

Wiley also publishes its books in a variety of electronic formats and by print-on-demand. Some content that appears in standard print versions of this book may not be available in other formats.

A catalogue record for this book is available from the Library of Congress

Paperback ISBN: 9781119740155; ePDF ISBN: 9781119740162;
ePub ISBN: 9781119740179; Obook ISBN: 9781119740186

Cover image: © Andrey_Kuzmin/Shutterstock, GaryAlvis/Getty Images
Cover design by Wiley

Set in 10.5/12pt SabonLTStd by Integra Software Services, Pondicherry, India

SKY10044474_031423

Contents

Contributors: "We Have Top Men [and Women] Working on It"

Nikolaj Kærslund Andersen holds a Ph.D. in Political Science from Aarhus University. His research and teaching revolve around international relations, geoeconomics, the rise of China, and the emerging world order. He is currently applying for funding for a massive research project on the weaponization of religious artifacts. The working title is "Shut your eyes, Marion: Weapons of Divine Destruction and Face-Melting," and the project is hiring curious student assistants for empirical experimentation.

Lance Belluomini did his graduate studies in philosophy at the University of California, Berkeley; San Francisco State University; and the University of Nebraska-Lincoln. He's recently published an essay on "Tenet" in *The Palgrave Handbook of Popular Culture as Philosophy* (forthcoming). He's also contributed chapters to *The Philosophy of Christopher Nolan* (2017) and the Wiley-Blackwell philosophy and popular culture volumes on *Inception* (2011), *The Walking Dead* (2012), *Ender's Game* (2013), and *The Ultimate Star Wars* (2015). Surprisingly, the iconic "Raiders March" theme isn't the first thing that pops into his head when someone mentions *Indiana Jones*. Instead, it's the cool ad-libbed lines by Harrison Ford in *Raiders*: "I don't know. I'm making this up as I go," and "It's not the years, honey. It's the mileage"—quotes that Lance would never use for he realizes Indy is the only person who's allowed to talk like that.

Matthew Brake is an adjunct professor at George Mason University and Northern Virginia Community College. He is also the editor the *Theology and Pop Culture* series from Fortress Academic and the co-editor (with A. David Lewis) of the forthcoming *Religion and Comics* series from Claremont Press. Matthew imagines a world where he, like Dr. Jones, can drop his teaching load at a moment's notice to go on an adventure, presumably paid for by his department.

Timothy Brown is the Dean of Southern Evangelical Bible College, and the Executive Editor of the *SES Christian Apologetics Journal*. He previously authored a chapter in *Disney and Philosophy* (2020), and courses he has instructed include Logic, Moral Philosophy, and Philosophy of Religion. Like Indy, he is a professor who has lectured in a bow tie and glasses, but unlike Indy he has his *mother's* eyes.

Matthew Crippen is a professor, who digs into history, cross-cultural value theory, and matters related to mind, and whips out articles in places like *Synthese*, *Topoi*, the *British Journal of Aesthetics*, *Environmental Ethics*, and *Transactions of the Charles Peirce Society*, also publishing a Columbia University Press book. He has collaborated creatively with his lifelong friend and co-author, Matthew Dixon, on music jobs, film projects, and popular philosophy pieces, which are small monuments to the long time they've known each other.

Matthew Dixon is interested in cultural studies and film, and works in the legal industry—where *ex*hibits very often do mark the spot. He has been involved in theatrical productions, music jobs, and short films, in addition to publishing on popular art. He has known his co-author, Matthew Crippen, since kindergarten and treasures their various entries on pop culture and philosophy as time capsules of their friendship, perhaps to be excavated by other like-minded people in the future.

Justin Fetterman lives in Montreal, where he works as a writer, editor, stage director, and creative designer for opera. He is simply passing through history, and making it up as he goes.

Duncan Gale is an adjunct professor of philosophy at San Bernardino Valley College, Riverside City College, and Chaffey College, all in the Inland Empire of Southern California. You can find his other articles on popular culture and philosophy in *Avengers Infinity Saga and Philosophy* (2020) and *Dave Chappelle and Philosophy* (2021). In his classes, he does not allow students to communicate via messages written on their eyelids.

Christopher Helali is a graduate student in cultural studies at Dartmouth College researching religion (Orthodox Christianity), nationalism, historical trauma, and war in modern Greece. Other research interests include philosophy (Marxism), imperialism, and national liberation struggles. Notable discoveries include the second known phone book belonging to Jeffrey Epstein, which was uncovered in December 2020 and revealed to the public in the summer of 2021. Chris shares with Dr. Jones a mutual hatred of Nazis: "Nazis. I hate these guys."

Louise Hitchcock has a Ph.D. in Aegean Bronze Age Art (UCLA 1998) and she's currently a professor of Aegean Bronze Age archaeology in the Classics and Archaeology program at the University of Melbourne. Her books include *Minoan Architecture: A Contextual Analysis* (2000), *Theory for Classics* (2008), and *Aegean Art and Architecture* (2000) (with Donald Preziosi), and she is the co-editor of *DAIS: The Aegean Feast, Aegaeum 29* (2008). When not dancing on tables in Aleppo, running away from rattle snakes, or jumping into lost tombs, Louise has found time to publish 100 articles about Aegean, Cypriot, and Philistine archaeology, gender identity, architecture, and theory. The Australian Research Council funded her excavations at the Philistine site of Tell es-Safi/Gath, where she collaborates with Aren Maeir. If adventure has a name, her name is Louisiana Hitchcock.

Alexander E. Hooke is a professor of philosophy at Stevenson University. His recent books include *The Twilight Zone and Philosophy: A Dangerous Dimension to Visit* (co-editor) (2018), *Philosophy Sketches—700 Words at a Time* (2nd edition) (2021), and *Alphonso Lingis and Existential Genealogy* (2019). He is to faculty meetings as Indiana Jones is to snakes. Unfortunately, he lacks Indy's fortitude and persistence to make the best of a bad situation.

Justin Kitchen teaches philosophy at San Francisco State University and CSU Northridge. His work centers around virtue ethics and virtue epistemology; it draws often from Stoic philosophy and early Buddhist philosophy. He hopes he never has to make a leap from the lion's head to prove his worth.

Dean A. Kowalski is a professor of philosophy and chair of the Arts & Humanities department in the College of General Studies at the University of Wisconsin-Milwaukee. He regularly teaches philosophy of religion, Asian philosophy, and ethics. He is the author of *Joss Whedon as Philosopher* (2017), *Classic Questions and Contemporary Film* (2nd edition, 2016), and *Moral Theory at the Movies* (2012). He is the editor of *The Big Bang Theory and Philosophy* (2012), *The Philosophy of The X-Files* (revised edition, 2009), and *Steven Spielberg and Philosophy* (2008); he is the co-editor of *The Philosophy of Joss Whedon* (2011). For him, attending Ripon College was the "X" that "marked the spot"; it was there he began "digging" for "the truth" (but he assures you that the ground floor of Lane Library remains safely intact).

Annalissa Lane has studied philosophy and religion at St. Olaf College and the University of Chicago. Her research interests include contemporary

American religions, racism, and the rise of Christian nationalism in the United States. She has tried to practice archeology and foil tomb raiders around the world, but mostly in her daydreams when she is not writing papers on the danger of nationalism or knitting a sweater.

Siobhan Lyons is a researcher in media, cultural studies and philosophy, having earned her Ph.D. in 2017. Her books include *Death and the Machine: Intersections of Mortality and Robotics* (2018), and *Ruin Porn and Our Obsession with Decay* (2018). She has also previously contributed chapters to *Westworld and Philosophy* (2019) and *Philosophical Approaches to the Devil* (2016), among other books. She shares Indiana's pursuit of fortune and glory, but has found that academia isn't exactly the best place to find it.

Aren M. Maeir is a professor of Biblical and ancient Near Eastern archaeology in the Department of Land of Israel Studies and Archaeology at Bar-Ilan University, in Ramat-Gan, Israel. For the last 25 years, he has directed the excavations at the site of Tell es-Safi/Gath (gath.wordpress.com), and kept himself busy with this and various other archaeologically related endeavors. Aren is a big believer in Kent Flannery's characterization of the profession: "Archaeology is still the most fun you can have with your pants on."

Robert M. Mentyka is an independent scholar who spends his days working as an average file clerk. Just as Indiana Jones hides his dashing character beneath the veneer of a seemingly mild-mannered professor of archeology, Mr. Mentyka utilizes such an unassuming position to further his philosophical expeditions into the deepest and most troublesome questions mankind has yet to pose. Primarily a student of ethics, personalism, and the history of philosophy, Mr. Mentyka received his M.A. in philosophy from the Franciscan University of Steubenville, Ohio. His previous contributions to the *and Philosophy* series include articles for *Bioshock and Philosophy* (2015), *Alien and Philosophy* (2017), *Lego and Philosophy* (2017), and, most recently, *Disney and Philosophy* (2019).

Edwardo Pérez is one of those Gen Xers who, influenced by Harrison Ford's Indiana Jones and John Williams' heroic theme, took a few archaeology courses in college. While they didn't help the GPA (because Mesoamerican archaeology on Wednesday evenings after marching band practice was a great time to nap), the courses did give Edwardo an appreciation for what real archaeology is all about (not the life and limb, but the folklore, to paraphrase Indy). So, while Edwardo might not be a swashbuckling obtainer of rare antiquities, he at least gets to be a dashing professor of English, keeping a brown leather jacket handy in case some rhetorical adventure demands a trip to the catacombs hidden deep below the Tarrant County College library in the legendary city of Cowtown, otherwise known (especially to those who don't speak Texan) as Fort Worth.

Robert Grant Price teaches writing and communications in the Greater Toronto Area. He is a professor … part time.

Kate C.S. Schmidt is an assistant professor of philosophy at the Metropolitan State University of Denver. So far, she has never jumped out a window to avoid meeting with students during office hours. (However, she has gotten lost on her own campus). She believes that historic objects belong in museums, is neutral on whips, and is absolutely making this up as she goes.

Robert Seddon is a moral philosopher who holds an Honorary Fellowship at the University of Durham, his alma mater, and is a member of its Centre for the Ethics of Cultural Heritage. Besides the kind of heritage archaeologists usually deal with, he has also written about heritage in outer space and heritage on the Internet. Where others want to be Indy, he identifies with the Staff of Ra: people keep wanting to know just how tall he is.

Pankaj Singh is an assistant professor at the University of Petroleum and Energy Studies (UPES), Dehradun, India. Although his formal research interests include philosophy of mind and existentialism, he loves writing about pop culture and philosophy. His publications include chapters in *The Expanse and Philosophy* (2021) and *The Palgrave Handbook of Popular Culture as Philosophy* (forthcoming). His thoughts and life philosophy mainly oscillate between doom and fortune and glory.

Tait Szabo is an associate professor of philosophy in the College of General Studies at the University of Wisconsin-Milwaukee. His specializations are in ethics and political philosophy. He has contributed chapters to *The Philosophy of Joss Whedon* (2011) and *Pornography and Philosophy* (2010). In his spare time, he practices judo and writes speculative fiction, for fortune and glory, kid. Follow him at taitszabo.com.

Charles Taliaferro is a professor of philosophy and the Overby Distinguished Chair at St. Olaf College. He has authored, co-authored, or edited over 30 books, including the *Cascade Companion to Evil* (2020) and (with Jil Evans) *Is God Invisible?* (2021). While Charles idolizes Indiana Jones, he looks and acts just like Marcus Brody.

Daniel Tilsley is a Ph.D. researcher in film studies and philosophy at the University of East Anglia (UK), with an interest in cult cinema, American horror, and existential philosophy. His research focuses on nineteen-fifties and sixties American horror and science fiction films and existential philosophy as culturally entwined. This all means that he really adores the silly aliens at the end of *The Kingdom of the Crystal Skull*—and is hopefully not the only one. He is also passionate about widening participation and inclusivity for young people in secondary and higher education in England, including young people with special educational needs.

Mia Wood is a professor of philosophy at Pierce College in Los Angeles, where she routinely conducts introductory courses across the philosophy curriculum. She has contributed essays to *Mr. Robot and Philosophy: Beyond Good and Evil Corp* (2017), *Westworld and Philosophy: Mind Equals Blown* (2018), and *Dave Chappelle and Philosophy* (2021). Among her research interests are personal identity and free will, causation, conditionals, philosophy of metaphor, and philosophy of death. As a child, Mia wanted to be an archaeologist—she sported a fedora and knew how to crack the bullwhip—but she hates snakes.

Acknowledgments: "We Can Discuss My Honorarium over Dinner and Champagne Tonight—Your Treat"

I would like to thank all the contributing authors. Each was a pleasure to work with, and many of them participated in voluminous email exchanges and provided multiple drafts. Unlike Major Eaton's disingenuous assurance, believe me that they are "top men and women," each of whom worked enthusiastically to share with you their respective appreciation for *Indiana Jones*.

The contributing authors and I acknowledge that this book would not have been possible if it were not for the visionary efforts of George Lucas, Steven Spielberg, and Harrison Ford (and their associates and co-workers); we thank them for bringing to life one of the greatest film characters of all time, but remembering to make him human and thus relatable. Perhaps they were making some of it up as they went, but we're no bureaucratic fools—all of us know very well what we have here.

Indeed, I am grateful for the efforts of many people on this project: Bill Irwin, who nearly 13 years after I first suggested this volume, surprised me with an unexpected and happy email one day in 2019, and then made the project a joy from start to finish; the College of General Studies Dean's office for awarding me a course release to finish the manuscript; Assistant Library Director for the College of General Studies Scott Silet for obtaining *Indiana Jones* research materials; UW-Waukesha Emeritus Professor of Music Craig Hurst for helping me paraphrase the beginning of Indy's theme; Ripon College Lane Library Director Andrew Prellwitz for providing me access to the Ripon College archives on past faculty members; and Ripon College Emeritus Professors of Philosophy Vance Cope-Kasten and Robert "Spud"

Hannaford for sharing their personal and professional recollections of their colleague William E. Tyree, many of which were incorporated into Chapter 10. Like Harrison Ford, I was a philosophy major at Ripon College, though unlike Ford I did not have the privilege of taking classes with Dr. Tyree.

While I don't know Harrison Ford personally, I think he is right about one thing: There is truth to be found "down the hall" on the second floor of East Hall. Like Harrison, perhaps, that is where I began my search. With great aplomb, Professors Cope-Kasten, Hannaford, and Doss masterfully set me on my path, and I couldn't be more grateful; it is to them that I dedicate this book:

To Vance, Spud, and Seale

Introduction: "Indiana Jones—I Always Knew Some Day You'd Come Walking Back through My Door. I Never Doubted That"

Dah da dah Dahhhh/Dah da Dahhhhh/Dah da dah Dahhhh/Dah da-dah Dah dah … Go ahead. You know you want to keep humming. I'll wait …

The Indiana Jones theme song is unmistakable. Harrison Ford cannot escape it, as he once remarked (tongue firmly in his cheek), "That damn music follows me everywhere. They play it every time I walk on stage, every time I walk off a stage. It was playing in the operating room when I went in for my colonoscopy" (*Time*, June 10, 2016). Beyond the music, Indy's leather jacket, brown fedora, and bullwhip are simply iconic, forever engrained in popular culture. We cannot escape Indiana Jones! (Not that we would want to, of course.)

Harrison Ford deserves credit for the character's popularity. His ability to subtly play up Indy's foibles while playing down the character's heroism, makes Indiana Jones relatable. Of course, Lucas and the screenwriters are also responsible, as they magnificently depict Indy battling antagonists seeking to possess mystical objects for world domination. But Indy is no mere action hero. He also struggles with unrequited love that lingers for decades, an estrangement from his overbearing father that lasts just as long, and a lifelong obsession with regaining an important object unfairly taken from him.

As we know, Indy doesn't always choose wisely, and if the *Young Indiana Jones Chronicles* are to be trusted, he made many missteps in his youth on the way to becoming the hero we know and love. Indy loses a fight as often as he wins, and when he wins, he doesn't always

Indiana Jones and Philosophy: Why Did It Have to Be Socrates?, First Edition. Edited by Dean A. Kowalski.

fight fairly. In fact, he stumbles so often, one might wonder why he persists decade after decade toward his goals. He's not getting any younger. What's the point? And, as he inexplicably trudges on, he—in the four films and various graphic novels—has many alleged encounters with the supernatural. He's not a religious person (at all), so what should he make of those? Should he take the leap of faith and become a believer? While we often see him conducting his highly unconventional fieldwork, spending an unusual amount of time in caves, he cannot completely ignore his "day job" teaching undergraduates and aiding their pursuit of knowledge. But why should archaeologists strive to put artifacts in a museum, or search for "fact," but not "truth" (and who is Dr. Tyree, anyway)?

The Indiana Jones character is expressive of the human condition, vividly illuminating our struggles and issues on the big screen. True, we don't have John Williams's orchestra filling us with pride when we manage to do the right thing or play the part of the hero. Still, no one would blame you if you imagined Indy's theme blaring in the background while rising to meet a challenge!

Have you started humming Indy's theme again? I hope you hear it many more times as you read through this volume and relive some of your favorite Indiana Jones moments. I'll get you going as you turn to the first chapter: *Dah da dah Dahhhh/Dah da Dahhhhh/Dah da dah Dahhhh/Dah da-dah Dah dah …*

Part I

"IT WAS WRONG AND YOU KNEW IT!": ETHICS AND VALUES

1

Acting Without Thinking: The Sagacity of Indiana Jones

Justin Kitchen

Indiana Jones gets the job done. He may stumble and fall along the way, but he picks himself up (or is forcibly picked up by a Nazi strongman) and keeps going without hesitation. What motivates a person who rarely hesitates? How does Indy make such confident decisions in the heat of the moment? The answer lies, not with a clear moral code or formula for how to behave, but with his character. Indiana Jones's confidence and spontaneity reflects his moral character. He's just a good person who is eager to be good.

Philosophy can help us elaborate on this idea: according to many ancient virtue ethicists, people with the *best characters* are those who are *most wise*—so-called "sages." Sure, Indy is a good person, but is he a sage? Once we get a handle on the quality of Indy's character and how he has become a good person, we'll be able to say whether he has attained sagehood or is at least heading in the right direction. Through it all, we can rest assured that Indiana Jones is at least a "hero," but maybe we'll be able to understand what that word amounts to by comparing it to the ideal of the sage.

Consequences or Character?

People adopt many different approaches when it comes to describing and justifying what's morally "right." By far, the most popular approach is one that looks at the consequences of actions. This is broadly called consequentialism: right actions are those that lead to good consequences. Another approach, instead, looks at the character of the moral agent. This is called virtue ethics: right actions are those performed by agents with good character, those who exhibit virtue.

Indiana Jones and Philosophy: Why Did It Have to Be Socrates?, First Edition. Edited by Dean A. Kowalski.

We'll be taking the virtue ethics approach because of its focus on the moral agent—the person doing the moral action—rather than the action itself. If we took the consequentialist approach and focused primarily on Indiana's actions (more precisely, the consequences of his actions), we might encounter some problems.

The character Amy Farrah Fowler from the CBS sitcom *The Big Bang Theory* expresses one such problem regarding Indy's role in *Raiders of the Lost Ark*:

> Indiana Jones plays *no* role in the outcome of the story. If he weren't in the film, it would turn out *exactly* the same. … If he weren't in the movie, the Nazis would have still found the Ark, taken it to the island, opened it up, and all died. Just like they did.[1]

Amy's argument is strong. In fact, we could make her argument even stronger by correcting the claim that the Nazis would have taken the Ark to the island regardless of Indy's interference. A major scene in *Raiders* centers around Indy and Marion trying to board the plane set to fly the Ark to Berlin. If Indy did *not* interfere in the Nazi's archaeological expeditions, the Nazis would have still found the Ark, taken it to Berlin on an unexploded airplane, and opened it up in the presence of the Führer or some other high-ranking officials. This is a hypothetical scenario of a fictional story, but the theory holds water. And it befuddles anyone who is taking a consequentialist approach—Indy actually might have produced worse consequences by redirecting the Ark and keeping more important Nazis out of danger! If Indiana's actions do not bring about good consequences or—worse yet—if they cause harm, then his actions are not morally right according to consequentialism. This is a problem for fans of the movie because the conclusion conflicts with our strong intuitions that Indy is really a good guy, if not a hero.

Indeed, our intuitive admiration of heroes, including Indiana Jones, does not seem to depend on any of this consequentialist arithmetic—adding up the harmful outcomes, subtracting that from the beneficial outcomes, and comparing the net total to some hypothetical scenario in which the action in question did not take place. The moral quality of Indy's actions doesn't actually hinge on hypotheticals at all. We admire Indiana Jones and his actions because of *who* he is, because of the good character he displays when he throws himself into the mix of things and tries to act rightly.

So if some smarty pants like Amy says to you that Indy is not really the good guy we think he is because he doesn't influence the outcome of events, you can point out the assumption she's making. Whether or not someone is a good person doesn't (exclusively) rely on the outcomes of his or her actions. Rather, moral goodness crucially depends on the quality of one's character revealed by that person's actions.

"I'm Making This Up as I Go"

Since we've settled on assessing Indiana Jones and his conduct using virtue ethics, we have to look at his words and actions in order to find evidence of good character. When we do this, we find a hitch in our plan. What matters to virtue ethics is not that you succeed in doing the right thing, but that you *try* to do the right thing. Although Indiana Jones seems to exert a lot of physical effort, someone might argue that in many cases, he doesn't appear to be trying very hard. That is, the decisions Indiana Jones makes throughout his adventures don't often appear well thought-out. We could cite three cases when Indy's lack of deliberation or planning is made very apparent:

[In *Raiders*]

INDY: Meet me at Omar's. Be ready for me. I'm going after that truck.
SALLAH: How?
INDY: I don't know. I'm making this up as I go.

[In *The Last Crusade*]

ELSA: What are you going to do?
INDY: Don't know. I'll think of something.

[In *The Kingdom of the Crystal Skull*]

MUTT: What's he gonna do now?
MARION: Ha! I don't think he plans that far ahead.

You would think that someone with good character would be more thoughtful about these serious life-threatening situations. This is especially problematic because what makes Indy so endearing is that he's spontaneous and that there's a confidence in his spontaneity. So, for us to be confident in our application of virtue ethics, we need to square these two thoughts. We'll have to get a better sense of what it means to have good character and be virtuous. Then we'll have to see whether Indy's "I'm making this up as I go along" attitude makes sense according to virtue ethics.

Winter Training

The word "virtue" is a common translation of the Ancient Greek word *arete*, which can also be translated as "excellence"—so we should say that if something is virtuous, then it's excellent. But, excellent at what? In Ancient Greece, famed philosophers Plato (428–348 BCE) and Aristotle (384–322 BCE) used the word to describe what makes *anything* excellent: a pruning knife is virtuous when it's excellent at pruning vines; a harpist is virtuous when they're excellent at playing the harp; eyes are virtuous when they're excellent at seeing.[2] These things are excellent at what they're meant for, what they're uniquely capable of. So, when ancient virtue ethicists called a human being "virtuous," they were saying that the person is excellent at being and doing what humans are uniquely capable of being and doing.

After Aristotle, the concept of virtue was elaborated upon in different ways. The ancient school of Stoicism continued to develop the virtue ethics approach up through the second century CE. The Stoics insisted that humans are uniquely capable of being rational *and* social. Thus, human beings are virtuous when they're able to exercise reason well and be congenial with each other.

Even if humans are prone to being rational and social, it still takes a lot of hard work to be excellent at being human. For starters, it takes many years for children to fully develop their rational faculties and social intelligence. And by the time they actually develop these capacities, they have been inculcated with values and beliefs that may be irrational or antisocial. If so, it would take a lot of hard work to recognize this and set themselves straight. But, as the Stoic Epictetus told his students, "No bull reaches maturity in an instant, nor do men become heroes overnight. We must endure a winter training and can't be dashing into situations for which we aren't yet prepared."[3] It makes sense that it takes a lot of hard work and preparation for someone to reach this state of "excellence"—we don't admire people who accomplish things that are easy.

Indy's "winter training"—when he undertook all the hard work that made him the hero we know and love—is the subject of *The Adventures of Young Indiana Jones* (also known as *The Young Indiana Jones Chronicles*). This television series showcases Indy's many adventures during his formative years as a child and young adult. Episodes mostly center around Indy becoming aware of his shortcomings and learning important moral lessons from various role models. Young Indiana's adventures fit well into what the Stoics described as the proper path of moral education.

Epictetus's teacher, Musonius Rufus (25–95 CE), introduced some popular analogies between moral education and other kinds of education:

> The doctor and the musician must each not only learn the principles of his own skill but be trained to act according to those principles. Likewise,

> the man who wants to be good must not only learn the lessons which pertain to virtue but train himself to follow them eagerly and rigorously.[4]

The Stoics insisted that moral education, as with proper medical and musical training, actually has two stages: a theory stage and a practice stage. As with medicine, we must first study a bit of theory. This just means examining our assumptions about how we should behave and making sure we have the right idea about what's good and bad, virtuous and vicious. This is what the prepubescent Indy does when he confronts his wrong assumptions or plain ignorance about life and learns from his mistakes with help of T.E. Lawrence, Teddy Roosevelt, Krishnamurti, and others. Here's a particularly poignant lesson that Indy learns, at least at the theoretical level:

KRISHNAMURTI:	I want you to think of something you want more than anything else in the world.
YOUNG INDY:	I want ... I want to live forever!
KRISHNAMURTI:	But everybody has to die. You cannot live forever. How does that make you feel, Indy?
YOUNG INDY:	I feel sad, I guess.
KRISHNAMURTI:	That is the answer to your question [about why people suffer]. You see, people want things they cannot have and that makes them sad and they suffer.[5]

After we get oriented with theory, then comes the more difficult process of really internalizing this information through practice. In medicine, this stage entails a long internship and residency under attending physicians. But in ethics, this entails life experience and honest conversations with other good people. This is what the teenage and young adult Indy does in fighting alongside revolutionaries, activists, and the allied forces of World War I. But, as Indy himself put it, "You don't start at the top. You work your way up, perfect your style until you *are* at the top."[6] Indy was referring to waiting tables as a college student, which requires less theoretical training, but the sentiment could apply to all kinds of human excellence including virtue.

By the time we reach the events in *Temple*, Indiana Jones has perfected his style and has achieved a noticeable form of excellence. I'm not talking about being an excellent archaeologist or teacher, but an excellent overall *human being*—excellent at being rational and social. He has cultivated his rationality by vetting his beliefs about right and wrong and addressing his prejudices. He has cultivated his sociability by relating to other people and sympathizing with their causes. And for the Stoics, this is what it means to be virtuous.

But how can we *really* tell that Indiana Jones has become virtuous? What has all his moral education and training amounted to? Again, according to the Stoics, we can distinguish a virtuous sage from a less-than-virtuous person by how they act and make decisions. So let's now examine how Indy makes decisions.

"Knowledge Was Their Treasure"

The Stoics said that someone who has become excellent—who has become virtuous—lives consistently or harmoniously (the Greek word is *homologomenos*). Such people live harmoniously with themselves because they're acting rational, free from contradictory beliefs and bias. They live harmoniously with others because they're being congenial, showing compassion toward other people and helping them when they can. This "harmony" is what led the founder of Stoicism, Zeno, to describe virtue as providing a "smooth flow of life."[7] Once someone has become virtuous, continuing to be virtuous and navigating through life should be as easy as swimming leisurely downstream—going with the "flow." Here's the Stoic Seneca (4 BCE–65 CE) describing this special person, what has come to be called the wise person or sage:

> he was always the same, consistent in every action, good no longer from policy but under the guidance of a habit that made him not only able to act rightly but unable to act other than rightly. In him we understood that virtue had been perfected. ... That man's orderliness revealed [virtue] to us, his seemliness and consistency, the harmony among all his actions, and his greatness in surmounting everything. It was thus that we came to understand happiness, the life that flows smoothly and is completely under its own control.[8]

Considering that Indiana Jones has gone through a very thorough Stoic-like moral education, we can see some sage-like qualities. This isn't in reference to his outward appearance, of course—he's obviously not the contemplative long-bearded sage we know from religious texts or kung-fu movies. Stoic sages live "harmoniously" and enjoy a "smooth flow of life" not because they're still and fluid in their motions and easily avoid every punch thrown at them. Rather, the "harmony" that sages experience is in their decision-making. Their good decisions flow out of them; they just intuitively *know* what the right thing to do is without having to deliberate.

Indy's quick, spontaneous, and confident decision-making—which always seems to be the right decision—is the key evidence for his potential sagehood. He appears to not hesitate (or even think!) when cornered into a tight spot: "Oh, the plane ran out of fuel and is careening towards a mountain? Everyone get in the lifeboat!"; "Oh, an atomic bomb is about to go off? Ah, here's a lead-lined refrigerator!" These examples may seem ridiculous, but instead of guffaws maybe we should be awestruck at how much moral education and training Indy has undergone—to the point where he can stay clear-minded and make the best choices possible (considering the circumstances) with little to no deliberation. In fact, we can add examples more commonplace but equally deserving of admiration: swinging on his whip or a vine, running off platforms or under doors, and even engaging in quick repartee with his sidekicks and love interests. Far from pointing to Indy's thoughtlessness and counting it against him we should admire him *more*, knowing that he has trained himself to be unencumbered by the thought process.

A more conventional way that virtuous people are described is by talking about the so-called cardinal virtues: courage, temperance, justice, and prudence. The Stoics insist that the cardinal virtues are just different ways to talk about the knowledge that people acquire through their two-stage moral education. Courage is knowledge of what should truly be feared and what is not to be feared. Temperance is knowledge of what truly should be desired. Justice is knowledge of what others indeed deserve—be it tangible or intangible. Prudence is knowledge of what someone actually should do when it comes to actualizing the other three virtues. The insight that Indy expresses at the end of *Crystal Skull*—"knowledge was their treasure"—can be appropriated and expanded by virtue ethics. Knowledge is *our* treasure! It is the most valuable thing a human can possess according to the Stoics—it not only underpins our beliefs it also allows us to be truly courageous, temperate, and just.

Indy has learned that not much is to be feared; he has a good sense of what's not dangerous and he seems to know how to navigate things that *are* dangerous. This manifests in the spontaneous acts of courage like the lifeboat and refrigerator examples. Indy has learned that not many things are desirable in themselves; he pursues valuable artifacts, but only because they belong in museums—where the public can appreciate and learn from them. This manifests as spontaneous acts of temperance when he runs through treasure chambers without a second glance, focused on the tasks at hand. Indy has also learned that people deserve more appreciation than a "fortune and glory" approach allows. This manifests as spontaneous acts of justice and compassion. An important example of this occurs in *Temple*: there's a remarkable moment when Indy first gets possession of the Sankara Stones and starts to make his exit from the underground temple when distant sounds of agony stop him in his tracks and compel him to investigate.

The fact that many of Indy's actions can be described as courageous, temperate, and just is important evidence for his virtue and potential sagehood. And just as important is that these actions flow out of him during his adventures confidently and spontaneously, without hesitation or deliberation. What initially seemed like a flaw becomes a crucial feature of a good person.

"Fortune and Glory" (… and Snakes)

What counts against Indy are the instances where his actions are not in line with the cardinal virtues, where he expresses irrational fear, irrational desire, or when he does not treat others in a manner they deserve. Let's rip the bandage off quickly: Indy is *not* a sage. He has learned and internalized a lot of moral knowledge. But he has also displayed some behavior that is not consistent with that of a sage.

Though courage is the most prominent cardinal virtue that Indy exhibits, we all know of one instance where he falters: yes, *snakes* … it had to be snakes. Indy's emotional reaction and hesitation toward snakes indicates that he has some work to do. Of course, snakes should be approached with caution, especially cobras and asps, which are very dangerous as Sallah reminds us, but they should not be feared to the point where one's rational decision-making is compromised. This seems to happen to Indy every single time he spots a snake (except when they are served for dinner for some reason), but in most cases they are relatively harmless boa constrictors, garter snakes, or rat snakes. In fact, recall in *Crystal Skull* when Indy insists that Marion and Mutt call the giant rat snake a rope. Only then (and only after closing his eyes) will he grasp it and be rescued from the dry sandpit (not quicksand pool) he is currently sinking into. In this encounter, like all the others, Indy gets through without a scratch. But all the snake encounters provoke a rare cowardly panic-stricken reaction in him indicating that he has not internalized some basic theoretical knowledge about snakes.

There are at least two moments that serve as examples of Indy's intemperance. During *Temple*, he plays a playful waiting game with Willie Scott in Pankot Palace. After 5 minutes is up and before he gets strangled by an assassin, he says to himself "She's not coming … I can't believe I'm not going." Though this comment seems innocuous, it reveals an internal conflict regarding what he should desire. In other words, it's a subtle sign of intemperance. Another, better-known, example occurs at the end of *Crusade*. Indy's brief flash of greed when he comes within reach of the Holy Grail seems to expose a rare shortcoming concerning his temperance toward artifacts. Perhaps he has not fully internalized the lesson that Krishnamurti taught him as a child—"everybody has to die. You cannot live forever"—or perhaps he has some false beliefs about how the Grail can help the relationship with his father. Regardless, that lapse in judgment is another sign of an irrational intemperance that wouldn't be found in a true sage.

Lastly, like many action heroes, Indy has some dysfunctions in his personal relationships that are inconsistent with the virtue of justice. It wasn't until the events of *Crusade* that he made amends with his father and it wasn't until *Crystal Skull* that he made amends with Marion. A sage strives for harmony with all people and though the term "stoic" brings images of a cold, unsympathetic, insensitive type, the ancient Stoics insisted that the sage is receptive to the concerns of others and exercises compassion whenever possible. In fact, the sage is especially effective at attending to the suffering of others because of his clarity of thought and lack of irrational biases. Indiana Jones is certainly responsive to the suffering of others, but he has needed work addressing the hang-ups in his relationships.

Overall, Indiana Jones is doing very well by the Stoics' standards. He might not be a sage, but he seems to be getting closer to sagehood after every adventure. Perhaps he has become a sage at the very end of *Crystal Skull*. We can't know for sure until we observe him in the fifth installment.

Our analysis here allows us to better appreciate Indy's off-the-cuff remarks about "making things up." Indy has earned the right to "make things up as he goes along." He has developed his intuitive know-how when it comes to being courageous, temperate, just, and prudent. He can appeal to that most of the time because he is very close to attaining the level of sagehood. And though he is not a sage, he is a hero in every sense of the word.

Our Hero

Because we can't yet label Indiana Jones as a "sage" in the ways that the ancient virtue ethicists used the term, I think "hero" is an acceptable term for someone who displays sage-like qualities. This is not a radical idea; the term hero is often used to describe someone in real-life who displays the qualities we have already highlighted in Indy: confidence, spontaneity, and a lack of deliberation when it comes to doing the right thing. As we've seen, this is a sign of good character and moral excellence similar to that of the sage.

The Carnegie Hero Fund awards a medal and monetary benefits to those who perform extraordinary acts of heroism. According to Carnegie, a hero is a person "who knowingly and voluntarily risks his or her own life to an extraordinary degree."[9] This definition emphasizes the external aspect of the hero—his or her heroic act. This makes sense because the Carnegie Hero Fund can only reward people when there are witnesses to their heroism and no one can witness a person's character directly. This is why we examined Indy's actions through this chapter—as a way to get at his character. But the Carnegie definition can be supplemented with our own common-sense beliefs and with empirical research on people who are considered heroes.

Research shows that those recognized as heroes by the Carnegie Hero Fund perform acts of extreme altruism *intuitively*, without thinking, and as a matter of habit: as the researchers put it, "the cognitive processes they describe are overwhelmingly intuitive, automatic and fast."[10] If this intuitive, thought-free behavior is the product of a thoughtful education, we can discuss the Carnegie heroes in the same manner as we discuss Indy and other heroes with similar qualities. They may have cultivated good character to the point that courageous actions can "flow" effortlessly from them in high-pressure situations.

Lastly, it's important to emphasize that this all aligns with our common-sense view of "heroes." The most vivid and common examples of heroes include firefighters who run into burning buildings and police officers or soldiers who run toward danger rather than away from it. At the time this chapter is being written, the COVID-19 pandemic has placed other occupations firmly in this group: in particular, doctors and nurses who often undertake the right actions quickly and intuitively despite knowing they are at risk of contracting the disease.

Though Indy is fictional, he is a model we can look at to better understand what it means to be a good person. Indy is good not because of the consequences he produces, but because of his character. He has oriented himself well through years of self-examination. He has strengthened his convictions and character through years of practice. Indy isn't perfect—he's not a sage—but he's close. He acts in accordance with what he knows is right, with courage and moderation and justice, and he acts without much if any deliberation. This is a mark of sagacity and sage-like heroism cultivated through a theoretical and practical education. Yes, Indiana Jones often acts without thinking and without planning far ahead. And that's admirable.

Notes

1 *The Big Bang Theory*, "The Raiders Minimization" (S07E04). *The Big Bang Theory* characters, who love *Raiders*, seem befuddled by Amy's theory, but they never suggest how Indy manages to save Marion's life; it's unlikely she survives Toht's interrogation.

2 See Plato, *Republic* 353a and Aristotle, *Nicomachean Ethics*, 1097b.
3 Epictetus, *Discourse*, trans. Robert Dobbin (London: Penguin Books, 2008), 1.2.32.
4 Musonius Rufus, *Lectures & Sayings*, trans. Cynthia King (London: CreateSpace, 2011), 6.
5 *Adventures of Young Indiana Jones*, "Journey of Radiance".
6 *Adventures of Young Indiana Jones*, "Young Indiana Jones and the Mystery of the Blues".
7 For example, see Diogenes Laertius, *Lives of Eminent Philosophers*, 7.88 (Text 101.88), in B. Inwood and L. Gerson, eds. and trans., *The Stoic Reader* (London: Hacket Publishing, 2008), 114.
8 Seneca, *Letters to Lucilius*, trans. Margaret Graver (Chicago: University of Chicago Press, 2015), 120.10–11.
9 Find examples of real heroes at: www.carnegiehero.org.
10 David G. Rand and Ziv G. Epstein, "Risking Your Life without a Second Thought: Intuitive Decision-Making and Extreme Altruism," *PLoS ONE* 9, no. 10 (2014).

2

Does It *Always* Belong in a Museum?

Edwardo Pérez

Blinding rain batters the *Coronado* on the Portuguese coast. As the nighttime storm rages, three sailors detain Indiana Jones. A man in a white suit carefully makes his way to the main deck. Donning a matching white Panama hat, the man announces, "Small world, Dr. Jones." "Too small for two of us," Indy drolly replies. Panama Hat reaches into Indy's belt for the Cross of Coronado and says, "This is the second time I've had to reclaim my property from you," to which Indy quickly retorts, "That belongs in a museum!" Growing weary of Dr. Jones, Panama Hat counters: "So do you! Throw him over the side." Just then, a giant wave slams into the ship, knocking everyone off their feet. The Cross skitters across the deck. Indy grabs it and jumps off the ship just before it explodes. Clutching the Cross—and a life preserver—Indy spies a white Panama hat floating away.

Indiana Jones's quest for the Cross of Coronado began 26 years earlier in 1912 Utah. That time, as a boy scout, Indy encountered Panama Hat's tomb-robbing henchmen, led by Fedora. (Indy never learned his name, either.) That was the first time Indy declared the Cross of Coronado belongs in a museum. Despite his clear conviction that artifacts like the Cross of Coronado belong in a museum, he never really explains why. What's more, he doesn't always act on his belief. In this chapter, we'll explore Indy's famous mantra and attempt to do what Indy never did, namely explain why it might be true and why he doesn't always take his own advice. As we'll see, it might not have anything to do with the artifacts themselves, but the good (or not) that comes of their being on public display for all—including scholars—to see.

Indiana Jones and Philosophy: Why Did It Have to Be Socrates?, First Edition. Edited by Dean A. Kowalski.

"Obtainer of Rare Antiquities"

The Last Crusade begins with a flashback to Indy's youth, where the late River Phoenix gives us a brief origin story, showing us how Indy eventually became the "eminent archaeologist" and "obtainer of rare antiquities" portrayed by Harrison Ford (as well as showing us why Indy fears snakes, uses a whip, and has a scar on his chin).

What's significant (other than Phoenix's memorable performance) is that Phoenix's Indy offers the closest thing to an explanation for the belief that artifacts belong in a museum. When encountering Fedora's men on top of the circus train, Phoenix's Indy reminds the bandits that the Cross of Coronado belongs to Coronado. Fedora corrects him: "Coronado is dead. So are all of his grandchildren." With that, Indy reaffirms that it belongs in a museum, which reminds us of the earlier—and much quieter—exchange between Indiana and his young friend Herman. Upon discovering Fedora and his crew in the Utah cave, Phoenix's Indy quickly assesses the situation: "It's the Cross of Coronado. Cortés gave it to him in 1520. That cross is an important artifact. It belongs in a museum." While referring specifically to the Cross of Coronado, Indy expresses an argument that pertains to all artifacts. He states the first premise: *That artifact [the Cross] is an important artifact.* He leaves the second premise unstated: *Important artifacts belong in a museum.* These two premises logically lead to the conclusion: *That important artifact [the Cross] belongs in a museum.* This is a start, but, unfortunately, Phoenix's Indy does not explain why he thinks either premise is true, so we are left guessing about his reasoning.

Still, two things remain clear: Indy has made a career of pursuing artifacts that certainly seem important, and he *almost* always believes that they belong in a museum. The viewer meets Indiana Jones in *Raiders of the Lost Ark*. Set in 1936, Indiana laments to Marcus Brody about losing the Golden Idol to the dastardly René Belloq: "I had it, Marcus. I had it in my hand." Brody is a curator at the National Museum, and not a teaching colleague at Marshall College, which explains Indy's follow-up point: "Look. I got these pieces. They're good pieces, Marcus." To which, Marcus replies, "Indiana, yes, the museum will buy them, no questions asked." There are two points here. On the one hand, Indy intends to spend that money on a plane ticket to Marrakesh, so he can retake the Golden Idol from Belloq, and then present it to Marcus and the National Museum. On the other hand, this serves as a reminder that Indy often deals with Brody and his museum.

Of course, Indy doesn't go to Marrakesh, but becomes focused on the Ark of the Covenant.[1] After Indy's meeting with the government men, he awaits their decision at his home. Indy apprehensively opens the door when Marcus arrives. His fears turn to elation when Marcus shares, "They want you to go for it. They want you to get a hold of the Ark before the Nazis do and they're prepared to pay handsomely for it." But Indy doesn't care about the money: "And the museum? The museum gets the Ark when we're finished?" When Marcus assures him of this, Indy reminisces, "[The Ark] represents everything we got into archaeology for in the first place." When Marcus reminds him that "for nearly 3,000 years man has been searching for the Lost Ark," and suggests caution due to the Ark's unknown secrets, Indy reminds him of his goal: "I'm going after a find of incredible historical significance. You're talking about the bogeyman." So, here, too, Indy pursues an artifact of obvious historical significance, solidifying its importance, with the goal of placing it in a museum, presumably to facilitate future study and enhanced appreciation.

"Fortune and Glory"

In between Indy's youthful pursuit of the Cross of Coronado and his search for the Lost Ark of the Covenant is the curious case of the Mayapore Sankara Stone. This is one time that Indy explicitly violated his "that belongs in a museum" credo.[2]

Temple of Doom is distinctive (infamous?) for its darker tone. It includes enslaving and torturing children, sacrificially pulling a still-beating heart from a man's chest, and drinking the mystical blood of the Kali Ma. It also casts Indiana Jones in a more dubious light. He intends to trade the remains of Nurhachi, the first emperor of the Manchu Dynasty, for an impressive looking diamond. Indy is very explicit about this. Lao offers him a small bag of expensive-looking gold coins, but Indy complains, "The deal was for the diamond, Lao." Indy goes so far as to threaten Willie Scott's life if Lao doesn't uphold the agreed upon terms. This makes Indy seem like a black-market dealer and not an archaeology professor intent on adding to Brody's Chinese collection.[3]

With some help from his assistant Short Round (and almost none from Willie), Indy narrowly escapes Lao Che's double-cross. Indy, Willie, and Short Round flee Shanghai on a cargo plane. But the plane is owned by Lao Che, whose pilots sabotage it, leading to the crash landing in India. The trio, drifting in their yellow life raft, come upon the Mayapore Shaman, who escorts them to his village. The village elders believe that Shiva brought Indy to their village so that he could rescue their stolen Sivalinga—a sacred rock that protected the village. The Shaman affirms, "We prayed to Shiva to help us find the stone. It was Shiva who made you fall from the sky. So, you will go to Pankot Palace to find Sivalinga and bring it back to us."

Although it seems like an incredible coincidence that an archaeologist who is an expert in the occult just happened to crash land near Mayapore, Indy is skeptical of any supernatural involvement. He calms Short Round by saying that the Shaman was telling a "ghost story." Indy becomes more sympathetic when he learns that in addition to the Sivalinga, the Mayapore children have also been stolen. When a young boy escapes Pankot that evening and informs everyone of their plight at the palace—and provides Indy with an ancient scroll depicting Shiva bestowing magical rocks to the priest Sankara—Indy agrees to travel to Pankot. But his intentions remain muddled, as he tells Short Round, "I think that somebody believes the good luck rock from this village is one of the lost Sankara Stones." When Short Round queries, "Who is Sankara?" Indy answers, "Fortune and glory, kid. Fortune and glory."

Of course, the Mayapore Sivalinga is indeed one of the fabled Sankara Stones, and Indy, Willie, and Short Round go to great lengths to rescue it from Mola Ram and his Thuggee cult. In the process, Indy frees the Mayapore children. On their return trip, they find Mayapore changed. What was once a destitute and desolate village is now a vibrant community teeming with hope and life. Indy returns the stone to the Shaman, who (rhetorically) asks, "Now you can see the magic of the rock you bring back?" To which Indy affirms, "Yes, I understand its power now." Willie reminds him of his original purpose: "You could have kept it." Without contradicting her, Indy replies, "Ah, what for? They'd just put it in a museum. It'd be another rock collecting dust." Willie further reminds him: "But then it would've given you your fortune and glory."

Indy suggests that his fortune and glory would have come from selling the stone to Brody's museum—and not selling it on the black market, as he seemingly did with Nurhachi. But Indy declined that opportunity and made his way to Delhi without the Sankara Stone. He doesn't fully explain his decision, but he seems to believe that more good would come from leaving it with the Mayapore villagers. That choice is better than the alternatives.

"… Right Down the Hall"

When attempting to determine what one ought to do, we often ask: What is best for everyone involved? Clearly, if an action will bring only pain and suffering and no positive results, that is excellent reason not to choose it. This sort of ethical thinking is called consequentialism because it stresses the consequences produced by our actions. Consequentialists believe that *only* positive or negative consequences—happiness and pain or suffering—matter morally speaking.

Jeremy Bentham (1748–1832) is a classic consequentialist who often spoke of the utility of one's actions. He defined utility as "that principle which approves or disapproves of every action whatsoever, according to the tendency which it appears to have to augment or diminish the happiness of the party whose interest is in question."[4] Contemporary scholar Philip Schofield further explains:

> The principle of utility was concerned with calculating the consequences of an action in terms of the pleasures and pains it produced on every individual affected by that action. [...] The question as to whether an action was right or wrong [...] was a question of fact—it would depend on the value, understood in terms of quantity, of the pleasures and pains which would be brought into existence by the act in question.[5]

For consequentialists like Bentham who apply the utility principle to each possible course of action, we ought to choose the one that produces the most good, that is, happiness or pleasure. For example, when Indy catches a very young and orphaned Short Round picking his pocket, he could turn him in to the authorities, send him to a local orphanage, or serve as a quasi-foster father. Presumably, he chose the third option because it would produce the best consequences for both Short Round and (arguably) himself.

Consequentialists are quick to remind us that we must take into account the happiness and pain and suffering of everyone affected by one's choice. Further, very rarely will an action bring about only happiness or only pain and suffering. Typically, every scenario involves a mixture of both. By becoming Short Round's foster father, Indy takes on a great deal of responsibility, which will require effort and include some hardship. Not everything will go smoothly, ranging from playing poker together to being held hostage by Mola Ram. Indy would suffer far less hardship if he simply turned Short Round in to the local authorities. However, he also benefits from Short Round's company—and Short Round's life is vastly improved compared to living on the streets as young orphan in Shanghai. Overall, Indy becoming his foster father is the best choice.

By stressing the consequences of one's action, consequentialists may deny that any acts—including murder—are inherently morally good or bad. This is controversial, but consequentialists are quick to remind us that some actions typically cause a great deal of pain and suffering, which allows for the existence of moral rules. As a rule, then, one ought to tell the truth or keep promises, because doing otherwise almost always causes more pain and suffering than happiness or pleasure. Still, consequentialists admit that, technically, any recognized moral rule can be overturned by carefully applying the utility principle to the circumstances at hand.

"If I Just Sit Down and Think ... the Solution Presents Itself"

Consequentialism offers a way to understand Indy's insistence that important artifacts belong in museums, which might also shed light on the reasoning that drives young Indy's implicit argument in *Crusade*. Indy perhaps believes that, as a rule, important artifacts belong in a museum because the general population can benefit by viewing and learning about them. When important artifacts are placed in a museum, scholars have ample opportunity to study them carefully, which enhances our understanding and appreciation of them. We better see their historical and cultural importance. Further, the museum will keep them safe and ensure their upkeep, so the general public can continue to benefit by learning about them for generations to come.

What's more, placing important artifacts in museums produces far greater positive consequences compared to keeping them in private collections. Private collections are viewed only by the owner and perhaps a very select few who the owner allows access. True, the owner benefits greatly, but the positive consequences they enjoy cannot compare to the positive consequences generated by thousands upon thousands of people enjoying them when placed in a museum. This explains why Indy was so keen on retrieving the Cross of Coronado. Yes, Panama Hat enjoys it as part of his private collection, but this is not the best option.

Consequentialism also offers an explanation for why Indy is more interested in the Ark being placed in Brody's museum than he is any monetary payment from the government for securing it. When the government alters the terms of the deal, but attempts to assure Indy and Marcus that the Ark will be held "somewhere very safe," Indy queries from whom it will be safe and complains, "Oh, the money's fine. The situation's totally unacceptable." Marcus adds, "The Ark is a source of unspeakable power and it has to be researched." The government men do their best to appease them: "And it will be, I assure you, Dr. Brody, Dr. Jones. We have top men working on it right now." Indy is thoroughly disgusted, as he later laments to Marion, "Bureaucratic fools ... They don't know what they've got there." Clearly, Indy believes that the government made the wrong choice by not allowing the public—and serious scholars—to have regular access to the Ark.

Yet, to be fair, the government is probably following the same logic as Indy and Marcus. They simply disagree with the two scholars about what is best given the situation. A restricted Area 51 warehouse might not be a museum, but isn't the Ark safer from the Nazis (or anyone else) if it's hidden in southern Nevada rather than displayed out in the open in Marcus's Connecticut museum? Certainly, given how the Ark remains tucked away in its "Do Not Open" dusty crate decades later in *Kingdom of the Crystal Skull*, it seems the government made the right call, one that fits the principle of utility insofar as it provided the best option for the Ark and for everyone involved (because after what happened to Belloq and Ernst Toht, what "top men" would really want to risk opening the Ark to study it?).

Indy, Marcus, and the government men disagree about the facts as they pertain to the happiness and pain or suffering caused by placing the Ark in a public museum as compared to hiding it away in a secret location. Some of these facts pertain to the future, so it's easy to sympathize with the two scholars. Still, it might be that Indy is not thinking clearly about the situation, which gets in the way of his seeing how the greater good is better served if the Ark is *not* placed in a museum. Perhaps the government is correct in its estimation that consequentialist thinking about the unique case of the Ark leads to overturning Indy's general rule about placing important artifacts in museums.

Notably, Indy made a similar decision about the Mayapore Sankara Stone. Indy doesn't divulge exactly how he weighs the facts, but his quip that if he took the stone back to Brody's museum, it would "just be another rock gathering dust" provides a helpful clue. It seems Indy recognized three options: (1) keep the stone and sell it to a private collector; (2) place the stone in a museum; (3) leave it with the Mayapore villagers. It seems that Indy never really considered (1) as an option. We don't know why, but it might be that by the end of the film he regains his sense of valuing the greater good over his selfish interests. So, the "fortune and glory" he initially sought was not to come from selling the Mayapore Stone on the black market to a private collector. Rather, fortune and glory would come to his career as an archaeologist by placing the stone in a museum. Still, it seems that he believes more good will come if he opts for (3) over (2). True, Indy himself would benefit more by opting for (2), but perhaps this is outweighed by a flourishing Mayapore village, where for generations to come the stone will protect its villagers and secure them constant happiness. Further, it might be that without the other Sankara Stones the Mayapore Stone would not garner that much interest from other scholars or the general public. This further explains his quip about it being just another rock gathering dust. All of this is difficult to know, but at least consequentialism provides a plausible story about why Indy made the choice he did, and why he overturned his general rule about placing important artifacts in a museum.

"I Don't Know, I'm Making This Up as I Go"

Fans have long noted the apparent inconsistency in Indy's decisions about placing artifacts in a museum. Sometimes he doggedly works to find and place artifacts in a museum, as he does with the Golden Idol, the Ark of the Covenant, and especially the Cross of Coronado. Sometimes he doesn't, for example, with the Crystal Skull, the Holy Grail, and especially the Mayapore Sankara Stone. Why? How might we explain this discrepancy? We've considered a plausible answer grounded in consequentialist ethical theory.

We should be honest and recognize that perhaps there is no single underlying perspective that neatly explains all of Indy's decisions. He is a fictional character written and filmed by numerous people, with diverging artistic goals. Of course, we don't know for sure that consequentialist thinking can explain all of what we see when watching Indy trapse across the globe looking for artifacts. But consequentialism does explain why Indy struggles against the Nazis in *Raiders and Crusade* and Mola Ram in *Temple*: If the Nazis or Mola Ram successfully wield occult objects for world domination, that would cause extensive pain and suffering; almost any other alternative would be better for all those involved. It also helps to explain why Indy believes that important artifacts belong in a museum, and why when he breaks his own rule he might not be inconsistent.[6]

Notes

1 As it turns out, Indy resumes his quest for the Golden Idol in the wider Indyverse of the comic books. See "The Gold Goddess Chapter 1: Xomec's Raiders" and "The Gold Goddess Chapter 2: Amazon Death-Ride!" in *The Further Adventures of Indiana Jones* (vol. 1, nos. 9 and 10: September and October 1983).

2 It's true that Indy did not strive to secure either the Holy Grail or the Crystal Skull a place in a museum, but it's also not clear that he had explicit intentions about them one way or the other. In both cases, his explicit goal was rescuing someone he cared about (his father and Harold Oxley).

3 The junior novelization attempts to smooth out this apparent wrinkle in Indy's character by claiming that the diamond is an important artifact; it is called the "Peacock's Eye" and once belonged to Alexander the Great. See Suzanne Weyn, *Indiana Jones and the Temple of Doom* (New York: Scholastic, 2008).

4 Jeremy Bentham, *The Works of Jeremy Bentham*, ed. John Bowring (Edinburgh: W. Tait, 1843), 2.

5 Phillip Schofield, "Jeremy Bentham, The Principle of Utility, and Legal Positivism," *Current Legal Problems* vol. 56, no. 1 (2003), 25.

6 For a non-consequentialist account of Indy's actions, please Chapter 4 by Mia Wood in this volume.

3

The Virtues that Made the Man, and the Man Who Became the Legend: The Adventures in Philosophy of Young Indiana Jones

Robert M. Mentyka

During the 1990s, the *Indiana Jones* franchise was maintained in the form of the live-action television series *The Adventures of Young Indiana Jones*. Chronicling Indy's tumultuous past alongside the historical backdrop of the early twentieth century, the show was meant to be a semi-educational experience for the entire family, and it won several Emmy Awards during its three-season run.

The expanded format of a television series allowed for increased character growth and exploration, while the tighter budget necessitated fewer high-octane stunts in favor of thematic discussions and world-building. Although the franchise was known for its emphasis on history and archaeology, *The Adventures of Young Indiana Jones* broadened the scope of Indy's interests. The episode "Passion for Life," for instance, saw Indiana thrust head-first into the tumultuous world of art inhabited by figures like Pablo Picasso and Edgar Degas, before shifting gears entirely and introducing Indy to the natural conservation efforts of none other than Theodore Roosevelt.

The episode "Travels with Father," takes a more reflective turn. After trading ideas and baseball cards with Leo Tolstoy in Russia, Indy and his family venture to the inspiring vistas of Greece, on their way to a cliffside monastery that houses ancient manuscripts vital to his father's research. As both Henry Jones, Sr. and Jr. get caught up in a series of misadventures while traveling to this monastery, the two strike up a conversation about Aristotle (384–322 BCE) and the birth of Western

Indiana Jones and Philosophy: Why Did It Have to Be Socrates?, First Edition. Edited by Dean A. Kowalski.

Philosophy. Using the lessons learned from this discussion, the two are able to successfully arrive at their destination and grow together as father and son.

Building on the foundations established in the episode "Travels with Father," this chapter considers Aristotle's approach to ethics, with its emphasis on character development and virtue. Along the way, we'll discover what *The Adventures of Young Indiana Jones* can teach us about what it means to be good, and how human beings can overcome their personal weaknesses.

Hollywood Follies ... on a Television Budget

Although *The Adventures of Young Indiana Jones* played an important part in keeping the franchise in public awareness prior to the release of *Kingdom of the Crystal Skull* in 2008, the television series has fallen out of the limelight since then. The entire production was released on DVD in 2007, but shifting rights and licensing agreements have made this collection the only reliable way to watch the series. Little in the way of official merchandise or marketing has been dedicated to the show, making fan websites and internet forums the most reliable source of information about the series.[1]

The show began as *The Young Indiana Jones Chronicles*, a series produced for the ABC television network, first airing in March of 1992. It was pitched as a cost-effective way of continuing the franchise following the original trilogy's success. The shift to television would also allow the production company to take some risks, testing new filming techniques and special effects options in a relatively low-risk environment that wouldn't bankrupt the company if they didn't succeed.

In its original run, the series would feature Indy at three different points in his life, as a troublesome youth from Princeton, NJ traveling the world with his parents, as an idealistic young man fighting for his beliefs before settling down for a college education, and as a garrulous retired professor eager to share his stories with anyone who would listen. Each episode was roughly 45 minutes long and would be bookended by the elderly Dr. Jones providing context for the exploits of his younger self. The adventures themselves alternated between the preteen "Junior" and adolescent "Young Indy," with episodes tending to be more educational while Indy was in grade school before ratcheting up the action during his later teenage years.

The production itself was a collaboration of many different writers and directors. Although Indy was accompanied by a small cast of recurring characters, each self-contained episode featured a revolving door of special guest appearances and hundreds of region-specific extras. This constantly evolving cast allowed the show to feature numerous prominent historical figures, staying true to its marketing pitch that audiences would encounter "All the action, all the intrigue, all the exciting exploits of the young man who not only witnessed history, he made it."[2]

Although the show was a critical success, general audience reaction was lukewarm. Many found the stories too focused on education, and sequences with the elderly Dr. Jones were panned for failing to capture the essence of the hero in his twilight years. The series' numerous writers and directors resulted in a wide variation in episode quality, and the travel costs required to film each episode made the production prohibitively expensive for long-term success. The show's first season was cut short, but it did manage to return for a second season that focused almost exclusively on the more action-packed stories of Indy's late teens and early twenties. *The Young Indiana Jones Chronicles* finished its production run as a series of four television movies created for the Family Channel after having been canceled outright by ABC.

This change in format would prompt George Lucas to reevaluate the entire series, heavily re-editing episodes in order to create 23 television movies collectively called *The Adventures of Young Indiana Jones.* Each of these features would essentially be two episodes tacked together, with varying degrees of success for how seamlessly one episode would transition into another. Segments featuring the elderly Dr. Jones were cut entirely. Subsequently, this version was released to home video, and this new format would serve as the only way the series would be discussed in official capacities moving forward. Accordingly, it will be the version examined in the rest of this chapter.[3]

My First Adventure ... in Philosophy

Within philosophy, ethics is the field of critical discussion about the nature of human action, about the good that our actions should strive for, and how we can hope to attain that good. For Aristotle, ethical discourse is the natural extension of his theories about the nature of reality, a logical outgrowth of his conclusions about existence and human knowledge. So, in order to discuss Aristotle's ethics, we need to consider his influential work on the principles of causality.

Indeed, this is where a young Indiana begins his exploration of Aristotle's ethics in the episode "Travels with Father." Having already discussed logic with his father, Indy is introduced to Aristotle's thoughts on causation by the Greek writer Níkos Kazantzákis, who says "Look at it this way. Aristotle said, 'Nature does not act without a goal' and that sprang from his theories of causality, right?" When Indy questions him about the definition of "causality," Níkos answers by having the young adventurer push an orange on the cover of a tilted book, observing how this action leads to the orange rolling down onto the table. Causality focuses on the relationship between cause and effect; it's the exploration into why a certain item or state of affairs occurs the way it does.

In modern times, causality is usually reduced to a single aspect, the scientifically measurable force that directly causes a certain effect to come into being, such as the push that Indy gives to the orange in order to get it rolling. However, Aristotle looked at things differently, seeing four interlinked causes that must be examined in order to truly understand why a certain effect occurred. The first of these is the material cause, the stuff out of which something is made. The second, the formal cause, deals with the overarching structure or form that makes a thing recognizable as what it is. The efficient cause, the third type, focuses on who or what made a certain effect. (It's what most people think of when they discuss causality these days from a scientific perspective.) Fourth, is the aptly named final cause, which is the reason why that particular item or set of circumstances exists at all.[4]

This fourfold examination is clearer when applied, so let's consider what Aristotle would say are four the causes of *The Adventures of Young Indiana Jones*. The series' material cause is everything that went into its production, the performances given by its actors, the extensive sets and costumes created by its fabrication department, and anything else needed to bring such an epic adventure to life on the television screen. Its formal cause is similarly multifaceted, consisting of the episode scripts, the vision of each episode's director, and the camera and editing work needed to shape each part of this series into a cohesive whole. The show's primary creator was George Lucas, but, in a sense, everyone whose hard work and effort went into bringing Indiana Jones's early story to life could be listed as part of the production's efficient cause. As for the final cause, we've already mentioned that George Lucas's motive in creating the series was to capitalize on the success of the *Indiana Jones* film trilogy and keep audiences interested in the franchise.

Although all four of these causes need to be considered when investigating the nature of a certain object, Aristotle stressed the importance of a thing's final cause. While the other causes are necessary to explain an object's existence, the final cause goes further, giving that object meaning and orienting it toward the end it was made to accomplish. The final cause governs the role a particular object has to play in the grand drama of reality, and it serves as the ultimate measure by which that object is judged.

Passion for Life ... and Its Highest Good

The idea of a final cause links Aristotle's ideas about causality with our primary investigation into the field of ethics. For Aristotle, the question of good and evil is directly tied to humanity's final cause, and the answer to our original question turns out to be a relatively simple affair. The good, according to Aristotle, is whatever aids us in achieving our final cause, while evil is that which impedes us from this goal.

Of course, Aristotle still has to explain what this final cause actually is if he hopes to provide us with a definitive guide to human action. In order to do this, Aristotle examines our day-to-day choices, looking at our goals and trying to find one that directs all the others. He reasons that our final cause, being so important a part of our existence, must be something that all rational people aim at, even if they don't always achieve this lofty goal.

Aristotle argues that our final cause can be found by determining the ultimate goal of all human action, the one thing toward which all of our efforts are directed. In the episode "The Phantom Train of Doom," Indy and his comrade-in-arms Remy are separated from their World War I unit and get embroiled in a series of crazy escapades alongside a rag-tag group of elderly British forces specialists. They blow up a train, hijack a hot-air balloon, and kidnap German commander Paul von Lettow-Vorbeck, but all of their actions are motivated by their overarching goal of getting back to their regiment of the Belgian Army. The pair have many goals throughout the episode, but only one ultimate end that inspires and guides all of their decisions. Similarly, Aristotle believes that humankind's final cause is the underlying goal that motivates all other action, the one thing we always aim at and which is never undertaken merely as a means to some other end.

Possible candidates for such an ultimate end to all human action include things like wealth, power, pleasure, and any other good that a large number of people claim they need. Yet human history bears witness to many cases of people possessing these goods, only to find themselves miserable and unfulfilled. Young Indiana Jones gives us a prime example of this in the episode "Demons of Deception," where a lurid affair with the infamous spy Mata Hari helps Indy learn that there is more to love than mere carnal pleasure. Though he enjoys his nights of passion with Mata Hari, his inability to trust her and the flippancy with which she regards their relationship leaves the young adventurer bitter and unhappy.

Aristotle reasons that the final cause of all human activity is happiness itself. The Ancient Greek term he used was "eudaimonia (εὐδαιμονία)," which is imperfectly translated into English as "happiness." The Greek word expresses a more nuanced idea than the English translation implies. Eudaimonia is not mere contentment, or the absence of misfortunes, but a real, authentic realization of the fullness of human life, perhaps better expressed in modern English by the terms "flourishing" or "fulfillment." The desire for eudaimonia informs all that we do, but achieving it is extremely difficult. This is where Aristotle turns his attention to the notion of virtue and the pivotal part it has to play in helping people to become good.

The Winds of Change … for Good

Virtue, for Aristotle, is a type of readiness in being that enables us to consistently make good choices. Translations often use the term "habit" to describe this state of moral preparedness, but whereas habits are often thought of as mindless, automatic responses to specific stimuli, Aristotelian virtue requires vigilance, constantly remaining alert for opportunities to choose and act appropriately. Indy often adjusts his trademark fedora, taking it off when in polite society, but this sort of ingrained habit isn't what Aristotle means when he refers to virtue. Rather, the virtues are more akin to the special care Indiana Jones takes to make sure that he always goes back for his fedora, constantly aware of its location and willing to risk life and limb in order to retrieve his beloved headgear.

Aristotelian virtue is a type of excellence, a level of expertise that one achieves through hard work and diligent practice. Much of the storyline of *The Adventures of Young Indiana Jones* shows Indy slowly beginning to develop and hone the skills that would one day define him as a hero, including his whip and lasso work. Young Indy's attempts to employ such tools come across as amateurish at best. He even cuts himself, by accident, when he tries to use a whip in the flashback sequence from *The Last Crusade*. Apparently, it took a lot of time and effort for Indy to become as proficient with these items as he's portrayed in the movies.

Although Aristotle agrees that we must work hard in order to become virtuous, he famously dismisses the idea that virtue is a type of superlative excess. The excellence of virtue, he argues, is that it exists as a middle ground between two opposing extremes. In Aristotle's words:

> It is moral virtue that is concerned with emotions and actions, and it is in these we have excess and deficiency and the mean. Thus it is possible to go too far, or not far enough … and the excess and the deficiency are alike wrong … wherein excess is all error and deficiency a fault, while the mean is successful and praised, and success and praise are both characteristics of virtue.[5]

Courage, for example, is not the complete lack of fear, but the appropriate mean seen in action between the deficiency we call cowardice and the excess we call recklessness. Achieving the mean we call courage is difficult and takes practice. *The Adventures of Young Indiana Jones* shines as an exploration of Aristotelian virtue, as the evolving plotline of the series constantly shows us how Young Indy swings back and forth between his passions as he slowly grows in wisdom and maturity. In the episode "The Spring Break Adventure," the first half of the tale shows Indy desperately trying to get out of the danger his current girlfriend, Nancy Stratemeyer, seems intent on getting them embroiled in. Then, in the latter half of the episode, Indy completely throws caution to the wind, joining up with Pancho Villa's revolutionaries in Mexico before setting sail to enlist as a World War I soldier. While this inconsistency in character might not make for the best television, it nails the trial-and-error approach to personal growth that so many people experience in their youth, and illustrates how, slowly, Indy begins to learn from his excesses to take a more measured and mature response to the situations in which he finds himself.

Travels with Father ... and Many Others

If living virtuously is the key to becoming good, how can we grow in virtue? Aristotle's answer to this question is twofold, the first aspect of which was already hinted at. Growth in virtue requires an unflagging dedication to constantly direct our efforts toward better living. Now, this doesn't mean that we always make the right choices or succeed with the good intentions we set out with, but that, even when we mess up and give in to our baser inclinations, we have the strength to pick ourselves back up and keep on trying. Virtue requires its practitioners to have the humility to admit their mistakes, the wisdom to learn from their failures, and the fortitude to carry on in full knowledge of their personal weaknesses.

The second part of Aristotle's answer includes the resources we find in others. Like many other Ancient Greek thinkers, Aristotle believed that humans are inherently social creatures, who can only truly flourish when they exist as active members of a society. If we truly wish to grow in virtue, we need to surround ourselves with virtuous men and women, whose example and companionship can help us when the going gets tough.

Again, a story from *The Adventures of Young Indiana Jones* provides the perfect illustration. One of the few constants connecting all of Indy's disparate adventures is the reliance he places on those around him. The series' supporting cast, consisting of Indy's parents, his tutor Miss Seymour, and his best friend Remy, form the core of this community and are the principal agents of Indy's moral growth. They are the ones who most often support the young hero through his challenging struggles, and they are the teachers who impart to him the foundational lessons that help shape his moral character.

This connection is not limited to his immediate friends and family, however, and the show's focus on famous historical figures helps to highlight the influence that all of our interpersonal relationships can have on our growth in virtue. Through his interactions with famous individuals, Indy is given striking examples of how one can succeed or fail at living a life of virtue. Whether it's learning about the value of human life from Albert Schweitzer, arguing about romance with Ernest Hemingway, or encountering evil in its most diabolical form while running from the ghost of Vlad the Impaler, Young Indiana Jones's encounters with such characters helps to inform his own moral development.

Such connections and the lessons he learns ultimately define Indiana Jones as a character. While *The Adventures of Young Indiana Jones* and the first two movies are content to focus primarily on Indy, his later exploits in *Crusade* and *Kingdom of the Crystal Skull* shift audiences' attention to those closest to the adventurous archaeologist. We see Indy repair the relationship with his estranged father and finally take responsibility for the son he didn't know he had. The later movies are clear in their message that Indiana Jones can only fully become the hero we know him to be when he accepts the roles proper to him as the member of a family.

Tales of Innocence ... Setting the Stage for the Actions of a Hero

Looking at Indy through an Aristotelian lens provides important insights. First, ethics is not some extraneous burden or set of rules placed on us by others. Indiana Jones isn't searching for treasures simply because the Nazis are goading him on at gunpoint. He's searching for those artifacts because of the inherent value he sees in them, acting out of a desire to make sure that such treasures don't fall into the wrong hands. Similarly, we don't strive to make good choices just because we're told that we have to do so. The desire to grow in virtue comes from within, and it is necessary for finding true happiness and fulfillment.

Second, if we're serious about living virtuously, we have to be prepared for our fair share of difficulties. It's easy to swing back and forth between extremes, but the discipline required to approach every situation with a level head and to act appropriately within it will probably take a lifetime to achieve. Indy's growth through three seasons of television and four feature-length films shows that one doesn't become a virtuous hero overnight.

Finally, growth in virtue is only attainable in communion with others who are dedicated to achieving it. While it's up to each one of us to take responsibility for our actions and try to live the best lives we can, those around us can help to shoulder the burden of virtuous living, picking us up when we fall and guiding us when we've lost our way. Although the tagline of *The Adventures of Young Indiana Jones* claims that these stories are "The adventures that made the man, and the man who became the legend," it was actually the virtues that he picked up along the way, and the people who supported him through struggles, that shaped Indiana Jones into the icon he became. In navigating our own adventures in life, we would do well to follow Indy's lead.

Notes

1 This entire section is indebted to "The Young Indiana Jones Chronicles" hub at theraider.net (accessible at http://www.theraider.net/films/young_indy/index.php). Theraider.net is arguably the premiere website for information regarding Indy's televised adventures.

2 This tagline is taken from the trailer for the series that was included on the VHS releases of several of the episodes in the late 1990s. The trailer itself is available on several video-hosting platforms, for example, https://youtu.be/V-pnJWXze5s (accessed June 1, 2020).

3 George Lucas is notorious for his insistence that later, reworked versions of his creations are what he considers the canon product. Given Lucasfilm's almost complete rebranding of the series as *The Adventures of Young Indiana Jones*, it seems natural that we should focus on this edit as our primary source material.

4 Christopher Shields, "Aristotle," in *The Stanford Encyclopedia of Philosophy*, ed. Edward N. Zalta, December 21, 2016, at https://plato.stanford.edu/archives/win2016/entries/aristotle (accessed May 15, 2020).

5 Aristotle, *Nicomachean Ethics*, trans. James Welldon (New York: Macmillian Press, 1897), Book 2, ch. 6.

4

Raiders of the Lost Kant: Indy Meets the Categorical Imperative

Mia Wood

Clutching a golden statue, a man in a brown fedora stumbles as he runs from a gigantic boulder menacingly gaining ground. Narrowly escaping death, he leaps through the cave entrance and rolls down the hill covered in cobwebs. He's met by a hostile band of natives and a man wearing a tan safari hat, who smugly states, "Dr. Jones. Again we see there is nothing you possess which I cannot take away." As the man extends his open palm, and the natives ready their spears, arrows, and poison darts, Dr. Jones hands over his revolver … and the statue. "Too bad the Hovitos don't know you the way I do, Belloq," Dr. Jones mutters. "Yes, too bad, Belloq sarcastically replies. "You could warn them, if only you spoke Hovitos." Belloq turns to display his prize and the Hovitos bow their heads. Dr. Jones opportunistically sprints off into the jungle, and Belloq directs the Hovitos to pursue. As Belloq's cackles echo through the trees, Dr. Jones shouts to someone named Jock to get the plane ready for takeoff.

After the iconic first 12 minutes and 48 seconds of the film, all we really know is that some smarmy guy with a French accent named Belloq took something that didn't belong to him. The Dr. Jones guy did all the dangerous work to obtain the prize, only to relinquish it when Belloq arrived with some local muscle. That probably makes Belloq the bad guy. But the statue doesn't belong to Dr. Jones either. He took it out of the cave, avoiding all the boobytraps that are supposed to dissuade small golden statue stealers. So, are they both bad guys?

Indiana Jones and Philosophy: Why Did It Have to Be Socrates?, First Edition. Edited by Dean A. Kowalski.

Talking about good guys and bad guys leads to considerations of right and wrong—ethics, a subject about which the German philosopher Immanuel Kant (1724–1804) had a lot to say. As we'll see, Kant's notion of duty and his famous categorical imperative shed new light on the shadowy figure who became a cinematic hero despite his moral shortcomings.

Kant and the Categorical Imperative

Kant believes that we are morally praiseworthy only if we do the right thing for its own sake. In other words, we ought to do what is right simply *because* it is the right thing to do. If anything else motivates us to do what seems right, then we act for improper reasons. In this, Kant distinguishes between actions that conform with duty and those that are done from, or out of respect for, duty. For example, although it seems that Belloq did the right thing by attempting to rescue Marion from the Nazis twice—first at the Well of Souls and second on Katanga's ship—he is not to be commended for these choices because he was acting out of self-interest and not because it was the right thing to do.

Kant believes that an action is wrong (or right) not because of its consequences, and not whether it causes pain (or produces happiness), but due its very nature—the kind of act it is. In Kant's words, "A good will is good not because of what it effects or accomplishes, … but good just by its willing, i.e., in itself."[1] Because we are rational beings, the morality of our actions is determined by respect for reason. This respect is characterized by doing our duty as rational beings, or as Kant puts it, "Duty is the necessity of an action from respect for the law."[2]

For Kant, the moral law is expressed by the categorical imperative: "Act only according to that maxim through which you can at the same time will that it become a universal law."[3] A maxim is the implicit general rule corresponding to one's specific action. When Belloq waited for Indy outside the cave, his implicit maxim was (something like): When you are able to take what doesn't belong to you, especially if you really want it, you should do so. But Belloq cannot reasonably accept that *everyone* should act as he does. A world in which everyone takes what isn't theirs is a world with no possessions at all. That scenario, however, undermines Belloq's reason for taking the Golden Idol from Indy in the first place. Belloq's maxim makes sense only if he makes an exception for himself. It's okay *only* for him to take what doesn't belong to him; everyone else must refrain (lest they take Belloq's possessions, leaving him with nothing). In this way, Belloq's maxim cannot become a universal law for everyone to follow equally—it fails the categorical imperative. This makes his action morally impermissible. Not only for him, but for anyone—including Indy—who might choose to take what doesn't belong to them.

When reason demands that one act a certain way, and someone fails to do so, then that person fails to respect himself or herself—and every other person—as a rational being. Put another way, to make an exception for yourself is to put yourself above others. But it's intuitive that all rational beings have equal moral worth, insofar as the moral law applies equally to all of us. This leads to Kant's second formulation of the categorial imperative: "So act that you use humanity, in your own person as well as in the person of any other, always at the same time as an end, never merely as a means."[4] People are not instruments or props to be used for any specific or selfish purpose. Doing so treats a person as a mere thing, which is another way to make an undeserved exception for yourself. All persons possess inherent dignity and must be treated as such. All are deserving of respect equally.

Belloq, Indy, and Marion

Belloq commits (at least) three notable violations of the Kantian categorical imperative. The first is that he almost certainly deceived the Hovitos about the Golden Idol. He took advantage of his knowledge of Hovitos to lead them to believe that he would help them protect the Idol from treasure hunters. But it was a ruse. Belloq gained the Hovitos' trust and used them merely as a means for his selfish purposes of selling the Idol on the black market in Marrakesh.

The second violation occurs when Belloq deceives the Nazis into aiding him in his quest to use the Ark as "a radio for speaking to God." When Nazi commander Dietrich clearly expresses his discomfort with the Jewish ritual Belloq prescribes, the sly look Belloq gives suggests he has anticipated this concern. He redirects: "Let me ask you this: Would you be more comfortable opening the Ark in Berlin, for your Fuehrer? Finding out only then if the sacred pieces of the Covenant are inside? Knowing only then whether you have accomplished your mission, and obtained the one true Ark?" Belloq's questions are clearly rhetorical. He walks away—smiling to himself—without waiting for Dietrich's reply because he knows his ploy will succeed. He has preyed upon Dietrich's fears of failure—using him as a mere instrument—to guarantee his personal desire to open the Ark and have an audience with the divine.

Belloq commits a third Kantian violation in treating Marion as a prized *possession* and not a *person* worthy of respect. He is guilty of this throughout *Raiders*, but the most obvious affront occurs in his tent at the Tanis dig site. He begins with an apology about how the Nazis have treated her. With a mouthful of bread and eyeing up the plate of fresh fruit, Marion retorts, "No food, no water. What kind of people are these friends of yours?" Belloq (not surprisingly) corrects her, claiming the Nazis are not his friends, but are "necessary evils" to accomplish his work "at this particular time and place." He then presents Marion with an elegant white dress, obtained through his Nazi connections. Marion agrees it is beautiful, which prompts Belloq to share, "I would very much like to see you in it." She plays along. He forewarns her that he can keep the Nazis at bay for only so long—as he uses his desk mirror to ogle her as she dons the dress. He hopes that she will provide some information about Jones to placate the Nazis, but his true goal is to seduce her with the help of wine, food, and fine clothing. If downing a bottle of wine, and the resulting impaired judgment, will facilitate this, so be it. Belloq treats Marion like a mere thing for information and his sexual pleasure—all in the hope that the Nazis will allow him to keep his prized possession.

By Kantian standards, Indy also has his failings, and two of them involve Marion. We learn about Indy's first moral error as the film unfolds. After being visited by the government men, Indy sets out to find the Staff of Ra medallion before the Nazis do. He believes (as do the Nazis) that his University of Chicago mentor Abner Ravenwood currently possesses it. As Indy packs his bags, he asks his friend and colleague Marcus Brody, "Suppose she'll still be with him?" Marcus knowingly replies, "Possibly, but Marion is the least of your worries right now." Arriving in Nepal, Indy indeed finds Marion in a remote tavern. Wasting no time, he states, "I need one of the pieces your father collected." Marion replies with a right-cross to Indy's jaw, and quickly adds, "I learned to hate you in the last ten years." Rubbing his face, Indy claims, "I never meant to hurt you." Marion is not appeased. "I was a child," she replies forlornly, before switching to the plaintive lament, "I was in love." Then she lands the moral blow: "It was wrong, and you knew it." But Indy is not so easily shamed. "You knew what you were doing," he responds dismissively. "Now I do!" she retorts, and continues, "This is my place. Get out!" Not finished, Indy redirects: "I did what I did. You don't have to be happy about it, but maybe we could help each other out now."

This fraught reunion hearkens back to when Indy, while studying with Abner, initiated a romantic relationship with Marion. She was 16.[5] Marion believes Indy took advantage of her back then; Indy *used* her for his selfish purposes. He had his fun with her—"looted" her heart—and then cast her aside. Indy (lamely) attempts to defend himself by asserting that Marion consented to their romantic tryst, fully aware that it could end abruptly. Indy claims that he and Marion entered into the relationship as adults and without deceit or deception, despite Marion's tender age. Marion denies it, claiming she knows *now* how to respond to Indy's overtures, even if she was too immature to properly understand them *then*. At the heart of their argument is whether Indy demeaned Marion by treating her like a prop or plaything.

What's more, now that Marion is an adult, Indy is reluctant to accept responsibility or show genuine remorse for leading her into a romantic relationship, when she probably wasn't ready for one, only to break her heart. Marion suggests Indy had a debilitating effect on her journey into adulthood, lamenting, "Do you know what you did to me, to my life?" Annoyed, Indy affirms, "I can only say I'm sorry so many times." Another impasse. At least he says the words, but it's unclear whether he means them. If Indy's actions had the demeaning and debilitating results Marion claims, Indy owes it to Marion to make amends. For Kant, there is no moral offense worse than treating persons as mere things.[6]

Indy doesn't learn his lesson about treating Marion with proper respect very easily. Later in the film, but before Marion's wine-infused encounter with Belloq, Indy discovers Marion bound and gagged in Belloq's tent. Believing her to be dead, he is elated to find her alive. They passionately kiss and he instinctively moves to cut her loose. But he stops: "I hate to do this, but if you don't sit still and keep quiet, this whole thing is going to be shot. I'll be back to get you." Jones, having discovered the true location of the Well of Souls, puts the value of finding the Ark above Marion's life. Here, Indy acts for the greater good of obtaining the Ark and keeping it out of Nazi hands. In this, he treats Marion as a mere means to this end. Kant would object because persons have priceless inherent value. No number of positive consequences, regardless of how great, may take ethical precedence over a person.

Consequentialist approaches to ethics have some intuitive appeal, but Kant was staunchly opposed to them. Desiring positive consequences often gets in the way of doing the right thing. In addition, consequentialism requires us to strive for things beyond our control. We can only be held responsible for those things we can control, which is why Kant requires us to follow the demands of reason as articulated via the categorical imperative, regardless of any positive consequences produced by our actions. As he puts it:

> If despite its greatest striving it should still accomplish nothing, and only the good will were to remain (not, of course, as a mere wish, but as the summoning of all means that are within our control); then, like a jewel, it would still shine by itself, as something that has its full worth in itself. Usefulness or fruitlessness can neither add anything to this worth, nor take anything away from it.[7]

It is always within our power to follow the ethical demands of reason. There is no worthier end.

Kant and the Curious Case of Lying

In *Crusade*, the Nazi co-conspirators—especially Walter Donovan and Elsa Schneider—are duplicitous, and certainly more subtle than Belloq or Major Toht. They fool both Indy and Henry by deceiving the Joneses about their true intentions. Donovan duped Indy's father into becoming the Grail project leader by not divulging his actual motivations for obtaining the Grail or his alliance with the "scum of humanity" (as Henry would say). He duped Indy into searching for Henry under similar pretenses, in addition to not telling Indy that *he* kidnapped Henry. Elsa became romantically involved with Indy to gain his favor and for effective cover about her true intentions regarding the Grail. She deceived Henry, at least initially, via similar methods.

When Elsa finally reveals her true intentions and allegiances to Indy in Castle Grünwald, he is crestfallen. Elsa tells Indy, "Don't look at me like that. We both wanted the Grail, I would have done anything to get it. You would have done the same." Indy demurs, "I'm sorry you think so." Elsa used Indy as a mere tool for her goal of obtaining the Grail, and Indy believes she was wrong in doing so. Kant, of course, sides with Indy. Kant believes that some acts are *inherently* impermissible and cannot be made permissible by associating them with positive consequences. Indy seems to agree. Most of us would side with Indy, and Kant provides the reasoning why. There are some things that you simply ought not do to another person, including deceiving someone into believing that you care for them.

A similar situation occurs in *Raiders*, but the tables are turned. Captain Katanga offers Indy and Marion safe passage on the *Bantu Wind*. The Nazis stop and search the ship. They find the Ark—and Marion—and move to take both back to their submarine. But they want Indy, too. "What about Jones?" shouts Dietrich. In the attempt to protect his two passengers, Katanga grabs Marion and coolly states, "Jones is dead. I killed him. He was of no use to us. This girl, however, has certain value where we're headed. She'll bring a very good price." Katanga lies to Dietrich about Jones's whereabouts and his intentions regarding Marion. His ruse does not prevent Dietrich from kidnapping Marion (again), but we approve of the attempt. Most of us would agree that Kantanga's lie is justified in these dire circumstances, but not Kant.

Kant believes that we have a moral obligation to *always* tell the truth, regardless of the circumstances, including when lying to "the scum of humanity" in the attempt to help someone defeat them.[8] Lying is impermissible because it fails the test of the categorical imperative. On the first version, it is permissible to lie only if you can reasonably accept that everyone be dishonest. But if everyone were to lie, then no one would believe anyone, including you. Because the whole purpose of lying is for you to be believed, you cannot rationally accept that everyone lies. Thus, lying is impermissible. On the second version, when you lie to another person, you use them as a mere prop or tool to achieve whatever purpose you wish the lie to achieve. Kant would add that Katanga's goal, namely aiding Indy's escape from the Nazis, is simply not within his control. The fact that Indy does escape hasn't been guaranteed by Katanga's lie, for things could have gone differently, as they did for Marion. Again, our ethical obligations are kept to those things we can control. Thus, we *never* ought to lie. A moral person is one who acts from respect for the moral law, full stop.

Kant's moral absolutism—that our moral obligations always hold, without exception—is one of the more controversial features of his ethical system. Intuitively, it seems that there are some exceptional circumstances where lying might be permissible. After all, "a little white lie" is often considered acceptable. It suggests that even if lying is typically wrong, it is not always wrong, especially if no harm comes of it. But recall that Kant staunchly opposed the idea that consequences dictate right and wrong.

Shadowy Reflections

Indiana Jones is framed in shadow quite a lot in the first half of the first film. In fact, during the opening scene, we don't see Indy's face for 3 minutes and 15 seconds, when he comes out of the shadows to disarm the traitorous Barranca. Even then, half of his face remains shadowed. The effect creates doubt about his character. Is he a good guy or not?

When Indy visits Marion in Nepal, we see his shadow on the wall, looming over Marion, indicating the large but shady role he played in her life a decade earlier. At the end of the bar scene, when Marion tells him to come back tomorrow if he wants the medallion, most of Indy's face is cast in shadow as he walks out the door. Intriguingly, he pauses in the darkened doorway and intently looks back at Marion. This reinforces the idea that Indy had wronged Marion in the past and did little to redeem himself after their first meeting in 10 years. He knows it, and he remains a shadowy figure to Marion.

Consider also the cantina scene, which strengthens the parallels between Indy and Belloq. Indy believes that Marion has perished in a fiery explosion. As Indy drowns his sorrows in a bottle of whiskey, Belloq's associates bring the two together. When Belloq greets him, the right side of Indy's face is in shadow. Indy mutters, "I ought to kill you right now." As smarmy as ever, Belloq muses, "Not a very private place for a murder." Belloq insists that Indy join him at his table. Indy sits and his face is again framed in shadow in a very close camera shot. Belloq begins pontificating (again): "You and I are very much alike. Archaeology is our religion, yet we have both fallen from the pure faith. Our methods have not differed as much as you pretend. I am a shadowy reflection of you. It would take only a nudge to make you like me. To push you out of the light." Ironically, Indy is the one who is framed in shadows, more so than Belloq. Yes, Belloq is the bad guy, but Indy's moral character is also questionable. That is the whole point of putting Indy in shadows. What's more, Belloq seems correct that Indy might be tempted to stay in the shadows now that Marion is presumed dead.

Recall that the original title of the first film is simply *Raiders of the Lost Ark*. It is not *Indiana Jones and the Raiders of the Lost Ark* (unlike the subsequent films, each of which begins with "Indiana Jones and"). At the start of *Raiders*, Indy is not yet the hero we now know him to be. Indeed, he seems to be one of the interested parties raiding the Ark of the Covenant. A raider is someone who plots to take something that doesn't belong to them through aggressive or hostile means. The Ark belongs to neither Belloq nor Indy. (it obviously doesn't belong to the Nazis.) And just as it was with the Golden Idol, both Belloq (with an assist from the Nazis) and Indy employ aggressive or hostile means to obtain the Ark. Indeed, concerning the Ark, Belloq claims, "Men will kill for it. Men like you and me." Kant provides us with persuasive reasoning why both theft and murder are impermissible. When Indy takes what doesn't belong to him or kills someone, he, too, acts impermissibly.

Cue the John Williams Music

Of course, Indiana Jones is no boy scout (even when he *was* a boy scout in 1912 Utah). That, too, was obvious from the very first viewing of *Raiders*. But it also seems intuitive that he is not on the same level as Belloq (to say nothing of Major Toht). Indy eventually redeems himself at the end of *Raiders* by rescuing Marion. Still, he remains imperfect.

As we now know, he does not fully redeem himself in Marion's eyes until the end of *Crystal Skull*. Further, in *Temple of Doom*, he uses Willie Scott as a prop in order to persuade Lao Che to honor their bargain, and he initially seems more interested in fortune and glory than he does in helping the Mayapore villagers. But in the end, he rescues not only Willie and Short Round but all the Mayapore children who were enslaved by Mola Ram. In *Crusade*, he risks his own life to save his father. He similarly strives to find and rescue his old friend Harold Oxley—and accepts the responsibility of being a father himself—in *Crystal Skull*. In the latter three films, Indy is not framed in shadow.[9] He manages to leave the shadowy aspects of his character behind and does a much better job of living by the Kantian idea that there are some things that a person does not do to others.[10]

Notes

1 Immanuel Kant, *Groundwork of the Metaphysics of Morals*, trans. Mary Gregor (Cambridge, UK: Cambridge University Press, 1998), 9. For an analysis that stresses the ethical importance of consequences, see the chapter by Perez in this volume.
2 Kant, *Groundwork*, 13.
3 Kant, *Groundwork*, 33.
4 Kant, *Groundwork*, 41. Kant seemingly believed that the first and second formulations were logically equivalent—asserting the same thing but in different words. This is controversial.
5 James Luceno, *Indiana Jones: The Ultimate Guide* (New York: DK Books, 2008), 14–15.
6 Indy does better by offering to make Marion his partner, one who will be paid $5,000 for her services, and she consents. This is contrasted with Toht's "offer" to torture her for the information. Kant would approve of Indy and disparage Toht.
7 Kant, *Groundwork*, 10.
8 See Kant's "On a Supposed Right to Lie from Philanthropy," in Mary Gregor trans. and ed., *The Cambridge Edition of the Works of Immanuel Kant: Practical Philosophy* (Cambridge: Cambridge University Press, 1999), 605–616.
9 The one notable exception is *Temple of Doom*, when Indy is framed in shadow as he harms Willie Scott and Short Round. Because he is under the influence of the "black sleep of the Kali Ma" and merely an instrument of Mola Ram's evil intent, this exception only bolsters the use of shadow discussed here.
10 Thanks to Dean Kowalski for helpful comments on earlier versions of this chapter.

5

Feminism and *Indiana Jones*: A Field Guide

Kate C.S. Schmidt

With his charisma, courage, and curiosity, Indy is the protagonist I want to take on my movie adventures. I am far from alone—one 2015 poll found Indiana Jones was the most popular movie character of all time.[1] It's not hard to see why. Indiana Jones is a symbol of bravery, perseverance, and masculinity.

My love for the *Indiana Jones* series might seem to be incompatible with my feminist commitments, though. After all, the movies can be callous, cliché, and sexist. It would be unrealistic, however, to expect the movies to succeed fully on feminist terms. And actually, some strengths of the series come into view when we look through a feminist lens.

"I Cracked a Nail!": Portrayals of Gender

The *Indiana Jones* series is inundated with messages about gender. It's hard to think of a movie franchise that has had a more significant impact on portrayals of masculinity. As the lovable rogue (not a perfect gentleman, but also not a bad boy), Indy represents a distinctive expression of masculinity whose impact still echoes today.[2] The franchise is successful because of the charms of the main character. The adventure feels fun, and the stakes feel real because we (the audience) care about Indy.

Yet aspects of Indiana's masculinity become problematic when they're paired with rigid stereotypes about femininity. The movies sometimes reinforce damaging stereotypes about what it means to belong to a particular gender.

Indiana's masculinity is usually contrasted with his female companion (Marion, Willie, Elsa) in a movie. This contrast often reinforces the

Indiana Jones and Philosophy: Why Did It Have to Be Socrates?, First Edition. Edited by Dean A. Kowalski.

value and significance of masculine traits (relative to feminine traits), which reinforces the sexist view that masculinity is inherently more valuable than femininity. Consider the opening scene of *Temple of Doom*, where Indy uses Willie as a human shield. Her stereotypical reaction is to complain, "He put two holes in my dress from Paris!" While Indy is cleverly calculating a way to get what he wants (payment), Willie is disproportionately emotional and ditzy, often used simply as a prop during the action. She spends a great deal of the movie screaming, while Indiana is focused and in control of his actions. Nothing ruffles Indy. When they find themselves in a plane without a pilot, Indiana says, "How hard can it be?" but Willie, of course, exclaims, "I'm gonna faint."

Sexist portrayals in *Indiana Jones* reinforce stereotypes that women (as a category) are passive, helpless, dumb, and emotional. In contrast, the man is idealized as active, resourceful, intelligent, and logical. Stereotypes reinforce social oppression because one's membership in a social group is linked not only to perceived negative traits but also to social hierarchy; sexist stereotypes reinforce a worldview that says men are more valuable than women.

Movies that send sexist messages work contrary to feminist goals. Movies are anti-feminist if they function in any way that encourages and enforces women's oppression. The goal of feminism is to end women's oppression, and this project is so multifaceted that some writers refer to "feminisms" to highlight the variety of perspectives.[3] While there are many different feminist perspectives, there are two essential shared commitments: (1) women are treated differently than men, and (2) the ways women are treated differently than men constitute a moral wrong.[4] Feminists argue that it's morally necessary to work toward ending gendered oppression. For example, political theorist Iris Marion Young (1949–2006) writes:

> The culture and society in which the female person dwells defines woman as Other, as the inessential correlate to man, as mere object and immanence. Woman is thereby both culturally and socially denied by the subjectivity, autonomy, and creativity which are definitive of being human and which in patriarchal society are accorded the man.[5]

Feminists affirm that women deserve to be represented in society, have value separate from their association with men, and deserve autonomy within their lives.

"I'm Your Goddamn Partner": Gender and Autonomy in Film

Individuals have the right to autonomous control over their lives, regardless of their gender. Thus, stereotypes are harmful when they restrict autonomy and constrain the people who are stereotyped.[6]

If women are seen as helpless and emotional, they will be overlooked and excluded from various social or economic activities. Historically, women were not allowed to study philosophy at universities, because schools were only for educating men. Today, women remain underrepresented in various fields (including philosophy), and gendered expectations partially explain this disparity.[7]

One way to examine feminist themes in movies is to see how gender and autonomy interact on screen. Men are typically portrayed as leading characters making their own choices and guiding the course of their own lives. In the universe of *Raiders of the Lost Ark*, for example, almost everyone (protagonist, villain, sidekick, or background) is a man. Rather than looking at gender expression in a movie, we can look at how women characters function as agents, specifically how they influence (or fail to influence) the plot. For example, the "sexy lamp test" is designed to criticize stories where a woman could be replaced with a sexy lamp without any change to the story.[8] This test highlights stories where women serve as objects rather than agents. Even portrayals of women with positive traits can be oppressive if they perpetuate the idea that women should be passive elements in a story, rather than agents capable of making their own decisions.

Throughout the *Indiana Jones* series, there are instances where female characters are treated as props to advance the storyline of the male protagonist, rather than as characters with their own desires and motivations. Women in the *Indiana Jones* films are treated as uninteresting and insignificant when they primarily serve as background information, or as a set-up for male characters' actions. For example, in *Raiders*, the camera pans slowly across Dr. Jones's class to show a sea of fawning female students. A student in the front row distracts Indy by batting her eyes at him. This young woman, whose eyelids read "love you," isn't treated as a multidimensional character, or even treated as a student—she is only on camera to show that Indiana Jones has sex appeal. Throughout the series, women seem to exist only to fall in love with Indy.

"Why Don't You Give Your Mouth a Rest? Okay, Doll?": Feminism and Flawed Media

Despite these sexist elements, I still love the *Indiana Jones* franchise. At first glance, this seems to be a case of contradicting commitments: affirming feminism means rejecting non-feminist things. Am I contradicting myself in the same kind of way as if I enjoyed a hamburger while also declaring myself vegetarian? Maybe not. My commitment to feminism informs my other core values and commitments: I value equitable treatment of the genders and support things that end women's oppression while opposing things that perpetuate women's oppression. To remain consistent with these values, I devalue media that is sexist. However, enjoying art with sexist elements is not the same as enjoying the sexist elements themselves, and watching a movie doesn't directly contribute to gendered oppression.

I enjoy movies, and I want to avoid being placed in the awful position of having nothing at all to watch. One way to assess the feminist value of a film is the Bechdel Test, designed as a set of minimum requirements for female representation.[9] A film passes the Bechdel Test by meeting three criteria: (1) There are at least two named female characters, (2) that speak to each other, (3) about something other than a man. This test seeks to ensure that a story contains at least two women who are characters capable of speaking about things other than male characters. In *Indiana Jones* there is usually only one woman with a significant speaking part, and all the films in the series fail the Bechdel Test.

The *Indiana Jones* series is far from alone in this failure: half of all best-picture-winning-films fail the Bechdel Test. Feminists claim gendered oppression is pervasive in our society, and so it should not be surprising to find upon closer analysis that many (if not all) movies include some form of sexism in their narratives, character representation, or production.

The Bechdel Test looks at representation in a film, asking whether women are real characters in a story or mere background. Still, representation isn't the only way to measure the feminist commitments of a movie. Movies might be sexist not by excluding women, but by portraying women as mere supporting characters to others, lacking the dimensionality usually given to male characters. Along these lines, the Pierce Test requires that a movie has (1) at least one female character, with (2) an authentic multi-dimensional story, (3) who desires what she pursues, and (4) whom the audience can understand and empathize with. Another way to articulate this requirement for fully realized women characters (via the Landau Test) is that a woman in a film should not exist merely because she "causes a plot problem for a male protagonist." Movies are feminist when they affirm that women have worth (to the plot, to the audience) separate from association with a man.[10]

Regardless of the type of feminist stance taken toward a movie, most films will be mixed cases with some feminist and some anti-feminist components. In *Raiders*, Marion Ravenwood can be considered a feminist character in some ways: she's aggressive (verbally and physically) in ways that conflict with a stereotypical portrayal of women as damsels in distress. She is also resourceful and exercises agency in making her own choices, as when she attacks a henchman with a cast iron skillet. In *Kingdom of the Crystal Skull*, Marion disregards Indy's advice and drives the car/boat (or "duck") over a cliff, ultimately helping the gang of protagonists to escape. However, she also has desires that are difficult to separate from Indiana's and spends most of her time helping him pursue his goals. In *Crystal Skull*, it's difficult to identify whether Marion has any significant goals or desires separate from Indy's, and her role in that movie seems mostly designed to cause plot problems for Indiana to solve as the movie progresses.

Colonel Irina Spalko in *Crystal Skull* is shown in a position of leadership, and she is not defined by her association with any man. However, her character is not fully realized and authentic. She does not have her own story arc. Rather, she spends the whole movie seeking to obtain the skull on behalf of her organization, and in the end she dies. There is no character development for her; the main role of her character is to chase and direct the progress of Indiana Jones through his narrative. When she gives monologues about her goals, she uses the term "we," so the audience is unable to distinguish her own desires from those of the organization she serves (except, perhaps, for her dying words, "I want to know").

The most intriguing example, and strongest female character, is Elsa in *The Last Crusade*. In some ways her character demonstrates feminist values—she's competent and powerful. However, she's also a villain who is conventionally attractive and uses sex appeal as one of her main tools. It's a fairly sexist trope to portray an attractive woman as socially manipulative, using sex for power, and lacking morals. The portrayal reinforces that a woman's value is constituted by her physical characteristics and sexual appeal to men. Elsa reinforces gendered expectations in those ways and contributes to sexist stereotypes. However, there are also feminist elements to her character, namely that she demonstrates autonomy over her own life. Elsa has motivations separable from other main characters, makes her own choices, and dramatically influences the plot. The Mako Mori Test asks if a film (1) has at least one female character, (2) with an independent plot arc, that's (3) not about supporting a man.[11] Elsa and *Crusade* pass this test and pass the aforementioned Pierce Test for authentic female characters. Despite Elsa's strong desire for the Grail, we see her resolve to ally herself with the Nazis (and Donovan) weaken throughout the film. She cries at the book burning in Berlin and very nearly rushes to Henry's side after he is shot. Ultimately, she (purposely) hands Donovan the false grail, killing him. Despite her regrets over the methods of her allies, she never stops pursuing *her* goal. It would be overly simplistic to argue either that she's merely a sexist prop, or that she's a feminist icon—the truth is somewhere in between.

Enjoying Imperfect Media

Art is valuable for many reasons, not solely due to its feminist representations. I enjoy the stories of Indiana Jones for what they are: a mixed bag of sexist and feminist features. I can love the *Indiana Jones* franchise without endorsing sexist stereotypes. It's cringeworthy when Indy refuses to apologize to Marion for his role in a relationship with her when she was underage. Marion argues, "It was wrong and you knew it," only for Indy to brush her off repeatedly, including saying, "I did what I did. You don't have to be happy about it." But that's not the central element of the movie for me. While feminists should be committed to recognizing media that creates and supports gendered oppression, we need not commit to hating all sexist action movies. Film and literature are imperfect, and we can be true fans without being blind to sexist flaws.

Flawed movies can still be valuable for the enjoyment they provide or for the other moral values they represent. Overall *Raiders* is about courage, the pursuit of knowledge, and resistance to fascism against all the odds. Indiana Jones isn't defined by his occasionally sexist actions either—he's a rebel. He can take a punch, endure betrayal, and come up with a plan no matter what situation he faces. What makes him so lovable is his ability to get back up and persevere in the face of any problem. We can love the whole without endorsing all the parts of the series.

Rejecting Toxic Masculinity in Crusade: "He Chose ... Poorly"

The rebellious spirit of *Indiana Jones* is one of the reasons I love the franchise. Indy doesn't conform to societal expectations, he doesn't back down from a fight, and he sticks to his ideals. The most feminist movie of the series is *Crusade*, for its portrayal of masculinity that questions, undermines, and overcomes traditional stereotypes about gender. In fact, *Crusade* contains transgressive and transformative depictions of masculinity, with the movie's emotional heart centered around Indiana and his relationship with his father. His masculinity is transgressive because it resists the narrow confines of classic stereotypes about manhood, in ways that show the audience a broader picture of masculinity. The film celebrates personal relationships and emotional growth above societal or professional success, showing how it is transformative for Indiana to move beyond narrow definitions of male achievement. At the climax of the movie Indy has to let go of a need to succeed no matter the cost. In contrast to Elsa, he has a support network to help him make the right choices. Tellingly, Indy's relationship with his father saves his life.

Toxic masculinity refers to features of stereotypical masculinity that are emotionally stunting, individually limiting, and socially corrosive. For example, portraying men as sexually active and aggressive while women are passive undermines the ability for individuals of any gender to establish healthy sexual relationships. One stereotypical element of toxic masculinity is "boys don't cry," a way to prioritize coldness, while also falsely portraying emotional expression as fragile and feminine. These stereotypes of masculinity appear, but are undermined in *Crusade*. Donovan is violent and aggressive, but these traits result in his downfall when he thinks (falsely) that he can accomplish everything through force rather than through reflection and consultation with others.

Indy is, at times, a violent character, willing to fight and kill to get what he wants. Indeed, his outward aggression includes fistfights and whip wielding. *Crusade*, though, reveals the origin of Indiana's use of a whip—he grasps one in desperation to defend himself from a lion during a chase scene on a train. Indiana's aggression was developed as a form of self-defense, as an adaptation to the environment in which he finds himself. Suggestively, Indiana actually cuts himself the first time he uses the whip, a nod to the ways aggression and violence can hurt those who wield them.

Crusade also comments on gender stereotypes through the actions of its characters. Elsa can successfully seduce and betray Indiana by playing the part of a blonde and innocent love interest. But Indy is genuinely surprised by her use of sex appeal to deceive, showing that he hadn't seriously considered that she would be disingenuous. For Indiana, gendered expressions and stereotypes don't need to define you—individuals should be judged by their beliefs and their actions. Elsa appeals to an ends-justify-the-means argument to defend her deception, saying, "You would have done the same." For her, the emotional fraud (partly through gender expression) is inconsequential compared to her ultimate goal. Indiana disagrees, and replies, "I'm sorry you think so." This scene shows that while gender expression can be used as a social tool, it's not the defining feature of someone's personality. Instead, Indiana judges people based on their beliefs and commitments, including judging Elsa harshly for her association with Nazis.

Following Elsa's betrayal, Indiana doesn't fall back on a posturing sort of masculinity: a different action hero might have hidden his pain and remained emotionless. In the castle, Indy's betrayal happens right in front of Donovan and Henry Jones, Sr. Rather than acting tough in front of his rival and his father, Indiana is focused on Elsa and openly shows he's been hurt. The stereotypical male hero is relentless, aggressive, and successful. Instead, Indiana is vulnerable. To its credit, *Crusade* depicts Indy's emotional sensitivity as tied to his integrity and strength of character, rather than as a weakness. Indiana genuinely liked Elsa and is wounded by her behavior.

Celebrating "Feminine" Values: The Power of Relationships

Crusade is feminist not primarily because of its portrayal of women, but because of its counter-stereotypical portrayal of men. Both Henry and Indiana display stereotypically feminine traits, without the traits being portrayed as weak or embarrassing. Henry is awkward, nerdy, and not good with his hands. While these traits are played for laughs at times, they do nothing to undermine the respect he receives from other characters, and they don't impact his autonomy. In fact, his intelligence and aversion to violence are portrayed as strength of character. Henry Sr. saves the day when he scares a flock of birds into the propeller of a plane shooting at him and Indiana. Savoring the moment, he says: "I suddenly remembered my Charlemagne, 'Let my armies be the rocks and the trees and the birds in the sky.'" Both Indiana and Henry show emotion, which is usually reserved for women in action movies. For example, James Bond keeps a calm and cool exterior no matter who is killed in front of him, and Han Solo faces death without much acknowledgment of his own emotions. More broadly, and importantly, *Crusade* follows the emotional development and reconciliation of Indiana and Henry Sr. as the central conflict of the film.

The most substantial feminist element in *Crusade* is the way the story embraces values central to feminist ethics generally, and care ethics specifically. Care ethics is an approach to morality that argues moral value is best understood by looking at personal relationships and compassionate "care." Contemporary scholar Carol Gilligan articulated this perspective after researching the ways that women and girls spoke about morality, arguing that we must "recognize for both sexes the central importance in adult life of the connection between self and other, the universality of the need for compassion and care."[12] Following Gilligan, feminists also critiqued how some theories overemphasize "masculine" traits such as reasoning through obligations, rather than "feminine" traits such as empathy. If the care ethics approach is right, then moral value and moral obligation are rooted in personal relationships.

In line with care ethics, Indy drops everything he is doing to search for his father and works to keep him safe throughout the movie. His father's disappearance is the instigating event; the search for his father drives much of Indiana's movement. The importance of this goal overrides any of Indiana's other commitments—and it should. Toward the end of *Crusade*, Donovan shoots Henry Jones because he knows it's the only way to motivate Indiana. No matter Indiana's stubborn refusal to help, regardless of the abhorrence of the Nazi agenda, he *will* walk into the unknown for his father's sake.

Throughout *Crystal Skull* as well, Indiana is motivated by family; his actions are often reactions to someone being kidnapped or threatened. However, this feels reductive when the side players lack their own characterizations distinct from Indiana and are used as props to move the plot forward. The relationships in *Crystal Skull* also feel more superficial because they are less likely to trigger emotions in Indiana, who maintains his confident swagger regardless of who is being held at gunpoint. While we are shown a wedding in *Crystal Skull*, we don't get to see Indiana feel romantic and emotional as he does in *Raiders*. In contrast, in *Crusade*, Henry Sr. is a more fully developed character. Both he and Indiana adapt over the course of the film to achieve and maintain their relationship. When Indiana is able to show his emotions, and must sacrifice his own desires for others, the relationship feels more real to the audience.

Importantly in *Crusade*, the value of family is not portrayed as weak or misguided, but instead as the morally valuable choice to make even at the cost of losing one's other desires. At the climax of the movie, Indiana chooses family over greed and success because of his father's urging—"Indiana. Let it go." Henry Sr. uses Indy's chosen name for the first time, and with that act of care Indiana is able to see for himself that he must let go. Indy is called back from the brink, to pursue his next adventure, rather than succumbing to a singular focus on achievement. When Indiana rides into the sunset, he doesn't have the Grail, but he does have a family.

Crusade fully embraces feminist insight about the power and meaning of personal relationships. Both Henry Sr. and Indiana develop as people throughout the film, because of the reconciliation in their relationship. Indiana gains perspective, realizing that his way is not the only way to view the world, while Henry is pulled out of his shell and into action. Feminists argue that personal relationships are an important source of meaning and morality. Dramatically, the relationship between Henry Sr. and Indiana facilitates their ability to fight the Nazis and to make the right decisions in their lives. Ultimately, their relationship improves each of them individually and gives additional meaning to their lives. Through its storytelling, *Crusade* shows the importance of community—that all of us have our own identity because of our interrelatedness with others.

Loving Imperfect Movies, Loving Indiana Jones

Indiana Jones has yet again narrowly escaped the clutches of the Nazis when his plan suddenly goes awry. Indy reassures his father to "relax," but a German henchman has boarded the airship and is scanning the crowd, looking for him. In classic style, Indy dons a disguise to get close, before punching the Nazi and throwing him overboard. Turning to face the gaping crowd whose attention has been drawn to the spectacle, Indiana scoffs: "No Ticket." The passengers are aghast and frantically display their tickets.

That scene makes me laugh every time. I love it. I really do, and that doesn't make me (or you) less of a discerning viewer—or less of a feminist.[13]

Notes

1 Becket Mufson, "Poll: Indiana Jones Is the Most Popular Movie Character Ever," *Vice*, June 24, 2015, at https://www.vice.com/en_us/article/kbngz9/poll-indiana-jones-is-the-most-popular-movie-character-ever.

2 J.D. Reed, "The Sexiest Man Alive '98 ... Harrison Ford," *People Magazine*, November 16, 1998, at https://people.com/archive/cover-story-the-sexiest-man-alive-98-harrison-ford-vol-50-no-18.

3 Unfortunately, there's not enough space in this chapter to look at the representation issues with sexual orientation or race, despite that they're intimately bound up with the goals of feminism.

4 Noëlle McAfee, "Feminist Philosophy," in *The Stanford Encyclopedia of Philosophy* (Fall 2018 edition), ed. Edward N. Zalta, at https://plato.stanford.edu/archives/fall2018/entries/feminist-philosophy.

5 Iris M. Young, "Throwing Like a Girl: A Phenomenology of Feminine Body Comportment Motility and Spatiality," *Human Studies* vol. 3 (1980): 137–156.

6 Iris M. Young, *Justice and the Politics of Difference: Five Faces of Oppression* (Princeton: Princeton University Press, 1990).

7 Sarah-Jane Leslie, Andrei Cimpian, Meredith Meyer, and Edward Freeland, "Expectations of Brilliance Underlie Gender Distributions across Academic Disciplines," *Science* vol. 347 (2015): 262–265.

8 "Kelly Sue DeConnick Talks Captain Marvel, Pretty Deadly, and the Sexy Lamp Test," *IGN*, June 20, 2013, at https://www.ign.com/articles/2013/06/20/kelly-sue-deconnick-talks-captain-marvel-pretty-deadly-and-the-sexy-lamp-test.

9 "100 Women: How Hollywood Fails Women on Screen," BBC, Entertainment and Arts, March 2, 2018, at https://www.bbc.com/news/world-43197774. Alison Bechdel, "The Rule," DTWOF, at https://dykestowatchoutfor.com/the-rule (accessed June 2020).

10 For more on the Pierce and Landau tests, see Terri Waters, "7 Tests (that Aren't the Bechdel Test) that Measure Movies for Gender Equality and Representation," *The Unedit*, at https://www.the-unedit.com/posts/2018/8/20/7-tests-that-arent-the-bechdel-test-that-measure-movies-for-gender-equality-and-representation (accessed June 2020).

11 See Lena Wilson, "*Pacific Rim* Inspired the 'Mako Mori Test'; *Uprising* Gives the Character a Far Less Inspiring Arc," *Slate*, March 23, 2018, at https://slate.com/culture/2018/03/pacific-rim-uprisings-disappointing-treatment-of-mako-mori-spoilers.html.

12 Carol Gilligan, "In a Different Voice: Women's Conceptions of Self and of Morality," *Harvard Educational Review* vol. 47 (1977): 481–517.

13 Special thanks to Elizabeth Shrumm for her thoughts on feminism and assistance with this chapter.

Part II

"… BUT CHOOSE WISELY": EXISTENTIALISM AND AUTHENTICITY

6

The Absurd Hero: Indiana Jones, God, and Sisyphus

Justin Fetterman

In a television episode appropriately titled "The Raiders Minimization," *The Big Bang Theory* laid out a concise criticism of *Raiders of the Lost Ark*: "Indiana Jones plays no role in the outcome of the story. If he weren't in the film, it would turn out exactly the same ... the Nazis would have still found the Ark, taken it to the island, opened it up and all died, just like they did."[1] Indiana Jones is literally tied up while the power of God defeats them. If anything, Indy's actions help the Nazis find the Ark faster: he leads them to the medallion, he locates the Well of Souls, and he goes ahead and unearths the Ark for them. Things might've turned out better if he wasn't involved at all, and they certainly wouldn't have turned out worse (expect, perhaps, for saving Marion from Toht, but that's for another time).

What's the upshot of all Indy's effort? The Ark is deposited in a mysterious government warehouse, all the proof of its existence and power locked away. It's highly likely no one would believe his story, and he has nothing to contribute to the museum. Dr. Henry Jones, Jr. is not much of a "hero" by traditional definitions. However, by viewing his adventures sequentially and alongside the existentialist writings of Søren Kierkegaard (1813–1855) and Albert Camus (1913–1960), we can see Indy as an appropriate hero for an absurd world.

"Archaeology is Our Religion"

In his four big screen adventures, Indiana Jones finds very little success. The only valuable artifact we see him definitively donate to a museum is the Cross of Coronado, early in *The Last Crusade*. Yes, the ending of *Temple of Doom* is successful, as Indy returns the children and one

Indiana Jones and Philosophy: Why Did It Have to Be Socrates?, First Edition. Edited by Dean A. Kowalski.

Sankara Stone to the village—but even then he has lost two other stones in the river and completely overlooked the last two nearby in the wall of the mine.[2] Additionally, the Shanghai exchange at the beginning of *Temple* falls apart extravagantly; Jones loses the Golden Idol at the beginning of *Raiders;* the Ark never makes it near a museum; the Holy Grail disappears down a bottomless chasm in *Crusade;* and all evidence of the extraterrestrials in *Kingdom of the Crystal Skull* ends up either in a different dimension or at the bottom of a massive new lake. Indiana Jones's legacy as a discoverer of important relics is almost nonexistent.

Indy *has* sold some recovered materials to the museum, even sometimes "good pieces" (as Marcus Brody confirms in *Raiders*), and earned a teaching post in archaeology. His knowledge is enough that Brody and the US Army turn to him for assistance. But while Indy dreams of pursuing a massive find like the Ark, Brody has to convince the army intelligence officers to let Jones "go after it." They were only coming to him for information, not to do fieldwork. And why should they? Nothing in his history suggests that Indy is the one to uncover a world altering artifact. Even Brody doesn't seem terribly confident in Indy's abilities, politely demurring when Jones claims he can retrieve the Golden Idol that Belloq walked away with in the prologue.

In *Raiders* alone, Jones suffers myriad failures: Satipo dies; Belloq takes the Golden Idol; Jones is captured at the dig site; he escapes to unearth the Ark but Belloq takes it and leaves Jones to die; then he escapes *that* but the boat he leaves on is intercepted by the Nazis! Indy tries to be heroic on the way to the island, but can't bring himself to destroy the Ark, so is tied up with Marion, completely helpless to stop the ritual. The Nazis are ultimately killed by, as Jones describes it, "the power of God, or something" when the Ark is opened—remember which would have happened whether Jones was involved or not—and then the Ark is hauled off to the government warehouse instead of a museum.

Yet Indy persists, pursuing each step with the same zeal. This constant seeking with no fulfillment is an absurd situation, seemingly untenable. Jones is experiencing despair, a persistent existential crisis Søren Kierkegaard detailed in *The Sickness Unto Death*. Despair is a nearly universal sickness, but one of the spirit rather than of body or mind. The affliction comes from living an existence that is out of sync with, or unaccepting of, one's true self. Though not directly tied to fate or purpose, Kierkegaard treats the self as an innate element of all individuals, created and maintained by a greater Power.

Jones suffers specifically from the despair of possibility due to a lack of necessity—he can imagine all the things that may arise from his adventures, but is actually unable to effect those ends, creating a disconnect in his understanding of himself. Repetitive failure counterintuitively strengthens this disconnect. As Kierkegaard explains, "Possibility then appears to the self ever greater and greater, more and more things become possible, because nothing becomes actual."[3] Each time Indiana fails, it does not convince him that he should give up, but rather that his success is always just around the corner. Like a gambler with a 1-in-100 chance, Indy is willing to try 100 times because each failure must be bringing him closer to that singular triumph.

Over time, Jones begins to believe he is a great archaeologist, but this image exists only within his mind. In this way, he pulls away from the real world, losing other necessary and fulfilling elements of life, like his relationship with Marion. The disconnect he experiences within himself has external consequences, as his self-understanding conflicts with how the wider world sees and treats him.

Kierkegaard, however, has an answer for Indiana Jones and for all those in despair: faith, which is a person's relationship to the divine. In order to reconcile the disconnects within one's self-understanding and relationship with the world at large, Kierkegaard says that a person must place himself or herself before the singular Christian God. Since God is the creator of the self, it is God alone who can reveal its truth and repair one's relationship with it. If Indiana Jones can accept and practice faith in God, he can gain true understanding of his self, eventually overcoming his despair.

"You Will, Dr. Jones, Become a True Believer"

If anyone has good reason to have faith, it would be Indiana Jones. In explaining that Jones is superfluous to the ending of *Raiders*, it's easy to breeze past the amazing revelation of the climax: the Nazis are killed *by the power of God* via angels of death. Up until that ending, Jones deals with clues, booby-traps, and an astounding laser-beam lighting trick in locating the Well of Souls, but nothing sets up the revelation that real mystical powers are stored within the Ark, presumably by God, Himself. Indy is driven by an archaeologist's imperative to uncover, understand, and share knowledge of history. At no point is he out to prove the existence of God, but that might be exactly what he does (though only he and Marion survive with direct experiential proof).

Temple explains why Indiana Jones isn't completely overwhelmed by the mystical power of the Ark. The disappearance of one sacred Sankara Stone from the village of Mayapore spurs the main adventure in *Temple*. While investigating, Indy witnesses the actions of the Thuggee cult and their mystical powers: Mola Ram removes the still-beating heart from a still-living man and the Maharaja controls Jones with a voodoo doll. At the climax, Indy invokes the name of Shiva against Mola Ram, causing the Sankara Stones to become burning hot; two fall from Jones's bag into the river below while the third burns Mola Ram's hand enough that he loses his grip and plummets to his death. In the events of *Temple*, occurring prior to the events of *Raiders*, Indiana witnesses and even utilizes magical powers. By the time angels, lightning, and fire are flying out of the Ark, he's learned to expect the unexpected and be prepared for the dangers of the supernatural, aware enough to shut his eyes (and warn Marion) so the Ark's powers don't kill him, too.

It's important that the mysticism in *Temple* has absolutely nothing to do with Christianity. The Thuggees worship Kali, and Jones activates the stones by invoking Shiva—both of whom are Hindu deities. While Kierkegaard had plenty of complaints about the way Christianity was practiced and preached in his day, his philosophy permits only a single God before whom each person must stand revealed. But in *Temple*, Jones witnesses the power of two gods, and neither of them the Christian God or even an Abrahamic God.

When at last Indiana witnesses the power of the Ark (or at least its direct aftermath upon reopening his eyes), it is not *an* example of *the* God's power, it is merely *another* example of *some* god's power. Jones later quips (in *Crystal Skull*) that "it depends on who your god is." Even the healing power of the Holy Grail, in *Crusade*, doesn't offer clarification: the Ark signifies God's covenant with the Jewish people, while the Grail attests to His promise through Jesus Christ, whom the Jewish faith does not recognize as God. The sum of Jones's experiences suggests that any of the deities may be valid; what matters is the actions of a god and their followers as witnessed in life on earth. In *Raiders*, Indy warns his students that folklore is an impediment to archaeology, the beliefs and practices getting in the way of the work. Doctor Henry "Indiana" Jones, Jr. is a man of science. For him, the facts of the Ark must be added to the facts of the Thuggees and the Sankara Stones, information about the supernatural but not necessarily information in support of faith.

Indeed, in Kierkegaard's philosophy, no information can or should be used to rationally support faith. Though he never used the phrase directly, the popular Kierkegaardian concept of a *leap of faith* is appropriate. He did say that "the whole of Christianity hinges upon this, that it must be believed, not comprehended [and] I regard it then as a plain duty to admit that one neither can nor shall comprehend it."[4] The relationship formed with God by faith is not one of understanding, because God is unknowable, forever distant from humanity as the great creator who exists before and above his creation. The human being stands before God in need of revelation: through faith God will reveal truth of the self to the believer. There is no accrual of knowledge to gain comprehension, only a persistence of faith returned as revelation.

"Archaeology is the search for fact ... not truth," as Jones explains to his students in *Crusade*. An archaeologist painstakingly pieces together a web of details to discern what is most likely the case. Indiana Jones diligently ponders clues, follows leads, and draws conclusions. The singular event of the Ark's opening, which could be interpreted as a moment of revelation, is not enough to suddenly throw Jones into faith, not after his previous mystical encounters. The supernatural effects of the Sankara Stones and the Ark of the Covenant both exist outside of Jones's scientific, historical concept of the world. His success in *Temple* did demonstrate necessity—he plays an important role in the successful outcome of the story—but Indy remains in an existential crisis because he cannot square his concept of himself and his understanding of the universe with his direct experiences. Rather than Kierkegaard's despair, Jones now finds himself confronting absurdity, as Albert Camus calls it.

"You Lost Today, Kid. That Doesn't Mean You Have to Like It"

At the beginning of *Crusade*, the young Indiana Jones has retrieved a valuable artifact, later revealed as the Cross of Coronado, from grave robbers. He flees at first on foot, but soon comes to a small ledge and whistles for his horse, who dutifully takes up position awaiting its rider. As Indy jumps down, the horse steps forward and leaves Indiana crashing into the dirt. Rather than a leap of faith, he has taken a tumble to absurdity.

Why should the horse move at that exact moment? It came as called and stood exactly where it was needed, free from danger. Presumably, the two had done such a maneuver previously; Indiana seemed confident it would work. But such is the way of the world, exactly as the absurd man sees, experiences, and understands it.

For Kierkegaard, despair is humankind's problem: not understanding or accepting the self, and not having proper faith in God to receive the revelation of truth. Kierkegaard would see Indiana Jones as a person with potential (with much he *wants* to achieve) but no necessity (with little he *actually* achieves). Indy has an internal issue, a problem with the way he sees and relates to himself and to God. The proper path is one of subservience before God. Henry Sr. attempts to impart this lesson by admonishing his son that the Grail's true purpose transcends archaeology (and slapping him for blaspheming). Thus, Indy's desires and goals must be secondary to larger forces (even if Indy never quite submits). The kind of faith championed by Kierkegaard operates similarly, with God as the supreme force lording over life and purpose.

Existential absurdity, the kind Camus writes about, depicts a universe that appears to be understandable—filled with natural laws and patterns—but which repeatedly proves unpredictable and indifferent. Human actions are absurd because of the disconnect between their intentions and the reality encountered in the world. Indiana Jones wants to understand how the universe functions, and to operate within those bounds to achieve his personal ends. But too often he tumbles as he did when trying to get on his horse. Indy, for instance, is able to retrieve the Cross of Coronado only by undertaking a fraught smuggling mission that destroys a ship and the many lives onboard it. Indy's belief that artifacts "belong in a museum" is a moral stance based on dedication to knowledge rather than religious faith, and he is willing to do whatever it takes to further that goal—in spite of a universe that cares not a whit for right, wrong, or good intentions.

Camus's most well-known image of the absurd person is Sisyphus, a Greek king whose afterlife punishment was to repeatedly roll a boulder up a hill, only to have it always rolls back down to the bottom to be done again. His torment is effort without reward, inexhaustible repetition, continual trying without hope of success. Indiana Jones can relate. *Crusade* is a clear example of recurrence in Indy's life. As in *Raiders*, Indy is tasked with chasing a Judeo-Christian artifact in a race against the Nazis. Once again, Marcus Brody is involved and Sallah is called upon to help. Jones leads the Nazis to the artifact, which they wouldn't have located without him, and ultimately the power of the artifact destroys the enemies while Jones helps save his companions. Indy is arguably as superfluous here as he is in *Raiders* (except, perhaps, for saving his father's life as he did Marion's). His efforts are again more in assistance to the Nazis than against them, and the holy relic is again lost, although even more permanently this time.

Crusade and *Raiders* result in disappointments. As an archaeologist, Indy has largely failed, but he should be used to that by now. And in that "getting used to it," Indy becomes an absurd hero. Throughout his many adventures, Jones has become conscious of the absurd world he inhabits. Like Sisyphus, he continues in the same repetitive effort despite no obvious payoff. Camus imagines Sisyphus with a strong inner life, seizing on that brief moment when the dead king stands at the top of his hill, watching the boulder roll back down to its starting place. For that instant, Sisyphus stands literally and figuratively above his task, able to survey his world and his absurd situation holistically enough to seize a fleeting feeling of happiness. Indeed, Camus says, "The struggle itself toward the heights is enough to fill man's heart. One must imagine Sisyphus happy."[5]

Indy's rejection of Kierkegaard's *leap to faith* is based in his training as a historian and social scientist. While he cannot reason through the powers of the Ark, the Sankara Stones, and the Holy Grail, neither can he reconcile them with a singular God. There is, however, little proof that Jones has ever sought such explanations. The brief glimpses of his classroom show a teacher interested in the methods and records of archaeology but not one concerned with the conclusions offered by those findings. He repeatedly presents the details of what others believe—the legends of the Sankara Stones, the biblical record of the Ark—but what does he believe beyond the importance of placing artifacts in museums to be studied?

Indy values experience. In *Crystal Skull*, he advises one diligently bookish student that "if you want to be a good archaeologist, you've got to get out of the library." This recontextualizes Dr. Jones's seemingly dry classroom lectures on site excavation and his rather destructive enthusiasm for following clues to the Holy Grail's location. Artifacts belong in a museum, but an archaeologist belongs in the field, foregrounding direct experiences of the world as the path to knowledge. Indy understands that "there is but one world." It may be confounding, frustrating, and repetitive, but it is the only world he has and he will strive to stand at the top of his hill and survey it.

"Why You Gotta Do Everything the Hard Way, Jonesy?"

Irina Spalko, the Russian antagonist in *Crystal Skull*, has the incorrect picture of Jones-as-scientist. "You've spent your entire life searching for answers," she says, thinking she can entice him by offering a path to those answers. But she is only projecting her own search for "power over the mind of man." At the climax, face-to-face with interdimensional beings with unfathomable knowledge, she repeats "I want to know." Ultimately, the information is beyond her comprehension and overwhelms her mind and body, disintegrating all but her boots. If only she, like Indy, had wanted to know less.

"Sin is not so much knowing as wanting to know," says Camus, and "for the absurd man it is not a matter of explaining and solving, but of experiencing and describing."[6] Too often, striving for understanding takes one away from the immediate experience of the world. Popular images depict a professor standing before students in the lecture hall or holed up in study and contemplation. Ironically, such professors want so badly to understand the world, that they have withdrawn from it. For her part, Spalko ventures out in pursuit of a shortcut to understanding, hoping to gaze into the eyes of the crystal skulls and thus unlock all her mental faculties. But Indiana Jones is not a professor content to examine and lecture, nor is he one to seek the easy road to understanding.

What he wants, most of all, is to be out in the field, experiencing life firsthand in all its absurdity. Indy's life is one of action, of doing. He has causes, mainly protecting those close to him, but he doesn't have an ironclad moral code. He certainly hates Nazis, but many of his actions actually *help* them, right up to the point that an external factor intercedes. Jones shows essentially zero caution in his dealing with Nazis, going so far as to sleep with Elsa (in *Crusade*) before doing any research into her past or character. Elsa is smart, beautiful, interested in his archaeological knowledge, and attracted to him sexually, so why should he think any further? That she turns out to be Nazi is disappointing, but does not negate the experience. Neither does he think twice about entering into relationships with Marion (despite her youth and connection to Indiana's mentor) or Willie (despite the distracting direness of their situation). Like the repetition of his archaeological exploits, Indiana experiences repetition in romance.

Kierkegaard surmised that repetitive failure heightened the disconnect of despair in a negative manner. By contrast, Camus sees value in repetition, especially as a way to heighten engagement with absurdity. Sisyphus experiences an eternity of repetition: push boulder up hill, watch boulder roll back down hill, walk down to begin again. This is a torment, certainly, but to be aware of the repetition, of the futility, to accept the disconnect between your desires and your reality, and to keep trying anyway is the victory of the absurd man. Camus sees Kierkegaard's leap of faith as a form of giving up, a choice not of accepting ourselves and God, but of denying our immediate experience and saying we cannot trust our senses and our own thoughts. The absurd hero is strong enough to look at the disconnects of the universe, to experience the repetitive torments it puts upon him, and to still continue on, refusing to be defeated or defined by the external.

So Indiana Jones persists, a modern Sisyphus armed with whip and fedora (and sometimes a pistol, being the cautious fellow he is). At every opportunity, he is willing to undertake dangerous missions to save valuable artifacts from enemy hands or passionately embrace the alluring woman before him, even though each adventure and relationship will almost certainly fail.

Camus concludes that "what counts is not the best living but the most living ... The present and the succession of presents before a constantly conscious soul is the ideal of the absurd man."[7] For Camus the best life is not a matter of virtue or pleasure. Rather, the ideal for the absurd man is *the most living*. This means being conscious of the world, recognizing in each moment that the universe is absurd, and continuing to live regardless of this situation. An absurd hero must, like Sisyphus, continue to act and observe in each and every moment, fully conscious of the ridiculousness and futility of their existence.

Indy lives a most absurd existence. The series of events is almost endless. For example, his signature whip is gained when he falls into the lion's trailer of a circus train while being pursued by grave robbers. In Shanghai, after supposedly watching a surreal dance performance that involves a troupe of blondes performing in a room that cannot be witnessed by anyone in the audience, he gets in a fight where he kills a man by throwing a skewer of flaming kebab meat though his chest before escaping behind a rolling gong. He survives a nuclear bomb test by hiding in a lead-lined refrigerator. Though agitated in the moment, Jones ultimately takes each event in his stride, accepting the evidence of his experience without searching for anything except the next event. He never even seems to comment upon or refer back to these singularly extraordinary events. These things simply happen to him. In true Sisyphean fashion, Indy spends his whole existence ready for the next challenge, even when that challenge is essentially the same as before. The only promise is that each adventure will expose more absurdity.

"Your Persistence Surprises Even Me!"

The stories of Indiana Jones are called adventures for a reason. They are invitations to unique, exciting experiences that reaffirm life, outcomes be damned. It may be tempting to wonder why *Crystal Skull* was necessary, why Indy would go on that or any other expeditions so many years removed from his original grand adventures. But Jones would not ask why. Camus explains, "When [he] glances backward over his life," the absurd hero, "contemplates that series of unrelated actions which become his fate, created by him, combined under his memory's eye and soon sealed by his death."[8] Whether the next adventure is grand or glorious or futile or preposterous, it does not matter. Indy will almost certainly fail at each quest, and he must succumb to death in the end.

Jones is not a mythic hero, but an all too human hero—a hero worthy of admiration. He almost never succeeds in the missions he sets out upon, and he is nearly sure to make the situation worse before it gets better, and even then it only gets better because of "the power of God, or something." Indy suffers the despair that all people suffer, and he wrestles with faith as nearly all people do. In light of his religious father and contact with the supernatural, it may have been the easy path to submit to some vision of God and hope that revelation could save him.

In the end, though, Indy comes to perceive the world as few do. He becomes conscious of the absurdity and repetition in his life and in the world at large. He not only accepts but embraces this condition and rises to meet it. Because he grasps absurdity and has the strength to confront it, Indiana Jones is a shining example of how Camus would have us all live: facing and acknowledging the absurdity of our world, seizing each opportunity no matter how repetitive or insurmountable, and always seeking the moments where we can stand against the absurdity to proclaim ourselves fully alive.

Notes

1 Season 7, episode 4; CBS, October 10, 2013.
2 James Luceno, *Indiana Jones: The Ultimate Guide* (London: Dorling Kindersley, 2008).
3 Søren Kierkegaard, *Fear and Trembling and the Sickness unto Death*, trans. Walter Lowrie (Princeton: Princeton University Press, 1941), "The Despair of Possibility is Due to the Lack Of Necessity," 36.
4 Kiekegaard, *Sickness*, "Sin Is Not a Negation but a Position," 113.
5 Albert Camus, *The Myth of Sisyphus and Other Essays*, trans. Justin O'Brien (New York: Vintage Books, 1955), "The Myth of Sisyphus," 78.
6 Camus, *Sisyphus*, "Philosophical Suicide," 33 and "Philosophy and Fiction," 61.
7 Camus, *Sisyphus*, "Absurd Freedom," 42.
8 Camus, *Sisyphus*, "The Myth of Sisyphus," 78.

7

Indiana Jones and Existential Self-Affirmation

Daniel Tilsley

What is Indiana Jones looking for? Of course, we recall his quests for Ark of the Covenant and the Holy Grail and his self-proclaimed pursuit of "fortune and glory." Sometimes he searches for people he cares for, including his father and Harold Oxley. But he is also searching for something more personal—and philosophical: *himself*.

Indiana Jones and the Last Crusade shows us Indy's attempt at finding his father coinciding with their quest for the Holy Grail. Philosophically speaking, though, the film is also about *existential* discovery in answer to the question "Who am I?" For Indy, the real treasure of *Crusade*—and indeed of the whole saga—is his becoming "Indiana Jones." And as we'll see, the sort of existential self-affirmation Indy represents is a treasure that each of us can create.

Existentialists Say Yes to Life

Existentialism is a humanistic philosophy that is grounded in individual experiences of existence in the world. Focusing on anxieties about finitude and negation, existentialists explore how individual meaning and purpose can be constructed. The sense of self—the *who* of who one is—is the product of the individual's own creative authorship. Self-affirmation, in the existentialist sense, is the act of recognizing and celebrating oneself as something that is the product of one's own creation. To paraphrase the existentialist philosopher Paul Tillich (1886–1965), one crafts an individual sense of who one is by participating in the creative meanings that give one's life purpose.[1]

For Friedrich Nietzsche (1844–1900), self-affirmation manifests by saying "yes" to life—being willing to live it repeatedly in the "Eternal Recurrence."[2] This is a thought experiment where one is destined to

Indiana Jones and Philosophy: Why Did It Have to Be Socrates?, First Edition. Edited by Dean A. Kowalski.

repeat life in exactly the same way for all eternity. Persons who authentically love life and recognize the value of their experiences would actively agree to the Eternal Recurrence. There is no greater form of self-affirmation than to gladly will recurrence; according to Nietzsche, it is the supreme evocation of *amor fati*, which means "love of fate."[3]

Self-affirmation, for Nietzsche, obtains when one learns to love fate and becomes a "Yes-sayer" to life.[4] Fate is that which is done to us, but one is ultimately free to engage with fate and create oneself. Our hero's fate as "Indiana Jones" was determined by the formative experiences of his youth. For example, his path to becoming "Indiana Jones," in part, included the ways in which he related to both his father and the Cross of Coronado.

Becoming Indiana Jones

We readily recognize Indiana Jones's defining characteristics—for example, attachment to his hat and whip, being a swashbuckling treasure hunter, and displaying a nervous disposition around snakes. These elements are established through visual information within the first act of *Raiders of the Lost Ark*. However, more so than the other four films, *Crusade* addresses *who* Indiana Jones is and why he has become the heroic whip-cracking archaeologist who kicks ass and catalogues antiquities. *Crusade* offers a thorough uncovering—or archaeological excavation—of Indy's identity. In doing so, the film captures something more fundamental about the condition of human existence: One is who she becomes because of the way in which she relates to her own fate.

It is cinematic commonplace that the third film in a trilogy returns to the beginning, bringing the narrative full circle and returning our hero, now changed, home. True to form, *Crusade* begins in Utah, which in 1912 is where Indy and his father call home. The opening sequence follows a teenaged Indy as he attempts to recover the Cross of Coronado from a band of treasure hunters. We see Indy's philanthropic attitude toward artifacts emerge ("It belongs in a museum!"). Personality traits such as his fear of snakes and his skills with a bullwhip are also explained. We thereby see the character we know as "Indiana Jones" emerge before our very eyes.

Crusade's opening sequence also includes Indy donning a fedora for the first time—given to him by the treasure hunter simply called Fedora—as a reward for his brave but ultimately unsuccessful venture for the Cross. Fedora intends the hat as a consolation prize, saying,

"You lost today, kid. But that doesn't mean you have to like it." Indy could have rolled over and accepted defeat, being content with his new hat. Instead, and perhaps inspired by Fedora, he actively pursues the possibilities of a treasure hunter in an attempt to defy and overcome his defeat. Thus, the fedora embodies defeat—a reminder of Indy's fate—but it also signifies possibility in the existential sense of creating one's future, given one's past.

Indy's fedora thereby becomes a significant part of who he is. It represents the man that Indy has chosen to be. Why else would he risk his life to reach back for the fedora—repeatedly—from closing doors, collapsing ruins, and giant man-eating ants? The hat gives meaning to Indy's existence; his recurring choice to secure it is an act of existential self-affirmation as well as a commitment to his possibilities. And recall Indy similarly snatches away his hat from his son Mutt at the end of *Kingdom of the Crystal Skull.* Although no longer a young man, Indy is not yet ready to pass it along to Mutt as Fedora did to him. The fedora suits and stands for the heroic adventurer figure that Indy embodies. Thus, the 1912 sequence with Fedora uncovers Indiana's fate-as-history that facilitated the creation of the (married) man that he has become and his ongoing willingness to engage the corresponding existential possibilities of his future.

The Cross and Grail of Affirmation

The Cross of Coronado also represents existential importance for who Indy is, his chosen way of being and his becoming "Indiana Jones." Adult Indy eventually finds the Cross again in 1938, stealing it from a private collector (Panama Hat, the man who contracted with Fedora in 1912) on the ship fittingly dubbed the *Coronado*. It's significant that Indy's quest to recover it spans 26 years and continues well into his adulthood. Upon bestowing the Cross to Marcus Brody so that it takes a place of honor in Marshall College's Spanish collection, Indy (rhetorically) asks, "Do you know how long I've been looking for that?" To which Marcus (mindlessly) replies, "All your life." Indy wistfully reaffirms: "All my life."

Seeking and securing the Cross is an act of self-affirmation—an affirmation of "Indiana Jones." Recovering the Cross is, for Indy, a moment in which his chosen life-narrative has come full circle. That particular life-project, which first motivated the emergence of the man he was to become and the life he was to lead, has been completed. The recovery of the Cross brings a sense of authentic wholeness to Indy's life. It manifests his commitment to the life of treasure hunting—an actualization of the life-possibility that he has chosen to pursue. With that project completed, he embarks on a new one, finding his father as he seeks the Holy Grail.

Recall that when they find the Cross in Utah, the band of treasure hunters (grave robbers?) gleefully shout "We're rich!" For them, artifacts have a financial or material value as opposed to personal or existential value. This applies to the antagonists of the franchise generally. Belloq desires financial gain from the antiquities he finds and is willing to sell his services to the Nazis (even if his motivations regarding the Ark may be mixed). Mola Ram seeks the Sankara Stones for world domination (and pockets the gems the slave children unearth along the way). Donovan pursues the Holy Grail merely to extend his comfortable and affluent life. Irina Spalko seeks the Crystal Skull to subdue the Soviet Union's enemies and gain ultimate knowledge about the universe for herself. To say nothing of the double-crossing Mac, who is in it only for the gold (and loses his life as a result).

The antagonists of the *Indiana Jones* films invariably seek some external thing in the desperate hope of making their incomplete lives more satisfactory. Such pursuits are hollow at best. The antiquities they seek are merely instrumental to their desire for power or wealth. Again, according to Nietzsche, the person who lacks the ability to affirm his life on its own terms is unhappy or dissatisfied with such a life as it is.[5] Belloq, Mola Ram, Donovan, and Spalko all perceive their lives to be deficient in something—lack of wealth, power, time to live, or knowledge—which accounts for the particular brutality and desperation in their searches.[6] They crave the magical powers that these artifacts possess because they are ultimately dissatisfied with their individual lives. It is no wonder, then, that the artifacts they seek are always the means to their undoing.

Consider that Donovan seeks the Holy Grail in the hope of living forever. The Grail itself is merely instrumental to this goal. Of the cup itself, he cares little. Recall he entrusts Elsa to provide him with the correct cup among the many. He unwisely accepts her choice, saying, "Oh, yes. It's more beautiful than I'd ever imagined. This certainly is the cup of the King of Kings." This comment reveals Donovan's genuine lack of connection to the artifacts he collects. For him, Christ's divinity means that the famed cup would be a beautiful chalice, despite Christ's historical occupation as a humble carpenter. For Donovan, artifacts are purely materially pleasing objects that demonstrate and ensure his financial and cultural wealth.

This is not Donovan's only misstep. The Grail Knight reveals that the Grail cannot cross the Seal marking the temple's entrance. Remaining within the temple boundaries is the price of immortality. Donovan's possibilities would be bounded by the physical limits of the temple—thereby restricting what he could do with his eternal life. Donovan would undoubtedly rail against immortality if lived under this restriction. Although he tells Indy he "wants the Grail itself" he goes on to make his true intentions clear: "Hitler can have the world, but he can't take it with him. I'm going to be drinking my own health after [Hitler's] gone the way of the dodo." Living in the temple would forever bar Donovan from the sort of life he seeks. So, Donovan "chose poorly" not once, but twice.

By contrast, the Grail Knight accepts the honor of protecting the Grail, even though this means living out the rest of his unnaturally long life in the temple. He accepts his fate and makes this unending task his own project. It becomes the purpose of his life, which he affirms in perpetuity. The Grail Knight thereby represents an approach advocated in Albert Camus's (1913–1960) "Myth of Sisyphus."[7] Sisyphus is a mythological character who is cursed by the gods to push a large boulder up a hill, only to have it roll back down—endlessly. Sisyphus's task seems absurd and his life meaningless. But Sisyphus embraced his task and infused it with meaning. In turn, his task became the very thing that made his life meaningful. The Grail Knight similarly displays an authentic commitment to his life-project.

Indy invariably affirms his fate through authentically living it, which seems much closer to the Grail Knight than to Donovan. Indy does not seek artifacts for their supposed power. He seeks them (almost always) simply for the sake of becoming who he is—in affirmation of the life he chooses to lead on its own terms. Much as Sisyphus comes to see his task as a source of meaningfulness, so too Indy finds meaning in his search for artifacts. The Cross of Coronado is a prime example of how Indy's adventures are more existential than anything else. By pursuing such artifacts, Indy finds *himself*. Indy learns more about himself by living his life, and as a result of accepting that life, he shapes his character. This is self-affirmation. It comes from within, and not artificially or inauthentically from something external.

Indy affirms his chosen way of being by perpetuating it. Indeed, by continually choosing his life on its own terms, he comes to revel in it, even if he is not always immediately aware of this. Recall his impassioned lecture to the government men about the Staff of Ra. The government men were dumbfounded, but Brody just beamed. The look on Indy's face at 9:00 a.m. in the Tanis map room exuded reverence and awe (and, from the audience's perspective, perhaps more loudly than John Williams's orchestra). When finding the Sankara Stones, his eyes glowed brighter than the stones themselves. Furthermore, Indy's treasure-hunting adventures always relate back to the adventures of his youth, repeating the spirit of those events. By continuing to choose such adventures, Indy is indulging in his own legend and essentially saying "yes" to that youthful decision to pursue the Cross. His choices affirm his character as it propels him forward. Ultimately, Indy exemplifies the Nietzschean doctrine of loving one's own fate (*amor fati*), and his recurrent adventures evoke the Nietzschean Eternal Recurrence: He willingly repeats again and again the life that made him who he is—Indiana Jones.

The Illumination of Fathers and Sons

Of course, our hero's given name is not Indiana Jones. It is Henry Jones Jr., and Henry Sr. invariably refers to him simply as "Junior"—often derisively. As Henry (sourly) informs Sallah, "We named the dog 'Indiana.'" Although Indy has a lot of fond memories of that dog, it is difficult for Henry to see his son as anything other than "Junior." This is symbolic of Henry not recognizing Indy for who he has chosen to be, and it reflects Henry's desire to make another version of himself. Indeed, when Indy rushes to tell Henry about the Cross of Coronado in 1912, Henry tells him to wait and then to count in Greek. Henry is not interested in his young son; he is more interested in deciphering the Holy Grail legends. No wonder Indy chose the nickname "Indiana" from his dog and his fond memories of his faithful canine companion. This is another act of choosing who *he* wants to be. Taking the name "Indiana" is an act toward self-affirmation. He thereby affirms the man who *he* chooses to be—and *not* the man his father wishes him to be.

Yet *Crusade* is as much Henry's journey of self-affirmation and illumination as it is Indy's. As his son is attached to the Cross of Coronado, so Henry Jones Sr. is attached to the Holy Grail. He has devoted himself to the artifact, and finding the Grail is the completion of one of his life-projects. Furthermore, like Indy, Henry finds more than the Grail during his quest; he finds what he calls "illumination."

Theologically speaking, illumination refers to becoming aware of the need for divine guidance. Christ is often framed as the "guiding light" in both biblical and artistic depictions, and, in religious experiences, one often describes "seeing the light."[8] Henry alludes to this kind of illumination, saying (as he returns to his Grail diary and lets his teenage son fend for himself with the sheriff), "May he who illuminated this, illuminate me." Seeking the Grail, as Henry has most of his adult, professional life, is often referred to as a "crusade"—a holy mission. The quest for the Cup of Christ is thought to be an illuminating experience, but Henry's quest in *Crusade* seems to evoke illumination of an *existential* kind. For Henry, the Grail quest illuminates the man that his son has become, prompting his reconfiguration of his role as a father.

Henry's inability to recognize Indiana provoked their father–son estrangement in the first place. Henry was more focused upon his Grail diary than anything else (and, indeed, cared only about his medieval history research generally). Indy rebukes Henry about their life together, as he claims, "What you taught me was that I was less important to you than people who had been dead for 500 years in another country. And I learned it so well that we've hardly spoken for 20 years." Yet when Indy and Colonel Vogel plummet over a cliff at the climax of the tank chase, Henry comes to regret the lack of attention he has shown to his son, murmuring, "Oh, God. I've lost him. And I never told him anything. I just wasn't ready ... Five minutes would have been enough." Clearly, Henry wishes their life together would have been different.

Henry's changing attitude toward his son takes a drastic turn during *Crusade*'s climactic sequence. When Elsa reaches over the precipice to secure the Grail, Indy grabs her hand. He pleads with her to give up the Grail and grab his other hand. She refuses and falls into the abyss, almost taking Indy with her. Indy then (inexplicably) attempts to succeed where she failed. Henry, in turn, keeps Indy from falling into the abyss by holding his hand. Despite Henry's life-long pursuit of the Grail, he tells Indy to "let it go." The quest for the Grail has fostered a new sense of meaning for their relationship, in which Henry comes to rediscover—or, in fact, discover—who his son is. His pleas for "Junior" to "let it go" are initially ignored. Indy responds only when Henry finally calls him "Indiana." In doing so, Henry finally accepts his son as the man he has chosen to be. In this moment, Indy too attains a sense of self-affirmation as his father refers to him, for the first time, by his *chosen* name. He is recognized not as Junior—a copy of his father—but as Indiana.

Henry's most important find in *Crusade* is not the Grail; it is the man who his son has become. Of course, coming to acknowledge Indy was Henry's arc throughout the film. So, when Indy asks, "What did you find, Dad?" and he answers, "Illumination," this refers to coming to see his son in the proper light. Indy's relationship with his father was strained because Henry did not recognize the man that Indy had chosen to be. This is one reason why Indy rebelled against Henry. Therefore, the Grail quest also functions as an illuminative overcoming of the existentially oppressive dynamic between father and son. The father comes to accept and affirm the meaning of his son's life. Indy finds affirmation of who he is from his father.[9]

Crystal Skull revisits this sort of father–son dynamic, with Indy taking on the role of the less-than-perfect father. When a young man riding a motorcycle asks Indy if he will help him find Harold Oxley, one of Indy's friends from graduate school, they begin their own quest that takes them to South America. As they get to know each other, Indy learns of and initially countenances Mutt's decisions to quit school and become a motorcycle repairman. In fact, Indy asserts, "If that's what you love doing, don't let anyone tell you otherwise." When they meet Marion Ravenwood and she informs Indy that Mutt is their son, Indy's attitude immediately changes.

In fact, Indy's and Mutt's strained relationship is foreshadowed early in the film. Indy asks, "'Mutt,' what kind of name is that?" To which Mutt defiantly retorts, "The one I picked! You got a problem with that?" Just as Henry had difficulty accepting the name his son chose, preferring to call him "Junior" in the not-so-subtle attempt to express his expectations, Indy is taken aback by the name his new companion has chosen for himself. This foreshadowing is made explicit when Marion informs Indy that Mutt's actual name is Henry Jones III. Indy immediately demands that Mutt go back to school, showing us that Indy has assumed Henry's role as the father who has difficulty accepting the person his son chooses to be. Of course, Mutt assumes Indy's role from *Crusade* as he utterly rejects Indy and exclaims that he is nothing like Indy. The father–son arc of *Crystal Skull* is also similar to *Crusade* in that Mutt appreciates and indeed resembles Indy's more adventurous, treasure-hunting ways; he also comes to accept Indy's and Marion's past and countenances their future by participating in their wedding. The end of the film even suggests that the heritage embodied by the iconic fedora is due to transfer to Mutt in the future—well, at least perhaps someday, maybe—a suggestion of further cyclicality. Indeed, similar to Henry's illumination in *Crusade*, Indy's arc in *Crystal Skull* involves embracing the possibilities of becoming a proper husband to Marion and father to Mutt. Doing so requires him to accept the person each has chosen to be (and, of course, accepting that somewhere Mutt's grandpa is having a good laugh at all of this).

Living Like Indy

Crusade suggests that, existentially, one is who he determines himself to be through the way in which he relates to the world and his fate (or history). Indy affirms the life he has lived through his adventures. His clear love for and continual perpetuation of what he does indicates that Indy is affirming his life.

The *Indiana Jones* movies resonate with us in a profound and meaningful way because they tell a recognizably human story of self-affirmation and self-overcoming. Moreover, the protagonist—Indy himself—is portrayed as *human*. (Well, apart from the sort of physical indestructability not shared by German tanks.) Harrison Ford brings vulnerability to his roles and, this way, makes the characters he plays more relatable. This is especially true of his performance as Indy, who is perhaps the most human of Ford's action-film roles. And just as Indy revels in his adventures as he continues to choose them, it seems Ford's portrayal of Indy is a source of meaningfulness in his life. When the fifth film is released, Ford will be near 80 years old, with 40 years having passed since he first donned the iconic fedora. Clearly, portraying Indiana Jones is a part of who he has chosen to be as an actor, and in turn, continuing to choose it speaks to the kind of person he has become. If Ford could live forever in Nietzsche's "Eternal Recurrence," he would do so portraying Indiana Jones.

In this way, the *Indiana Jones* films offer existential lessons with real-world applications. Through self-affirmation, we live authentically. Each of us can live like Indy by affirming the creative life decisions that make us who we are. We should rejoice in the pursuit of our goals and possibilities—in the Nietzschean sense, we should love our fate. It is in such moments—in the commitment to purpose and possibilities—that we affirm who we are, because we are committing to our authentic selves. In this, and regardless of the adversity we face—from struggling against fascist regimes seeking supernatural military might to surviving giant Siafu ants—the *Indiana Jones* films remind us of our creative power over our own lives regardless of our age or station in life. They inspire us to live authentically with a love for that which makes us who we are.

Notes

1 Paul Tillich, *The Courage to Be*, 2nd ed. 1952. Reprint (New Haven: Yale University Press, 2000), 46–48.
2 Friedrich Nietzsche, *The Gay Science*, trans. Walter Kaufmann [1887] (New York: Vintage Books, 1974), S. 341.
3 Nietzsche, *The Gay Science*, S. 276.
4 Nietzsche, *The Gay Science*, S. 276.
5 Nietzsche (in *The Gay Science*, S. 341) suggests that such a person would "throw yourself down and gnash your teeth and curse the demon" who informed them of the hypothetical eternal repetition of life.
6 Typically, the search for knowledge is a noble pursuit, but in Spalko's case, she seems motivated by power and greed more than anything else.
7 Albert Camus, *Le Myth de Sisyphe* (*The Myth of Sisyphus*) (Paris: Gallimard, 1942).
8 See https://plato.stanford.edu/entries/illumination (accessed 24 April 2020).
9 Thus, we can interpret Henry, Indy, Sallah, and Marcus riding into the sunset at the end of *Crusade* in two ways. On the one hand, it signifies the end of the Grail quest (and perhaps the trilogy). On the other hand, it signals the beginning of a new project, namely Henry and Indy connecting as father and son, and accepting the corresponding existential possibilities of this new-found relationship.

8

Nietzschean Themes in *Raiders of the Lost Ark*: God May Be Dead, But Best Not Disturb His Corpse

Duncan Gale

Religion comes up a lot in the *Indiana Jones* films. But while Indy's exploits are undoubtedly intertwined with this subject, they are ultimately concerned with the nature of power—how it can be exploited, abused, and how only those who respect it will succeed. The German philosopher Friedrich Nietzsche (1844–1900), offers us some of the greatest sustained meditations on the nature of power. We'll see how Nietzsche's perspectives shed light on the primary players of *Raiders of the Lost Ark*—the Nazis, Indy himself, and, of course, God. Nietzsche is often misunderstood as advocating nihilism, a philosophy that values nothing. In fact, though, he warns us about the dangers of nihilism. By viewing *Raiders* through this Nietzschean lens we can see how the wrong reaction to nihilism can mean the difference between life and a grisly, divinely sanctioned death.

The Nazis and Nietzschean Morality

It's said that a movie is only as good as its villain. With all due respect to other villains in the franchise, things are just more exciting when Indy is squaring off against the Third Reich. Indy's first adventure features stereotypically militaristic Nazis like Colonel Dietrich as well as truly creepy representatives like the ghoulish Major Toht. These are the obvious villains of the film and, based as they are on actual villains

Indiana Jones and Philosophy: Why Did It Have to Be Socrates?, First Edition. Edited by Dean A. Kowalski.

from history, it is very easy for us to hate them. However, if we might engage in a bold philosophical thought experiment, let us temporarily bracket out our condemnation of Nazis and the atrocities committed by them and ask ourselves, how truly "bad" are they?

For Nietzsche, this question does not have a straightforward answer, and he might even object to the way it is posed. With his genealogical approach, he challenges fundamental assumptions concerning the way we see the world and the values we ascribe to it. Much like Indiana Jones, Nietzsche attempts an archaeological excavation of morality by exploring the origins of terms like "good" and "bad." He believes such terms cannot be traced back to some set of tablets bestowed upon us by God from above. Rather, they come from the cultural practices of human beings. Moral values commonly thought to be divine are in fact "human, all too human." This is similar to the point Belloq makes when he holds up a watch to Indy and says, "It's worthless. Ten dollars from a vendor in the street. But I take it, I bury it in the sand for a thousand years, it becomes priceless ... like the Ark." Belloq's perspective on the fluctuating nature of value as it relates to archaeological relics may strike us as cynical, but perhaps it can be seen as analogous to what humans consider to be morally good and bad.

Nietzsche began his career as a philologist, a field that overlaps with archaeology because it deals with the study of ancient languages. Drawing upon this training, Nietzsche notes that the term "aristocrat" derives from the Greek word *aristos*, which means "excellent" or "good." This bit of etymology provides the key to uncovering the origin of our supposed values. As Nietzsche observes, "The judgment 'good' did *not* originate with those to whom 'goodness' was shown! Rather it was 'the good' themselves, that is to say, the noble, powerful, high-stationed and high-minded, who felt and established themselves and their actions as good, that is, of first rank, in contradistinction to all the low, low-minded, common, and plebeian."[1] Nietzsche thus believes that our conception of moral goodness originated with terms the upper classes used to describe the qualities that earned them their place in the higher echelons of society. So understood, those members of society are "good" in so far as they are strong, aggressive, and effective in killing the enemy in battle. These would also seem to be the kinds of characteristics valued by the Nazis in general and those portrayed in *Raiders* in particular.

Consequently, in Nietzsche's warrior or "master" morality paradigm, the term "bad" is merely an afterthought, with no real positive content of its own. The warriors are so consumed with celebrating themselves that they do not bother to concern themselves with the other side of the dichotomy. So understood, "bad" becomes a synonym for weak, submissive, and ineffective. When Indy first encounters his friend Sallah, it comes as no surprise to him that the Nazis hired him since he is the best digger in Egypt, but Sallah replies that the Nazis care not a whit for his skills, saying, "They hire only strong backs and they pay pennies for them. It's as if the pharaohs have returned." The dismissiveness Sallah describes is completely indicative of this master morality in practice. The Nazis are incapable of appreciating "good" qualities in anyone outside of their social group, especially those who are essentially slave labor for them.

Speaking of masters and slaves, in Nietzsche's paradigm, the lower classes, or "slaves," see no option for themselves other than creating their own morality. What was "bad" for the masters gets redefined as "good" for the slaves. For them, it is good to be weak, humble, and submissive, and being aggressive and warlike is bad. However, within the slave mode of valuation, these qualities are not just bad but in fact *evil*. So understood, slave morality is fundamentally *reactive*. Whereas the masters develop their values purely from a celebration of themselves, the slaves develop theirs from a resentment of the masters. In fact, the slaves' feelings go beyond normal resentment. Nietzsche uses the French term *ressentiment* to refer to anger that cannot be expressed outwardly and must therefore go inward and gnaw at one's psyche.

Regarding the slaves, Nietzsche specifically explains who he is talking about:

> It was the Jews who … dared to invert the aristocratic value-equation … saying "the wretched alone are the good; the poor, impotent, lowly alone are the good … and you, the powerful and noble, are on the contrary the evil, the cruel, the lustful, the insatiable, the godless to all eternity; and you shall be in all eternity the unblessed, accursed, and damned!"[2]

Nietzsche is not referring to the conquering army of the Israelites we hear about in *Raiders* who wielded the might and wrath of God in the form of the titular object. Rather, Nietzsche is describing a later period in the history of the Jewish people where the era of Israelite dominance was a distant memory. His rhetoric also seems close to the anti-Semitic propaganda of the Third Reich. So, an obvious and superficial way to interpret Nietzsche's genealogical theory of morality is that he describes a situation in which there was initially a powerful group so confident in themselves that they did not even worry about those outside of their sphere. This group was then undermined by a weaker group, specifically identified as the Jews who no longer embody the warrior ideals of their distant Israelite past. They are now a disenfranchised group living in a world ruled by their conquerors, which leads them to use their frustration over their lack of power to sneakily subvert the pure morality of the powerful.

Of course, *Raiders* depicts a race between Indy and the Nazis to recover the Ark of the Covenant, an ancient relic crucial to the religion and early military success of the Jewish people. It seems a bit ironic that the Nazis are so eager to obtain an item that has its origins in the traditions of a people whom they despise. This is analogous to the historical reality of the Nazis trying to manipulate certain aspects of culture to their own twisted ends, despite lacking a full understanding of them—including Nietzsche's philosophy. The Nazis saw themselves as the masters and were determined to reclaim their power from the slaves who had taken it away. The Nazis resented the Jews, falsely believing the Jews had become powerful by secretly infiltrating European culture through financial and other cultural institutions. Notably and ironically, the Ark (in *Raiders*) and Nietzsche's philosophy (as a matter of historical fact) are cases of the Nazis fatally misinterpreting something that ultimately brings about their own destruction.

In *Raiders*, none of the Germans seem overly concerned with the profound bit of sacrilege they are about to commit, except for Colonel Dietrich. Recall his admission to Belloq: "Monsieur, I am uncomfortable with the thought of this ... *Jewish* ritual." Perhaps he merely expresses his distaste for all things Jewish. But perhaps he knows on some instinctive level the Nazis are meddling with forces they don't understand, which leads to his screaming in horror as his face melts off only hours later. The same is true, at least on a metaphorical level, of the Nazi's real-life misappropriation of Nietzsche. They adopted Nietzsche as their official state philosopher, which (allegedly) provided intellectual sanction to their naked plans of world ambition. After all, Nietzsche rejected objective, absolute values. The Nazis took this to mean that they could impose their resentful and intolerant values upon the world. The outcome of the Second World War proves just how wrong they were.

The Nazi's interpretation is a well-known but flawed misreading of Nietzsche's genealogical theory of morality. Admittedly, Nietzsche does paint a picture of an initially idyllic period where the powerful were free to create a morality without any sense of guilt or shame, only to be supplanted by a resentful, weak, and marginalized group explicitly identified as the Jews, but Nietzsche was no anti-Semite. The case for this was made most forcefully by the Nietzsche scholar and translator Walter Kaufmann (1921–1980), of German-Jewish ancestry himself. In his justly famous study, Kaufmann brings together extensive historical evidence to show that Nietzsche had a falling-out with his sister because she married a prominent member of the anti-Semitic movement, and it was only after Nietzsche's mental collapse at the end of his life that his sister began to dramatically rewrite his reputation. It was she who was the anti-Semite of the family, and there is even a famous photograph of Adolf Hitler shaking hands with her. In any case, Nietzsche did not fall prey to this prejudice of his times, and the overall tenor of his philosophy bears this out. As Kaufmann observes,

"*It does not follow from Nietzsche's 'vivisection' of slave-morality that he identifies his own position with that of the masters*. Nietzsche's own ethic is beyond that of both master and slave morality. He would like us to conform to neither and become *autonomous*."[3]

So, despite whatever apparently off-color comments Nietzsche might sometimes make about Jews, these are far outweighed by his explicit condemnations of the German people. Consider the following, which Nietzsche wrote in 1873 after the Franco-Prussian War, the war that effectively made Germany into a modern nation-state:

> Of all the evil consequences ... which have followed the recent war with France perhaps the worst is a widespread, indeed universal, error ... that German culture too was victorious in that struggle. ... This delusion is in the highest degree destructive...because it is capable of turning our victory into a defeat: into the defeat, if not the extirpation, of the German spirit for the benefit of the "German Reich".[4]

Such words are eerily prescient in light of the troubles that Germany as a nation would go through in the first half of the twentieth century, including defeat in World War I and economic collapse, all of which led to the Third Reich. In all tragedies, downfall results from the hubris of those who willfully ignore omens that suggest they are going against the natural order. Indeed, there is no better example of this than the Nazis, whether they are foolishly trying to harness the power of God Himself in *Raiders*, or trying to manipulate the views of a philosopher far too subtle for their crude interpretation of the will to power. Nietzsche's will to power states that the fundamental drive of all beings, even beyond survival, is to increase their power, but not in a simplistic sense of lording power over others and inflicting suffering. Rather, true power comes from mastering oneself.

Indiana Jones: Superman?

At first glance, *Raiders* appears to be within the tradition of old-fashioned movie serials from the Golden Age of Cinema. Such films feature square-jawed protagonists who bravely endure death-defying escapades without batting an eye. Yet Indy subverts this trope at every turn. When we see him at the beginning of *Raiders*, he is entering a sacred temple with the intention of stealing the Golden Idol. Initially, he is careful to avoid the temple's various boobytraps, but his confidence morphs into cockiness when he employs the half-baked scheme of replacing the Idol with a bag of sand. This of course sets off all the traps he was avoiding, and he barely escapes only to be outsmarted by the slimy Belloq, who steals Indy's hard-won prize. Indy cowers on the ground, pathetically covered in cobwebs. He narrowly escapes from Belloq and the Hovitos—only to endure a long and terrifying flight home with his pilot friend's pet snake in his lap.

What Indiana Jones lacks in terms of traditionally heroic qualities, he more than makes up for by gaining the audience's sympathy as a perpetual underdog. Indeed, there are times when Indy seems to be going up against almost the entirety of the Third Reich, so it is understandable that he may not always have the upper hand or the strongest position from which to gain an advantage. But Indy has other qualities, like his intelligence and cunning, that enable him to win out against seemingly impossible odds. So, just as we asked if the Nazis were truly "bad," we can now ask if Indiana Jones is truly a "good" character?

Once again, Nietzsche would object to the very premise underlying such a question, namely the existence of absolute moral values. Recall Nietzsche wants us to recognize that all valuations are ultimately the creations of human beings in particular cultural contexts, which invariably represent interests that have little to do with what we consider traditional morality. Nietzsche wants us to get beyond good and evil, and his term for the individual who is able to accomplish this is the *Übermensch*, originally translated as "superman" but later rendered as "overman" by Kaufmann in order to avoid certain distracting connotations. Indeed, the overman overcomes nihilism by creating new life-affirming values. As described in the most cryptic of Nietzsche's works, *Thus Spoke Zarathustra*:

> *I teach you the overman.* Man is something that shall be overcome. What have you done to overcome him? ... All beings so far have created something beyond themselves; and do you want to be the ebb of this great flood and even go back to the beasts rather than overcome man? What is the ape to man? A laughingstock or a painful embarrassment. ... Once you were apes, and even now, too, man is more ape than any ape.[5]

Such overt Darwinian language reminds us of Nietzsche's abuse at the hands of the Nazis. We can see how a facile interpretation of the above-mentioned passage could be used to promote all kinds of twisted theories of eugenics. Nietzsche is not actually talking about genetic development, though. Rather, he is calling for a fundamental change in consciousness.

Nietzsche's change of consciousness is the ability to overcome nihilism by boldly and confidently creating one's own values, no longer being a slave to the established values of an unquestioned tradition. This is as much destructive as creative. As he writes,

"Change of values—that is a change of creators. Whoever must be a creator always annihilates."[6] If this is the true spirit of the ideal of the overman, then Indy seems a very promising candidate indeed. His system of values is extremely flexible and improvisatory, as illustrated most memorably when he declares his intention to go after the truck in which the Nazis have stowed the Ark. Indy's faithful companion Sallah understandably asks, "How?" Indy responds, "I don't know, I'm making this up as I go." This could be Indy's slogan throughout the movie, regarding both his actions and perhaps his moral compass as well. While Indy is the hero, he is not above killing those who get in his way. The most striking instance of this comes during his frantic search for Marion in the Cairo marketplace. When he encounters an imposing warrior brandishing a scimitar, Indy pulls out his gun and nonchalantly shoots his adversary. The moment provides comic relief, but what are we to make of such unsportsmanlike conduct? Is this the conduct of a traditional hero? Perhaps not, but it could be the conduct of a new kind of hero, the overman.

Such a Nietzschean overman must be fully autonomous, which literally means able to generate one's own laws, and this is in fact the crucial distinction between Indy and his adversaries. The Nazi soldiers unquestioningly follow rules. The Nazi leaders may have created the rules and the repugnant values they represent, but they succumb to the dangers of nihilism to the extent that the values themselves are resentful and intolerant. By contrast, Indy creates rules based on life-affirming values. One of the US government agents delicately refers to Indy as an "obtainer of rare antiquities"—suggesting that he practices thievery. Still, Indy's primary concern is that his obtained antiquities be given to the museum. He is the Robin Hood of archaeology. This is why even his mousy colleague Marcus Brody can winkingly remark that all of his efforts accord with the International Treaty for the Protection of Antiquities.

The fact that Indy operates with such ethical flexibility leads Belloq to mistakenly believe that he and Indy are simpatico. At one point he says to Indy, "You and I are very much alike. Archaeology is our religion, yet we have both fallen from the purer faith. Our methods have not differed as much as you pretend. I am a shadowy reflection of you." Belloq may deliver these lines confidently, but they are wishful thinking. Deep down, he knows that he is fundamentally different from Indy. Beneath his bluster, Belloq has no true code of honor, no laws that he has generated for himself. Later on he takes advantage of this difference between them by calling Indy's bluff of threatening to blow up the Ark with a rocket launcher. Unlike Indy, Belloq may very well be a nihilist—he has no consistent values. Belloq's desire to believe that he and Indy are similar is as misguided as those who think that the overman is one who simply does what he wants without any concern for the consequences. Creating one's own values is like being your own boss—it requires an even higher level of self-discipline and commitment than is needed when one merely adheres to a pre-established set of rules.

Is God Really Dead?

Let's return to the overtly religious part of the plot. The climactic scene of *Raiders* features a brief but memorable "appearance" by none other than the Almighty Himself who orchestrates the demise of Belloq and the Nazis for opening the Ark. This naked display of divine power seems fundamentally at odds with the philosophical outlook of Nietzsche, the philosopher who proclaimed the death of God. But perhaps a closer look will yield some different insights.

Nietzsche's declaration that God is dead appears in a parable about a madman who seeks God and runs into the marketplace of a village ranting about his quest. The madman is ridiculed by smug atheists who find his quest amusing, which prompts him to launch into his portentous monologue:

> "Whither is God" he cried. "I shall tell you. *We have killed him*—you and I. All of us are his murderers. But how have we done this? How were we able to drink up the sea? Who gave us the sponge to wipe away the entire horizon? What did we do when we unchained this earth from its sun? Whither is it moving now? Whither are we moving now?"[7]

The death of God is not announced as some kind of celebratory liberation from religion, far from it. Because humanity has chosen to turn its back on the organizing principle of civilization, we are now faced with nihilism and the immense burden of having to replace God. The history of the twentieth century shows that the state was oftentimes used to fill the God-shaped hole of the collective consciousness. The Third Reich and the Soviet Union are two primary examples of this phenomenon. Unlike the Stalinists in Russia, the Nazis at least tried to maintain some continuity with the traditional Christianity of the German *Volk*. Their efforts were perfunctory, though, and did not accord proper respect to the shared traditions of Christianity and Judaism. Consequently in *Raiders*, the Nazis' presumption that they can simply harness the power of the holiest artifact of the ancient Israelites is what leads to their cinematic destruction.

The Americans of *Raiders*, by contrast, seem more respectful, even if not overtly religious. Indy is contacted by government agents who do not want the Nazis to get their hands on the Ark. Why exactly? This is unclear, and as Indy is explaining to them the historical power of the Ark, he even adds the qualification "if you believe in that sort of thing." The culture of 1930s America was one in which traditional religious ideas were beginning to erode, but not to such an extent that they could be replaced wholesale with something else. This *de facto* agnosticism coupled with an uneasy respect for Semitic religious tradition turns out to be the correct perspective to take toward the Ark, such that its seemingly unfortunate fate of being dumped in a vast warehouse may be the only workable solution. The bureaucratic apathy of the American government turns out to be preferable to the megalomania of the Nazis in the wake of the death of God.

And what of Indy's own views? Before he embarks on his quest, he tells Marcus Brody, "I don't believe in magic, a lot of superstitious hocus-pocus. I'm going after a find of incredible historical significance." At the end of the film, Indy does not appear to have undergone a dramatic change in his beliefs despite his experience. Yet, he was able to save himself from the power of the Ark because he at least had reverence for its *historical* value, and this kind of reverence seems to be enough for God to spare his and Marion's life, provided that they also do not look at Him. God may be dead, but that doesn't mean we should not respect His memory, and He can at least rest in peace knowing that His Ark is well protected from those who would use it for nefarious purposes.

The Will to Power Dramatized

Raiders uses the historical facts of the Third Reich's obsession with the occult and takes these to their logical conclusion. The philosophy of Nietzsche, with his idea of the will to power as the fundamental driving force of humanity, is the most plausible explanation for why the Nazis had such an obsession, but it also shows why the Nazis were destined to fail. They lacked the proper respect for the power they were trying to unleash and did not recognize that Nietzsche emphasized more than merely raw power. More importantly, he stressed the power of mastering oneself and affirming life. While Indy does not always exemplify this quality, he is at least able to win out against the Nazis by simply allowing them to be consumed by their own ambition and life-destroying values.

Notes

1 Friedrich Nietzsche, *On the Genealogy of Morals*, in *Basic Writings of Nietzsche*, trans. Walter Kaufmann (New York: Modern Library, 2000), 461–462.

2 Nietzsche, *Genealogy of Morals*, 470.
3 Walter Kaufmann, *Nietzsche: Philosopher, Psychologist, Antichrist* (Princeton: Princeton University Press, 1974), 297. Italics are in the original text.
4 Friedrich Nietzsche, *Untimely Meditations*, trans. R.J. Hollingdale (New York: Cambridge University Press, 1983), 3. Italics are in the original text.
5 Friedrich Nietzsche, *Thus Spoke Zarathustra*, in *The Portable Nietzsche*, trans. Walter Kaufmann (New York: Penguin Books, 1954), 124.
6 Nietzsche, *Zarathustra*, 171. Italics are in the original text.
7 Friedrich Nietzsche, *The Gay Science*, in *The Portable Nietzsche*, 95. Italics are in the original text.

9

Homeward Bound with Indiana Jones

Charles Taliaferro and Annalissa Lane

The adventures of Indiana Jones bring him into contact with strange characters all over the world, but his greatest challenge is coming home to himself and to those closest to him. Though he may not realize it, Indy works steadily toward this goal. Ultimately, he becomes at home with himself, at home with others, and at home with (or open to) the sacred. With his concept of creative fidelity, the French existentialist Gabriel Marcel (1889–1973) can help us see the philosophical relevance of Indy finding home.

Marcel Speaks (in French)

Being at home with oneself requires self-knowledge, and as Marcel explains, self-knowledge and commitment go hand in hand: "In principle, to commit myself I must know myself, but the fact is I really only know myself when I have committed myself."[1] By committing to oneself, one lives authentically. One is fully present to oneself in that one is free of self-deception about who one is and free of self-alienation about one's place in the world. And because one's experiences are dynamic, living authentically is a creative process: creative fidelity.

Indeed, Marcel believes that entering into committed relationships with others is crucial for being *truly* alive. This sort of commitment—being at home with others—requires a full-fledged placing of oneself at the disposal of another. As Marcel explains:

> It will perhaps be made clearer if I say the person who is at my disposal is the one who is capable of being with me with the whole of himself when I am in need; while the one who is not at my disposal seems merely to offer me a temporary loan raised on his resources. For the one I am a presence; for the other I am an object.[2]

Indiana Jones and Philosophy: Why Did It Have to Be Socrates?, First Edition. Edited by Dean A. Kowalski.

Marcel used the French word "avec"—meaning "with"—to describe the radical availability that is essential in a dynamic, enduring relationship. Again, fidelity needs to be creative because people, including oneself, change. Thus, being truly present or available to others needs to be a changing, dynamic process.

For Marcel, two people are truly with each other in his special sense of the term when each has internalized the life of the other so that the welfare of the other matters profoundly. Each person leads an authentic life in response to the other. We are not mere things, like pieces of furniture; we each have a presence that requires respect. Marcel writes: "When I put the table beside the chair I do not make any difference to the table or the chair, and I can take one or the other away without making any difference; but my relationship with you makes a difference to both of us, and so does any interruption of the relationship."[3] To be with another, then, is to profoundly impact the life of the other.

For many people, living in response to another involves religious elements. Marcel thought that living authentically at least allows for the possibility of being open to the sacred. To be at home with the sacred is to participate in a relationship, not with another person but with a divine presence.[4]

No single concept of the sacred runs through all the *Indiana Jones* films. There is Judaism in *Raiders of the Lost Ark*, Hinduism in *Temple of Doom*, and Christianity in *The Last Crusade. Kingdom of the Crystal Skull* has a science fiction backdrop, but it ends in a sacred rite, a marriage ceremony in a church. This sacred plurality fits with Marcel's views about religion. Though he was a practicing Roman Catholic, Marcel promoted a great, liberal openness about the sacred beyond Christianity. Indeed, his views influenced the Second Vatican Council (1962–1965).[5]

On the Path

Because *Temple* is the prequel to *Raiders* and we believe that Indy's journey toward being at home with himself, others, and the sacred develops over time, let's begin when we meet Indy in 1935 at the Shanghai Obi Wan nightclub. Donning a white tuxedo, Indy's sole interest is securing the diamond from crime lord Lao Che. He has a long way to go before he reaches home.

Indy must first obtain the antidote to the poison Lao tricked him into drinking and then escape Club Obi Wan. Young Short Round, wooden blocks tied to his feet, exclaims "Hold on to your potatoes!" as he steps on the gas. Singer Willie Scott, Indy's unwilling getaway car passenger, has the antidote hidden in her dress. As Indy desperately (and rudely) frisks her for the vial, Willie complains that she "is not *that* sort of girl." Short Round spies Indy in the rearview mirror and interjects, "Hey, Dr. Jones. No time for love! We got company!" With Lao Che's henchmen in pursuit, Short Round leads his two passengers to an airplane, and they flee Shanghai. Cue Indy's heroic theme.

The plane—owned by Lao Che—crashes in India. The Mayapore shaman finds them and leads them back to his village. He insists that they go to Pankot Palace to retrieve the sacred stone that protects the village. The shaman believes that Shiva made Indy's plane crash so that Jones could stop Mola Ram, the Thuggee high priest responsible for stealing it. Once Indy returns it, Mayapore will be revived.

On their journey to Pankot, we learn that Indy has, in a way, adopted Short Round. The boy's family was killed when the Japanese bombed Shanghai, and he has been homeless since he was four years old. Rather than having Short Round arrested, Indy made the youngster his assistant. Unfortunately, their relationship is not developed in any significant way, with one notable exception.

When Indy is under the influence of Mola Ram's black sleep of the Kali Ma, he strikes Short Round, knocking the boy to the ground. Undaunted, Shorty grabs a fire torch, and as he presses it into Indy's chest, exclaims, "Indy, I love you. Wake up! You're my best friend. Wake up, Indy!" Jones immediately snaps out of his trance. After battling Mola Ram's henchmen, Indy and Short Round reconcile. In a touching moment, Indy places Shorty's baseball hat on the boy's head. Short Round reciprocates by presenting Indy his fedora, and the two tenderly hug as Indy whispers, "I'm sorry." Despite this touching scene, it is not clear how available or "with" they are in Marcel's sense.

At Pankot Palace, Indy and Willie have an awkward near-romantic encounter. Indy knocks on Willie's door, offering her some fruit; after the dinner debacle, she is undoubtedly famished. While munching on an apple, Willie shares, "Maybe you could be my palace slave." Indy takes the bait and saunters into her room. She divulges that she sleeps wearing jewelry—and nothing else. "Does that shock you?" she queries. Taking a bite of his own apple, Indy confidently retorts, "Nothing shocks me. I'm a scientist." When Willie asks what sort of research Indy would do on her, he explains, "Nocturnal activities … Mating customs … Primitive sexual practices." They kiss (of course), but Indy quickly turns smug. Willie calls him a "conceited ape." Vanity consumes them and they begin bickering about who is more delusional about what was (or was not) about to happen. Indy strides out of Willie's room. Before closing her door, Willie asserts, "You'll be back over here in five minutes."

Sexual satiation is more important to Indy and Willie than establishing any sort of lasting relationship. Sadly, they do not take the first steps of becoming "available" or "with" the other in Marcel's sense. Indeed, Marcel might go so far as to claim that, at best, they offer each other "a temporary loan on their [sexual] resources," and, see each other as "furniture" for their personal erotic goals. Indy and Willie are not "present" to each other with the aim of establishing a mutually loving, intimate, enduring relationship.

Yet after defeating Mola Ram—which included Indy's acceptance of the Sankara Stones as sacred objects imbued with purpose and meaning by the Hindu god Shiva—Indy, Willie, and Short Round are portrayed as returning to Mayapore as a family. They reverentially greet the Mayapore shaman in traditional Hindu fashion. When the children they freed rush past into the loving arms of their parents, Indy embraces Short Round and Willie by putting an arm around each. Mayapore is re-established—its broken homes are repaired—and Indy presents the Sankara Stone to the shaman, professing belief in its power.

Still, it's not clear that the trio have become a family, with each member "available" or "with" the other in the senses appropriate for spouses, parents, and their children. True, Indy and Willie finally embrace and kiss in a more appreciable loving way, and Shorty is embarrassed to see them do this (as is any child when his or her parents publicly display their affection), but Willie has clearly had her fill of Indiana Jones and his "adventures." In fact, Indy uses his whip to lasso her back to him for that final kiss. Not an encouraging way to begin a committed romantic relationship. Neither Willie nor Short Round appear in future films; they disappear from Indy's life. So even if there are initial elements of Marcel's views about being at home, they are not well worked out at the end of *Temple*.

Setting the Foundations

We next see Indiana Jones a year later in *Raiders* where he remains far from home. In the jungles of Peru, Indy searches for the Golden Idol. After being betrayed by two of his traveling companions, Jones emerges from the tomb—having narrowly escaped the most famous boulder in all of cinema—only to meet his haughty adversary René Belloq and a band of Hovito warriors. Belloq takes the Gold Idol and Indy flees (yet again) for his life, this time from spears and poison darts. Cue Indy's theme.

Back at Marshall College, Marcus Brody escorts Indy to a large lecture hall to meet two government agents. The agents inform Indy and Marcus that the Nazis have located Tanis, one of the potential resting places of the lost Ark of the Covenant, and are seeking Abner Ravenwood, Indy's mentor at the University of Chicago, for something called the Staff of Ra. Indy explains, "Obviously the Nazis are looking for the headpiece to the Staff of Ra and they think Abner's got it." Indy's first stop in locating Abner is reconnecting with his daughter, Marion Ravenwood.

Indy finds Marion in Nepal, owning a remote tavern. She is no more at home there than Indy was in Peru. As she explains, Abner made a habit of dragging her "all over this earth looking for his little bits of junk" and now she is "stuck in this dive." Marion isn't surprised to see Indy again: "Always knew someday you'd come walkin' back through my door … Something made it inevitable. So what are you doing here in Nepal?" Jones describes the Staff of Ra medallion to her, hoping Marion knows where it is. She does, but she has some issues to work through first.

Marion lands a right cross on Indy's chin and exclaims, "I've learned to hate you in the last ten years … I was a child! I was in love! It was wrong and you knew it! … Do you know what you did to me, my life?" Indy is not fazed by her rebuke and rather callously replies, "You knew what you were doing. I did what I did. You don't have to be happy about it, but maybe we can help each other out now." After a decade apart, and with Abner now dead, Indy brazenly wishes to become partners with Marion again. He offers her $3,000 now and $2,000 more once they get back to the states if Marion hands over the medallion. The Nazis also come looking for the medallion, and her tavern goes up in flames, so she tells Indy, "Until I get my $5,000 back, you're gonna get more than you bargained for. I'm your goddamned partner!" Their partnership is one of convenience, but it is an important first step to being "with" each other in Marcel's sense.

Although we do not know all the details of their romantic past, we know that Indy was 26, Marion was 16, and the tryst lasted for only four months in 1925.[6] These details suggest that Indy was guilty of some self-deception about his intentions and that he did not make himself fully available to young Marion. Further, his lack of empathy for Marion a decade later is unsettling. He treated Marion like a mere object in 1925, and he doesn't do any better when they reunite in Nepal.

The relationship improves, however. Upon becoming partners, Indy and Marion *share* the adventure of chasing after the Lost Ark in ways that Indy and Willie never did in *Temple*. Indy shows genuine remorse when he believes that Marion dies in an explosion, and he's elated to find her alive. They share a touching moment on Katanga's ship, which allows for them to reconnect and rekindle their relationship as adults. Here they seem more committed to and "with" each other in Marcel's sense, even if Indy dozes off for a time. (Remember, it's not the years, it's the mileage.) Jones risks his life to rescue her when the Nazis capture her again, and he threatens to blow up the Ark if Belloq and the Nazis do not hand her over. Marion is no longer merely an object to Indy. He is fully present to her. When Belloq opens the Ark, Indy is immediately concerned for Marion's safety, telling her not to look upon it, "no matter what."[7] At the very end of the film, they are together, physically arm-in-arm, but also emotionally, as they walk down the steps. Indy and Marion are not fully at home with themselves and each other, but they make important strides toward this goal.

Restoring Family Relationships

Crusade gives us a glimpse of Indy's formative years with his father, Professor Henry Jones, Sr. Indy's mother had died tragically, and in 1912 the two Joneses live modestly in rural Utah. While on a boy scout expedition, Indy "obtains" the Cross of Coronado from tomb robbers, sprints home, and bursts into his father's study. Not looking up from his manuscript, Henry mindlessly says, "Out." When Indy assures his father that "It's important," Henry replies, "Then wait. Count to 20 … in Greek." As Indy quietly rehearses his Greek numbers, the sheriff pulls up. Indy closes the door to the study. Henry does not greet the sheriff and presumably doesn't know he's entered the house. Indy must fend for himself. Henry does not make himself available to his son, who is little more than another piece of furniture that the professor must navigate. Their house is not a home and they are not at home with each other.

In 1938 Indy has left Marshall for a position at Barnett College, where he doesn't quite seem at home—we see him collect his mail and then promptly escape through his office window rather than meet with students. Indy's brisk walk is interrupted by three serious looking men employed by Walter Donovan, an affluent antiquities collector. In turns out that Donovan has sponsored an expedition to seek the Grail, but the team leader has gone missing. Indy is skeptical of the Grail legend and says, "You've got the wrong Jones, Mister Donovan. Why don't you try my father?" Indy is shocked when Donovan informs him his father is the man who has disappeared! Donovan surmises: "Find the man and you will find the Grail."

Indy and Marcus speed to Henry's house. Marcus muses, "Your father and I have been friends since time began. I've watched you grow up, Indy. And I've watched the two of you grow apart. I've never seen you this concerned about him before." Henry's front door is ominously ajar. As they enter, Indy replies to Marcus's observations: "He's an academic. A bookworm. He's not a field man … He's in over his head." Henry's house has been ransacked. When Marcus notes that Henry's mail has been opened, Indy remembers the package he received from

Venice, Italy while in his office. It's Henry's Grail diary, containing every clue and tidbit about the Grail's whereabouts—a complete record of Henry's search for the Holy Grail. As Indy puts it, "This is his whole life," which then leads him to ask, "Why would he have sent this to me?" Indy and Marcus leave for Venice to find Henry and the Grail.

The Grail diary makes Indy and Henry partners, much as the Staff of Ra medallion did for Indy and Marion. Father and son get off to a rocky start. When Indy finds Henry, being held hostage by the Nazis—Indy really hates these guys—Henry is flabbergasted to learn that Indy brought the Grail diary back to Europe. "I should have sent it to the Marx Brothers," Henry scoffs. Indy is miffed that his father cares more about a vase that might be from the Ming Dynasty—one that Henry broke over Indy's head—than he does his son's well-being. Still, Indy and Henry escape. As they flee the Nazis and work toward finding the Grail, Indy gains a deeper appreciation of his father's "bookworm" research methods and Henry comes to see the value of being a "field man." They thus begin to be more present to each other.

Of course, becoming more available or committed to another can be a difficult process. One must come to grips with the person he (or she) was, for the relationship to move forward and grow—this is an important part of creative fidelity. For Indy and Henry, a vivid example of this process is their awkward conversation on the Zeppelin as they attempt to leave Germany. While Henry thumbs through his Grail diary, Indy muses that he had a milkshake the last time they enjoyed a quiet drink together. Henry detects a rebuke, but Indy expresses a regret: "It was just the two of us, Dad. It was a lonely way to grow up. For you, too. If you had been an ordinary, average father like the other guys' dads, you'd have understood that." Henry, putting aside his diary, sharply retorts, "I was a wonderful father ... I respected your privacy and taught you self-reliance." Indy calls out Henry's self-deception: "What you taught me was that I was less important to you than people who had been dead for 500 years in another country. And I learned it so well that we've hardly spoken for 20 years." Although the discussion is tense, it signals an important turn in their relationship.

As their adventures progress, Indy and Henry become more present to each other. This process is strikingly similar to how Indy and Marion reconnected in *Raiders*. Indy risks his life to rescue Henry when he is again captured by the Nazis. Henry is remorseful when he believes that Indy died saving him: "O God. I've lost him. And I never told him anything. I just wasn't ready. Maybe 5 minutes would have been enough." Henry is overjoyed to learn that Indy didn't perish (even if he soon regains his stiff upper lip). Indy risks his life again to heal his father's mortal gunshot wound; only the healing power of the Grail will save his life. Henry later pleads with Indy to let the Grail go—thereby prioritizing his son over his research—and calls his son not "Junior" but "Indiana" to express his commitment. Their Grail quest complete, an illuminated father and son ride off into the sunset to begin the new adventure of familial love and mutual respect. Cue Indy's theme.

Recovering Love and Embracing Fatherhood

In *Crystal Skull*, it's 1957 and Indy has recently returned to Marshall College. But it's the height of the "Red Scare," and Indy loses his job due to his involvement with double-agent George "Mac" McHale. As Jones packs his things, he commiserates with Dean Charlie Stanforth. Sitting at his desk, Indy laments, "Brutal couple of years, Charlie, first Dad and then Marcus." Stanforth replies, "We seem to be at the age where life stops giving us things and begins taking them away." Indy looks longingly at the photos of his father and Marcus on his desk. It's clear that he has lost something because of their passing, nothing like removing a chair from a desk. Indy and his father committed to each other in the years after their Grail quest, and even though they lived in separate houses, they became at home with each other.

As Indy boards the train headed for New York on his way to Europe, he wistfully looks back at the home he leaves behind. Just then, a young man wearing a black leather jacket rides his motorcycle on the train platform, signaling a new turn in Indy's life. He spies Indy in a passenger car window and shouts, "Professor, hello! Hey! Are you Dr. Jones? ... Are you a friend of Dr. Oxley's?" Indy disembarks the train and the two get better acquainted at a local malt shop. "The name is Mutt. Mutt Williams," the young man shares while shaking Indy's hand. Once Indy learns that Ox and Mutt's mother—Mary Williams—have gone missing and Indy deciphers Ox's last message, the two new acquaintances leave for Peru to search for them.

Like Short Round in *Temple*, Mutt begins as little more than Indy's troublesome assistant. But their relationship changes drastically when Mac and a band of Russian soldiers capture them after locating a mysterious crystal skull. Indy becomes better informed about Dr. Colonel Spalko's interest in the crystal skull. To motivate Indy's compliance in her plans, she threatens Mutt's life. Indy shrugs. She then presents her other hostage: Marion Ravenwood! Mutt yells, "Mom!" Indy is shocked, but recovers to muse, "Oh, Marion, you had to go and get yourself kidnapped." "Not like you did any better," she reminds him. "Same old, same old," is all Indy can say, shaking his head. But things between them quickly become different.

In the back of a Russian jeep, and with Mutt present, Indy and Marion enter into the same sort of difficult conversation that Indy and his father had on the Zeppelin in *Crusade*. They must take stock of themselves and their past—striving for self-awareness—before they can move forward. Marion reminds Indy that he broke off the engagement a week before the wedding. Indy claims, "I think we both knew, Marion, it wasn't going to work" and Marion immediately replies, "You didn't know that. Why didn't you ever talk to me about it?" Visibly upset, Indy yells, "Because we never had an argument I won!" Marion interjects, "It's not my fault if you can't keep up!" Exasperated, Indy shares, "I didn't want to hurt you!" But, of course, he did hurt her by leaving without sharing his feelings. Indy had succumbed to self-deception by believing that their relationship would never work and rationalized away any hope of success.

Perhaps picking up on Marion's honesty and her level of self-awareness, Indy redirects: "You should have told me about the kid, Marion. I had a right to know." Reminding him that *he* broke it off, she exclaims, "You vanished after that!" By the time Indy managed to write her again, Mutt was born and Marion had married someone else. Now it is Marion's turn to redirect: "I'm sure I wasn't the only one to go on with my life. There must've been plenty of women for you over the years." Indy sighs and reports, "Yeah, there were a few, but they all had the same problem … They weren't you." Indy finally comes clean. Recognizing his honesty, and as Indy begins to free them from their Russian captors, Marion beams. Although their discussion was heated and made Indy (and Mutt) uncomfortable at many turns, being honest with themselves and with each other allows Indy and Marion—and Mutt—to move forward.

Indy, Marion, and Mutt work together to return the crystal skull, demonstrating a degree of teamwork that Indy, Willie, and Short Round never did. Further, Marion takes action, serving as Indy's *partner*, in ways she did not in *Raiders*. For example, not only does Marion skillfully drive one of the ducks (truck-boats) through the jungle, she also courageously executes their escape. Carefully surveying a cliff and the water below, she drives back to rescue Indy and Ox from giant man-eating ants. With the Russians still behind them, Marion boldly guns the duck toward the edge of the cliff. Indy is alarmed: "Honey, you gotta stop or we'll go off the cliff!" Marion implores Indy to trust her (finally). The truck flies into a large tree growing in the cliff. Its branches slowly take them to the water below. Marion guns the accelerator again, and the duck takes them down river, away from the Russians and the ants. Indy mutters, "Don't ever do that again!" Beaming, Marion knowingly replies, "Yes, dear."

At the end of the film, Indy's and Marion's renewed partnership and commitment is cemented in two ways. The first is Indy's epiphany of self-awareness about his past with his father and his future as a father to his own son. Mutt is ready to venture into the jungle, away from Akator (and maybe Indy). Indy cautions him that night falls quickly and recommends: "Why don't you stick around, Junior?" Mutt recognizes the irony: "Huh. I don't know. Why didn't you, *Dad?*" Indy pushes his fedora back, looks toward the heavens and admits, "Somewhere your grandpa is laughing." Indy smiles—at himself and in recognition of himself—but also at Marion and Mutt. He is becoming available to each of them.

The second, and more obvious way, is that Indy and Marion—finally—are married, signaling their openness to being at home with the sacred. The minister announces, "Whom God hath joined together, let no one put asunder ... Congratulations, you may kiss your bride." But Marion is the one who kisses Indy! She has waited long enough for Indy to realize his true place by her side. As the small audience applauds, they *both* beam and lock arms. Indy "encourages" Mutt to add his arm, making a trio—each member is "with" one another in Marcel's sense of the term. Indy and Marion walk down the aisle and out the door, arm-in-arm as they did at the end of *Raiders*, but this time with the express purpose to walk the world *together*. Being present to one another, they are homeward bound wherever they go (even if Indy snatches his fedora from his son on the way out). Cue Indy's theme.

Finding Your Fedora

As Indy trapses over the globe, we see him grow as a person over multiple decades. We learn that home is not a place; it is a way to be—with yourself, with others, and for many of us, with the sacred. In this sense, wherever we go, we can be at home with ourselves and with others. But Indy shows us this requires work and a great deal of honesty. It is an adventure, one with many twists and turns, and strides and missteps, but one well worth the effort. Cue the heroic music.[8]

Notes

1 Gabriel Marcel, *Creative Fidelity*, trans. Robert Rosthal (New York: Farrar, Strauss and Company, 1964), 162.
2 Gabriel Marcel, *The Philosophy of Existentialism*, trans. Manya Harari (New York: Citadel Press, 1995), 40.
3 Gabriel Marcel, *The Mystery of Being Volume 1: Reflection and Mystery*, trans. G. S. Fraser (London: The Harvill Press, 1951), 181.
4 Charles has defended Marcel's view of persons in *Is God Invisible? An Essay on Religion and Aesthetics*, co-authored with Jil Evans (Cambridge: Cambridge University Press, 2021).

5 For more on Marcel, see his *Tragic Wisdom and Beyond*, trans. Stephen Jolin and Peter McCormick, ed. John Wild (Evanston, IL: Northwestern University Press).

6 Per James Luceno, *Indiana Jones: The Ultimate Guide* (New York: DK Books, 2008), 14–15.

7 Indy's choice not to look upon the Ark also conveys respect and arguably reverence for its sacredness, which suggests that he is at least open to the sacred.

8 We thank Dean Kowalski for his brilliant edits of earlier versions of this chapter.

Part III

"KNOWLEDGE WAS THEIR TREASURE": TRUTH AND EVIDENCE

10

Fact, Truth, and Evidence: A Lesson from Dr. Tyree

Dean A. Kowalski

A young bespectacled archaeology professor, donning a three-piece suit with coordinating bowtie, begins his lecture by declaring "Archaeology is the search for … fact." He emphasizes this point by writing "FACT" on the blackboard and underlining the word. Turning to face his class, he continues, "Not truth. If it's truth you're interested in, Dr. Tyree's philosophy class is right down the hall." His class knowingly chuckles at the reference, after which he resumes his lesson: "So forget any ideas you've got about lost cities, exotic travel, and digging up the world. We do not follow maps to buried treasure, and X never, ever marks the spot." Connecting this point with the need for careful scholarship, he finishes, "Seventy percent of all archaeology is done in the library. Research. Reading. We cannot afford to take mythology at face value." The bell rings, ending the lesson.

Of course, the archaeology professor is Henry "Indiana" Jones, Jr., who is known for his adventurous archaeological field work and the mantra: "It belongs in a museum!" But his classroom remark "archaeology is the pursuit of fact, not truth" is also noteworthy. In this chapter, with an assist from a certain philosopher "right down the hall," we'll attempt to decipher what Indy might mean by his puzzling statement about fact and truth. As we'll see, carefully exploring Indy's lecture about fact and truth leads to some intriguing insights about our favorite archaeologist and philosophy itself.

From Down the Hall Dr. Tyree Appears

In *The Last Crusade*, Indy's long-time friend Marcus Brody enters the classroom as Jones is finishing up his "fact, not truth" lecture. But imagine that the aforementioned Dr. Tyree—wearing an impeccably

Indiana Jones and Philosophy: Why Did It Have to Be Socrates?, First Edition. Edited by Dean A. Kowalski.

tailored suit and his trademark knitted scarf, and humming his favorite bars from Richard Strauss—was walking by Indy's classroom instead.

Tyree might poke his head in and say, "Jones, I heard your reference from the hallway," and, raising a bushy eyebrow, continue, "May I ask what you mean by 'fact' and 'truth'?" Taken aback by Tyree's bluntness, and perhaps feeling more like Tyree's student rather than a colleague, Indy might not know how to answer. (Such an exchange indeed would be déjà vu for Harrison Ford, who enrolled in at least three of William E. Tyree's philosophy classes at Ripon College from 1960 to 1964. For Ford to graduate on time, he needed to pass his senior-year second semester philosophy course taught by Robert "Spud" Hannaford. Alas, that did not happen, and Ford remains a few credits short of his degree.[1])

Tyree and Jones would probably soon settle on a straightforward account of truth, where a statement is true if it accurately describes how things are—if it corresponds to reality. A statement is false if it doesn't accurately describe how things are—if it doesn't correspond to reality. For example, the statement "William E. Tyree began teaching at Ripon College in 1950" is true because it correctly expresses actual states of affairs. And the statement "William E. Tyree retired from Ripon College in 1980" is false because it doesn't correspond to reality. Tyree actually retired in 1983.

If a statement is true because it corresponds to how things actually are, then we might say that a "fact" refers to some feature of reality. It's not quite correct to say that a fact is true, but a fact is some aspect of reality that makes a statement true, assuming the statement describes that aspect correctly. For example, the actual state of affairs consisting of Harrison Ford's being a philosophy major at Ripon College is the fact that makes the statement "Harrison Ford majored in philosophy at Ripon College" true. And because the facts do not include Harrison Ford graduating from Ripon, the statement "Harrison Ford is a Ripon College graduate" is false.

Tyree, becoming excited, as he often does when making some important point, might then resume his conversation with Indy by stating: "So, Jones, there is something curious about your statement 'Archaeology seeks facts, but not truth.' Presumably, you intended to make a true statement about archaeology, correct?" Although the question is rhetorical, Indy nods his head affirmatively. Tyree, now fully animated—the piece of chalk he was holding flying into the air—gestures toward Indy and inquires, "But if archaeology is not concerned with the truth, how can it be true that it is concerned only with facts?" In effect, Tyree points out that Indy's position seems self-defeating.[2]

Put another way, if facts are those aspects of reality to which a statement must correspond to be true, Indy claims that while archaeology seeks out how things actually are (or were), it is nevertheless not concerned with searching for the truth. But are there any college professors who are not keenly interested in true statements about their discipline? What, then, would be the point of conducting research? There is indeed something paradoxical about an academic who is not interested in seeking truths about his discipline.

Of course, Indy isn't a philosopher—as he might be brave enough to remind Dr. Tyree—even if he sometimes sounds philosophical. Jones may not be using words exactly as a philosopher would use them. He might also remind Tyree that not everyone has his older colleague's extensive vocabulary or exactness of expression. So, Indy might redirect the conversation and rely on common sense: what he means by "fact" consists of everyday, uncontroversial matters about the world in which we live. What Indy means by "truth" refers to controversial and not-of-this-world topics—about life after bodily death or the ultimate origins of the universe—those that Dr. Tyree, as a philosopher, explores. But such topics are not very relevant to people like Indy, who study and practice archaeology.

Indiana's intended message to his students, then, was that archaeology searches for physical things, namely the artifacts that humanity leaves behind, and by carefully examining those artifacts we thereby gain insights into human history. If his students want to search for that which cannot be found or learned about in burial chambers, pottery shards, or hieroglyphs, and scholarly books about them, then they should try studying philosophy—or another discipline, like mythology, perhaps, but not archaeology. Perhaps Indy is not denying the existence of abstract truths that philosophers like Tyree contemplate or the importance some people put on mythological beliefs, but Jones doubts their relevance to him, or to his professional endeavors. In fact, given his closing statement to his students about mythology, he thinks such perspectives may only impede proper archaeology.

Dr. Jones's (Blink of an Eye) Epistemology Primer

Leaving Dr. Tyree behind, Indy finds his outer office packed with students impatiently waiting to visit with him. He instructs his assistant Irene to put each student's name on a list, telling her that he will see them in the order they arrived. Jones quickly disappears into his private office where he sits at his ridiculously small desk, surrounded by cluttered artifact shelves and an antiquated boiler in the corner. He picks up his mail and sighs. There is a quick cut to the courtyard, and we see Indy exit his office from an open window. But what we don't see (let's say), is Tyree resuming their conversation about fact and truth.

Expecting Irene to bring in the first student, Indy is surprised to see Tyree enter. Careful to avoid soiling his pristine attire, Tyree takes a place next to Indy's desk and begins, "Jones, as I was finishing my lunch—I do love Yorkshire pudding, as you know—I began thinking again about our morning conversation. I agree we must search out the facts—as you say—but carefully, through established principles of evidence. We certainly cannot merely guess at them." Indy immediately recalls his impulsive attempt to gauge the weight of the Golden Idol. Had he properly measured its weight, he would have saved himself that harrowing rolling boulder experience! Tyree, getting wound up again, continues: "Often times, what seems to be the case, is not, upon further investigation." Indy nods affirmatively, as he thinks about Sallah's query when they opened the Well of Souls: "Indy, why does the floor move?" When Indy dropped a torch, they better saw that the floor wasn't moving; rather, it was covered with slithering snakes. "And in some situations," Tyree adds, "we ought *not* to trust our senses to help us identify the facts. A white wall will look blue if a blue light shines upon it, sirens on moving cars sound differently to pedestrians than they do to the driver, and some medications will disrupt memory and our reasoning faculties generally." Indy shudders as he thinks about how, under the influence of Mola Ram's "Black Sleep of the Kali Ma," he was sure that he was doing the right thing by sending Willie into the volcano pit.

Tyree might then remind Jones that we need not rely only on personal investigations when attempting to find the facts. Assuming that others are carefully exploring them and following established principles of evidence, we can trust their findings. Tyree would then probably explain inductive generalization: "And, Jones, we can also say that given past personal findings and those of others, we can expect similar results in future cases when the circumstances are similar." Putting these two points together, Indy readily agrees, and grateful that he didn't have to dodge another piece of flying chalk, cites a familiar archaeological example: "Yes, this is how we've come to know that artifacts found at a deeper dig level are older than those found at levels closer to the surface."

The two men might then discuss how scientists, including archaeologists, conduct their business. Scientists make observations, record their findings, form hypotheses to explain the data, and test those hypotheses by making predictions about future observations. Indy used such reasoning to infer that the Mayapore village rock was one of the Sankara Stones: if it were one of the Sankara Stones, then it would glow when placed near any of the other four Sankara Stones, which it did. Indy's hypothesis was confirmed by this successful prediction. But if new observations are inconsistent with what a hypothesis predicts, then scientists must revise or discard the hypothesis for another.

What's more, assessing the data—determining whether an observation conflicts with or supports a hypothesis—invariably involves background assumptions, which in turn require independent verification. Otherwise, we have no sure way to formulate informative predictions. Scientists also follow Ockham's Razor when articulating hypotheses to ensure that they are not unduly complex or require unnecessary assumptions when explaining a set of data. Sometimes, unfortunately, no hypothesis is deemed best at explaining the data; in such cases, we ought to remain agnostic until additional tests are conducted. Other times, though, scientists articulate and confirm a hypothesis, one that regularly makes successful predictions and thereby extends our knowledge about some subject. It all starts with making unbiased, careful observations and following principles of evidence.

At this point, Tyree, now ecstatic about their progress, would probably point out: "But, you see Jones, searching for the facts and doing archaeology properly require some background in philosophy, particularly in epistemology—the study of knowledge." Epistemology helps us devise principles for evaluating evidence, and these principles lead to justified beliefs about how the world actually is—that is, the facts.[3] Those principles point us to statements that are more likely true than not, which is to say that archaeology cannot divorce itself from the truth in the way Indy suggested in class. (Being shown—again—how his lecture requires revision, perhaps now we have the *full* story about why Indy felt the need to quickly exit his office window. Tyree, although an avid ballroom dancer and quite light on his feet, is not about to climb out of a window!)

... But Professor, You Said "X" Never Marks the Spot!

Upon emerging (escaping?) from his office window, Indy enjoys a brisk walk in the sunshine free of pestering students and Professor Tyree's pointed questioning, but it's cut short when he hears a car pull up and someone shout, "Dr. Jones!" He immediately worries that it's Tyree wishing to resume their "discussion," but that fear subsides when he sees the car is not parked laughingly askew. He is surprised, though, to see three unknown and imposing men get out of the car.

The three men take Indy to Walter Donovan's posh residence. Donovan apologizes for the abruptness of the visit. "I trust your trip down was comfortable, Dr. Jones," Donovan states and quickly continues, "My men didn't alarm you, I hope." Indy doesn't answer, but thinks to himself how glad he was that it wasn't Tyree driving—that man spends more time looking at his passengers than he does the road! Donovan and Indy then exchange pleasantries and shake hands.

Donovan begins sharing his passion for antiquities by presenting Indy a stone tablet bearing an early Latin text inscription. Intrigued, Indy begins reading aloud. Donovan pours glasses of champagne and waits for Indy to utter, "Where the cup that holds the blood of Jesus Christ resides forever." To which Donovan reaffirms: "The Holy Grail, Doctor Jones ... The cup that caught His blood at the Crucifixion and was entrusted to Joseph of Arimathea." Indy's disdain for mythology bubbles up again, as he replies cynically, "The Arthur legend. I've heard this bedtime story before."

Donovan ignores Indy's skepticism and shares another Grail "bedtime story," about three knights—brothers—who found the Grail during the First Crusade. Indy has heard this part of the legend as well, reminding Donovan that one of the brothers imparted his tale to a Franciscan friar. Donovan then surprises Indy with the friar's manuscript! Donovan shares some of the manuscript's details about the Grail, including tantalizing clues about its location, but laments the fact that his current project leader has gone missing. "Find the man and you will find the Grail," Donovan reassures Indy. But Indy replies, "You've got the wrong Jones, Mister Donovan. Why don't you try my father?" "We already have," replies Donovan and then divulges, "Your father is the man who has disappeared."

In Venice, Indy and Marcus meet Dr. Elsa Schneider, and the three visit the library where Indy's father, Henry, disappeared. The library is a converted church, and Indy quickly recognizes its large stained-glass window from his father's Grail diary. The window contains three Roman numerals: III (three), VII (seven), and X (ten). Indy begins to put the clues together. His father wasn't looking for a book about the knight's tomb—he was looking for the tomb itself! He finds "III" engraved on a stone pillar to the right of the window and "VII" engraved on a pillar to its left. However, Indy is unable to locate a corresponding Roman numeral X, that is, until he climbs a flight of stairs. He announces, "Ten," and while pointing at the floor, sheepishly admits, "X marks the spot." Indy bashes the floor and gains entrance to the catacombs underneath. He and Elsa navigate the dank tunnels, find *another* "X" on one of its walls, and crashing through it, gain entrance to a hidden burial chamber. They open an ornate sarcophagus, and Indy makes a rubbing of the knight's shield, which he immediately recognizes as the second Grail marker. (So, X marks the spot, not once, but twice!)

Later in the film, Indy and Marcus examine the shield rubbing and discover that it references the lost city of Alexandretta. The current city of Iskenderun is built on its ruins. This clue is the key to deciphering the Grail map that Indy's dad had painstakingly made from numerous other sources. They follow this map to the current location of the Grail.

The connections to Indy's classroom lecture are obvious. He traveled to Venice, an exotic city. He did some crude digging at a place marked with a large red X. He discovered a burial chamber, and made a rubbing of a previously unknown Latin text, which provided new knowledge of the Grail's whereabouts. Furthermore, Indy used a map only after identifying a lost city. What would his students say if they saw him now?

Interestingly, Henry, once rescued from the Nazis, offers Indy something else to ponder: "The quest for the Grail is not archaeology. It's a race against evil. If it is captured by the Nazis, the armies of darkness will march all over the face of the earth." Henry speaks of deeper truths associated with the Grail, many of which are seemingly later confirmed by Indy's own experiences in the Grail temple. He watches Donovan grow old and turn to dust in a matter of seconds because "he chose poorly," recalling the Grail knight's response to Donovan's drinking from a false grail. He witnesses his father's gunshot wound instantaneously and fully heal when he spills water from the Grail on it. Henry's being so restored certainly seemed miraculous, recalling how Marcus crossed himself at the event.

Yet Indy is notably dismissive of deeper truths about God and religion. In addition to his skepticism about the Grail legend, recall his (*Raiders of the Lost Ark*) conversation with Marcus about the Ark of the Covenant. Indiana reminds Marcus that the Ark "represents everything we got into archaeology for in the first place." When Marcus advises caution, Indy guffaws, and replies, "What are you trying to do, scare me? ... I don't believe in magic, a lot of superstitious hocus-pocus. I'm going after a find of incredible historical significance. You're talking about the bogeyman." The Ark of the Covenant indeed has great historical significance, and archaeologists are eager to discover it.[4] Still, Marcus's warning was prophetic. Further, given Indy's experiences in the first three films, one might question whether his persistent dismissiveness of deeper truths about religion (and perhaps philosophy) is justified. This includes a certain philosopher "right down the hall."

Tyree and Jones Share "Vacation" Stories

Although we see Indy simply riding off into the sunset after his Grail quest, we now know that he returned to Barnett College (briefly before moving back to Marshall). Tyree would no doubt seek out his young colleague. "Ah, there you are, Jones," Tyree begins and then adds, "I hope your time away from the classroom was worthwhile. *Another* vacation, I presume?" "I don't know if I'd call it a vacation ..." Indy replies, but Tyree interrupts, "I just got back from Hawaii myself; one of my favorite spots." Indy notices the odd tan line on Tyree's neck and surmises that he was in the tropical sun wearing his scarf (again).

It's not difficult to imagine Indy sharing the philosophical insights he gleaned during his "vacation." Indy might inform Tyree that he made a successful inductive generalization to predict the room where the Nazis were holding his father. In Indy's experience, people who wish to guard something put it in a room with an alarm on the door. Since Henry was valuable to the Nazi cause, Indy correctly surmised his dad's current location within the castle.

Indy certainly would speak of the invisible bridge. It spanned the chasm, but he couldn't see it; indeed, it appeared that the bridge didn't exist. Perhaps if Indy had more time, he could have devised other empirical tests for verifying its existence. After all, once he crossed, he spread gravel on the bridge, allowing Elsa and Donovan easy access. Lacking time, he guessed—or at least hoped—he would be able to cross the chasm, and luckily, especially for his father's sake, he did. Sometimes guesses are correct, but they (at the time) don't constitute knowledge of the facts.

More fantastic than the invisible bridge, though, was Donovan's demise and Henry's instantaneous recovery. Indy might confide, "I'm grateful that I chose better than Donovan and that my father was healed, but as a scientist, I have no way of explaining what I saw." Unlike Marcus, Indy resists divine intervention as a way to best explain his experiences. Having learned from Tyree's earlier epistemology lesson, Indy might express concerns about using a supernatural hypothesis to explain empirical observations.[5] The existence of the all-but-invisible bridge, a physical object, was difficult to verify, but how does one scientifically test for God's existence? Arguably, any possible naturalistic hypothesis, regardless of how unlikely, is at least as probable as a supernatural one, and this intuition is bolstered by Ockham's Razor, which advises us to avoid assumptions that cannot be empirically verified.

Beyond that, what sort of predictions does such a God hypothesis make? Without knowing quite a bit about God's intentions, which we cannot independently verify anyway, how could we rationally decide whether the God hypothesis is confirmed or falsified? Kazim believes that the Grail takes life from only the unrighteous, but the Grail Knight suggests all must choose wisely. Who is correct? Did Donovan perish because he was unrighteous or because he chose a false grail? Unless we have definitive and independently verified answers to these questions, the God hypothesis remains inconclusive, if not simply unworkable.

Attempts at evaluating supernatural hypotheses are particularly pertinent to Indy, given some of his past experiences. Why would God work through the Sankara Stones when Indy invoked the name of Shiva to defeat Mola Ram? Does this falsify the God hypothesis, leading Indy to believe that Shiva—not the Judeo-Christian God—exists? But what, then, of his experiences with the Grail or the Ark? These unresolved difficulties may very well account for Indy's reluctance to adopt metaphysical or mythological beliefs when explaining what he experiences on his adventures.[6]

All of this might lead Indy to inform Tyree: "Maybe I didn't phrase it very well, but this is why I prefer to follow the facts and not be overly concerned about 'the truth,' or at least philosophical or mythological accounts of how things are. Further, those who are steeped in what they take to be 'the truth' about such matters often have difficulty making impartial observations or assessments of the data."

From here, Indy might point out to Tyree that on his "vacation"—when he wasn't being shot at, escaping a watery grave, or going over a cliff on a German tank—he did many things that archaeologists do, and Indy's fieldwork, although sometimes unconventional, resulted in finding the Grail—"the greatest artifact in the history of mankind," as Donovan claimed to Marcus. That is, he found the Grail by doing archaeology (or what passes for such in his case). Indy is not steeped in Christianity, as Henry and Marcus seem to be (and as William Tyree was).[7] Nevertheless, by following the *facts*, he found the Grail—and his father—but he did so by putting aside Grail mythology and any deeper religious or philosophical *truths* about it.

Tyree absorbs all the details of Indy's "vacation." After acknowledging that it was *much* more exciting than his relaxing days in Hawaii, he might share, "Jones, some scholars, like me, do not affirm distinct divisions between theology, philosophy, and the other disciplines. In fact, my specialty field is 'philosophical theology'—I believe philosophical thinking should inform our most profound understandings, including what it might mean for humanity to come to fruition.[8] However, some philosophers believe theology and philosophy are importantly distinct in their methods and presuppositions, as are theology and other self-standing disciplines, like archaeology, perhaps." Indiana blankly stares at his older colleague, again feeling unsure of how to respond. "So, Jones," Tyree continues, "I suggest you explore the difference between what might be called 'methodological naturalism' and 'metaphysical naturalism.'"

Methodological naturalism is a stance that many scientists take when doing science. They assume that the world acts in regular and (statistically) predictable ways, and these ways can be known and utilized in extending our knowledge about things in the world. They do not assume anything about God, religion, or about any deeper metaphysical truth or mythological belief regarding such things as life after bodily death, the ultimate origins of the universe, or how humanity might achieve fruition. Those matters are kept separate from the domain of science.

When Indy is being careful, perhaps his words about fact and truth—and his dismissiveness about religion or "the truth"—are best interpreted as expressing his commitment to methodological naturalism. As an archaeologist, he uses the scientific tools of his trade to obtain artifacts and extend our knowledge about past civilizations by carefully studying those artifacts. Any deeper truths associated with them he keeps separate from his archaeology. But, as Tyree would probably remind his young colleague, Indy is not always careful. Sometimes his words suggest another perspective, namely metaphysical naturalism. Metaphysical naturalism holds that all that exists is somehow a part of the natural world. There are no transcendent or supernatural beings, including God. Whether Indy is a metaphysical naturalist is difficult to say, but, as Tyree might point out, his classroom claim that archaeology is about the pursuit of fact, not truth, does not require him to be. He might adopt methodological naturalism without also affirming metaphysical naturalism. Indeed, his inexplicable experiences in the first three films might lead him away from metaphysical naturalism—even if some skepticism about the supernatural remains.

Gaining Illumination about Philosophy

Indy tells his father that Marcus once got lost in his own museum. This may be an apocryphal story, the two of them poking a bit of fun at their friend and colleague. But it is not at all difficult for someone to get "lost" outside of one's primary discipline. Professor Tyree reminds Indiana Jones of this very fact. Indy is an archaeologist, not a philosopher. Perhaps Indy would be wise to follow Professor Tyree when he wades into philosophical waters and heed his wise counsel about avoiding self-defeating positions, brushing up on epistemology, and learning more about methodological naturalism and how it differs from metaphysical naturalism.

Each of us has had philosophical thoughts at one time or another, but the subject is difficult to master. William Tyree—or whoever the philosophy professor is down the hall at your (nearby) university—can help.[9]

Notes

1 Ford's *Crusade* "shout out" to Tyree resulted from his rewriting that part of the script himself. Tyree responds to it in the July 3, 1989 edition of *People Magazine*. Tyree passed away on January 2, 2016; he was 98.

2 For a slightly different interpretation of Indy's "fact-not-truth" lecture, see Chapter 24 by Brown in this volume.

3 For a helpful discussion of how epistemology pertains to archaeology, see Kenneth L. Feder, *Frauds, Myths, and Mysteries: Science and Pseudoscience in Archaeology* (New York: Oxford University Press, 2018), 16–43.

4 See Eric Cline, *From Eden to Exodus: Unraveling Mysteries of the Bible* (Washington, DC: National Geographic, 2007), 121–152.
5 For an accessible account of why supernatural hypotheses are epistemologically problematic, see Larry Shapiro, *The Miracle Myth* (New York: Columbia University Press, 2016), 29–56.
6 Indy would be dubious of any sort of Shiva hypothesis for similar reasons as a Judeo-Christian God hypothesis. For a different, but related, account of why Indy's agnosticism about such things seems justified, see Chapter 11 by Price in this volume.
7 Tyree served as a chaplain in World War II and was known to counsel Ripon College students in matters pertaining to their faith.
8 William Tyree earned a Masters of Sacred Theology degree from Union Theological Seminary and a Ph.D. from the University of Edinburgh. His education and writing synthesized aspects of theology and philosophy, including epistemology and the philosophy of history.
9 Thanks to Roman Ciapalo and Vance Cope-Kasten for their helpful comments on an earlier draft of this chapter. I am grateful to Kathy Babcock for sharing her personal recollections of William Tyree; Kathy knew Tyree as a Ripon College student and later as a family friend. Hannaford kindly offered extensive comments on an earlier draft that were influential in shaping the final version. I hope I haven't written anything that would lead Vance or Spud to revoke my William E. Tyree Prize in Philosophy!

11

Indiana Jones and the Quest for Agnosticism: What if All Stories Are True?

Robert Grant Price

Indy puts other archaeologists to shame, but there's something even more amazing about what he does than the artifacts he unearths. What really boggles the mind is the variety of myths, conspiracies, pseudo-histories, and religions that turn out to be factually, historically true in the world of *Indiana Jones*.

In *Raiders of the Lost Ark*, Indy locates the lost Ark of the Covenant and experiences the wrath of the God during an ancient Jewish ceremony reenacted by Nazis. In *Temple of Doom*, he watches a Thuggee priest mystically pull a beating heart from a man (without killing him), witnesses (and is subjected to) mind control on a massive scale, and becomes the target of voodoo practices. In *The Last Crusade*, he finds the Holy Grail, accomplishing what King Arthur could not, and seemingly confirms the divinity of Christ. In *Kingdom of the Crystal Skull*, with the help of his estranged son, Indy lends credence to ancient astronaut theories about the advancement of primitive cultures and beholds the reality of extraterrestrials (or interdimensional beings). And these are just the discoveries that appear in the films.

Things go even further in the officially licensed comic books and novels. In the comics, Indy (with the help of Plato's lost *Hermocrates* text) discovers the lost continent of Atlantis and navigates its powerful orichalcum technology. He encounters the golden fleece and its protector the goddess Hecate from Greek mythology. He uncovers the Covenant of Buddha, containing the words of Gautama Buddha, which would have united practicing Buddhists everywhere. Adventuring with his father, he learns the lance that pierced Jesus's side—the Spear of Longinus—is actually of ancient Celtic origin, with connections to faery-folk, and its possessor holds the fate of humankind in his or her hands. He witnesses the power of the fabled

Indiana Jones and Philosophy: Why Did It Have to Be Socrates?, First Edition. Edited by Dean A. Kowalski.

Philosopher's Stone as it turns base metals into gold and reanimates deceased Nazi soldiers from the grave—looking quite "zombified" as they give the Heil Hitler salute.[1] (How much would Indy hate *those* guys?)

In the novels, Indy finds other wonderous artifacts—including the Staff of Aaron—that verify various myths of multiple ancient civilizations. But some of his finds are quite surprising. He discovers Noah's Ark and is aided by Noah himself. He confirms the existence of Merlin the Sorcerer (who inspired Tolkien's Gandalf, in case you didn't know). Indy explores a realm under the Earth's crust, thereby conferring truth on the Hollow Earth theory. He experiences the reality of Druid, Wiccan, and voodoo magic, and must come to grips with (non-Nazi) zombies of the undead and chemically induced variety. And he also experiences the vast power of the Philosopher's Stone, but in ways contrary to his initial encounter from the comics.[2]

Despite the facts about religion and the supernatural that his adventures uncover, Indy remains agnostic about the truths they seemingly lead him to. As we'll see, though, agnosticism is not his only option. Thinking through those options with Indy can help us navigate our own world in which competing facts vie for our belief.

Questioning Truth Itself

Despite Indy's famed assertion that archaeology is about "the search for fact, not truth," truth cannot be ignored. Let's put aside mere matters of opinion posed by questions like "Is *Raiders* a better film than *Crusade?*" There are certain facts true for all people. Harrison Ford majored in Philosophy at Ripon College, though he dropped out before graduation. This is true, and if someone believes otherwise, they are simply mistaken. But what about more controversial statements of (alleged) fact? Many people believe it's true that Jesus is divine, but many others believe he is not. When beliefs conflict, one must turn out to be true and the other false, unless both prove to be false. People may believe different things, but truth cannot contradict itself.

That is, unless you are Indiana Jones. Somehow Indy's world does not collapse under its contradictions. Relativism results if there is no universal truth or standard—there are merely different truths and believing one is not any better than believing another. But does truth work like this? *Can* all stories be true? That seems to be a fashionable view in our world today. You can hear it in lines like, "Trust your own truth," or "Who am I to judge?" Even among some scholars, the idea persists that one story, or one history, is as good as another. Indeed, some even say that history is essentially a narrative—that is, a story, rather than a sequence of verified facts.

Trouble brews, however, when a group of people tries to recount the same story and each person remembers different facts and different sequences of events. Unlike in Indy's world, in our world these stories cannot all be true, especially if the stories contradict on critical details. At some point we have to make a choice: to say that somebody misremembered or lied. Or, even better, we can investigate for ourselves to determine which story is most accurate. Historians do this all the time when they fill in the gaps of the historical record. The justice system does it too: police work is premised on determining the facts of a crime and holding parties responsible for their actions.

Philosophically, the trouble with the world Indiana Jones inhabits is that all histories and all world views turn out to be adequately justified and true. We are supposed to believe according to the evidence, but Indy's world contains a fantastical overabundance of it. If we cannot epistemically value one account over another, then distinguishing between historical fact and mythic folklore or judging right and wrong becomes incredibly difficult, if not impossible, and this leads to all sorts of problems, philosophical and practical. As we know, members of a jury must have evidence that puts their beliefs about guilt "beyond a reasonable doubt" before they convict a defendant. To do otherwise is unethical and unlawful. But if all narratives about the crime are equally true and adequately justified, how should we proceed?

Similarly, a philosopher will find their job impossible if they cannot start with true statements. After all, philosophy is predicated on truth. Truth is like a squash court: it provides the hard surface that philosophers need to play the game. To philosophize, one must formulate statements, and their truth must be adequately justified before the philosopher can continue. Philosophizing without any truth is like a game of squash without the walls: the ball never comes back; questions *never* have answers.

Of course, people have disagreed about what is true since the beginning of time. These days, though, some people question the possibility of truth itself, and Postmodernism claims that no grand narrative can capture the truth. The postmodernist Jacques Derrida (1930–2004) formed his philosophy of deconstruction from the view that words do not hold any inherent meaning. Whatever meaning words appear to hold exists only in the consensus of the audience. According to Derrida, "As soon as there is language, generality has entered the scene and the idiom compromises with something that is not idiomatic."[3] In effect, we provide meaning to words by how we choose to interpret them.

It's tempting to extend deconstruction to truth. Rather than residing outside the audience and existing independent of the observer, this line of reasoning insists, truth exists among groups of people who make observations. It is "inter-subjective." And since we can only access truth through words, obtaining any real understanding of truth is impossible. What stands as truth, according to this method, is often enforced by power. All so-called truth claims, then, should be deconstructed to see what they reflect about the people and powers who make them.

Postmodernism is a radical school of philosophical thought. Some find it strange. How can a philosophical perspective be true when it denies truth? But the strange thing about Indy's world is that the squash ball *always* comes back. Rather than dissipate into the unknowable nothingness of relativism, or deconstruct into power relationships, each question implicit in Indy's quests is answered in the affirmative. Every story is historically true, and so is every god, theology, mythos, pseudoscience, and philosophy spinning out of these histories. How should Indy proceed? How would you?

Agnosticism, Skepticism, and Hinduism

Indy doesn't fully believe any of the myths he encounters. In *Raiders*, officials inquire about the picture of the Ark Indy shows them, asking about the ominous beams of light emanating from it. Dr. Jones replies, "Lightning ... fire ... [shrugging his shoulders] Power of God, or something." Indy has learned the stories—he presumably went to Sunday school—but he is ambivalent about the Ark's power. Further, when Marcus later reminds him that the Ark is not to be taken lightly because no one knows its secrets, Indy retorts, "Oh, Marcus. What are you trying to do, scare me? ... I don't believe in magic, a lot of superstitious hocus pocus. I'm going after a find of incredible historical significance; you're talking about the bogeyman." Indy's religious ambivalence persists even after the events on the secret Nazi island. Although Belloq and the Nazis have mysteriously disappeared, Indy is more concerned about where the Ark will be kept and who the "top men" are.

In *Temple*, the Mayapore shaman is convinced that Indy's crash landing in India is evidence that Shiva has answered the villagers' prayers. They prayed for the return of their Shivalinga—a mystical rock they believe to be one of the five Sankara Stones. It was fate, not chance, that brought Indy to them, so Jones must go to Pankot and bring the Shivalinga back to them! Short Round is shaken, but Indy reassures his young friend that the shaman was just telling a "ghost story." Later, Indy refers to the missing Shivalinga as the "good luck rock of the village." Even after Indy invokes the power of the Stones against Mola Ram, returns the Shivalinga to the villagers, and affirms that he understands its power now, he casually makes his way to Delhi without much additional thought.

In *Crusade*, when Donovan recounts the Arthurian Grail legend, Indy remains dubious, calling it a "bedtime story" and deriding the hope for eternal life the Cup promises as "an old man's dream." Indy embarks on a quest for the Grail, not for the sake of finding the Cup itself, but to find his father. Drinking from the Cup miraculously heals his father's gunshot wound—leading an awestruck Brody to acknowledge its religious significance by making the sign of the cross—but Indy shows no remorse about losing it in the Temple.

In the six-issue comic *Thunder in the Orient*, Indy travels throughout Afghanistan and China in search of the Covenant of Buddha, which is a tome like no other because it contains the words of Gautama Buddha. It harbors the power to unite all the different sects of Buddhism into one faith (and other more mystical powers, which is why it was hidden away). Locating it would go a long way to establishing the truth of the Buddha's teachings. When Indy and his sidekick Sophia Hapgood discover the scrolls, only after narrowly escaping the clutches of a nefarious Japanese army general and competing Chinese warlords, they absent-mindedly expose the ancient scrolls to the open air. The scrolls disintegrate in seconds. Indy is somewhat remorseful about his error, but not for reasons having to do with the Buddha or Buddhism.

Mola Ram contends that Indy "will become a true believer," but nothing Indy witnesses or finds leads him to become an overtly religious person. He remains ambivalent about any larger religious truth that might be attached to the facts of his experience. Decades later, when he and his estranged son Mutt are exploring a South American cave, they find pictographs of elongated skulls. Mutt doesn't understand the drawings. Indy explains, "Nazca Indians used to bind their infant's head with rope to elongate their skull like that … to honor the gods." Mutt objects, saying, "God's head is not like that." To which Indy replies, "It depends who your god is." Here Indy acknowledges that there are multiple beliefs about the gods and, more importantly, seems content with the idea that no belief about the divine is epistemically privileged over another. There are different stories about the gods, including the monotheistic God, and he remains agnostic about which, if any, are true.

Convinced there was not enough reason or evidence to either justify or deny that God exists, the English scientist T. H. Huxley (1825–1895) called himself an "agnostic." Agnosticism occupies the epistemological ground between theism, the belief that enough evidence exists to confirm the reality of God or gods, and atheism, the belief that there is enough evidence to conclude that God (or the divine) does not exist.

Agnosticism originated in scientific/religious discourse, but today the concept applies to many facets of life. A person might, for example, remain agnostic about which is his or her favorite coffee chain.

Indy must be the strangest agnostic ever. He is one of the few people who comes to his agnosticism through a *surplus* of evidence, rather than a lack of it. He can confidently claim that any number of myths and presumed pseudo-histories are factually true. So why doesn't he become a religious believer? He met Merlin, so he could become a practicing Druid, and he found the Holy Grail, so why not become a committed Christian? Similarly, the Sankara Stones appear to be gifts from Shiva to combat evil, and given that Indy activates them against Mola Ram at the end of the film, who could question Indy if he converted to Hinduism? He found the very words of Buddha, so why not become a practicing Buddhist? This opens an interesting question: How long should a person remain skeptical about a story that seems true?

Made famous by the French philosopher René Descartes (1596–1560), skepticism seeks truth through a method of doubt. "I think, therefore I am" is true because it cannot be doubted. But a skeptical mindset becomes destructive if it stubbornly refuses to cede to the truth. When Indy obtains convincing evidence, he should declare a matter settled. Indy's problem, though, is that he often encounters stories that claim exclusivity over history and truth. Think about it like this: In some of Indy's adventures, the myths he proves to be fact do not contradict one another. For example, in the extended franchise, Indy discovers Atlantis and finds Noah's Ark. Both these myths can be true without canceling each other out. They can occupy the same reality, odd though it may be. In the case of these stories, we might try to argue that by discovering the truth of Atlantis and the Great Deluge, Indy has uncovered a larger narrative that can coherently contain these two mythical stories. Similarly, the stories of the Ark of the Covenant and the Grail can co-exist in the same universe—in fact, many Christians believe in the veracity of both. Notably, Indy's discovery at the end of *Crystal Skull* about extraterrestrials does not necessarily contradict the veracity of the Ark and Grail (at least if one's monotheism has room for intelligent beings from other planets)—because one might believe that the Creator was responsible for their existence as well.

But some stories do not permit competing accounts. Consider Christianity's claim that Jesus is divine and is the second person in the Holy Trinity of the one and only God. When Indy encounters the Greek god Hecate or pagan gods, the Christian claim is challenged and perhaps disproved.

Hinduism presents another challenge, but also a potential way out for Indy. Hinduism is polytheistic, with Hindus believing in and worshipping Krishna, Shiva, and a host of other gods. Still, most Hindus believe that Brahman "stands behind" all that there is. On this account, Brahman is the supreme being and ultimate reality, not unlike the common understandings of most monotheistic conceptions of God as the singular, generative, and sustaining force in the universe, including Christianity's God-the-Father. So, on one level, Shiva and Krishna exist and are to be worshiped, but the deeper truth is that all is Brahman. Might Indy find a way out of his epistemological predicament by adopting the overarching Hindu narrative about Brahman? Perhaps, but it would only take him so far. A new contradiction would emerge: In Christianity, ultimate reality (God) is personal and approachable. Christians are taught to worship God as father, but in Hinduism Brahman is non-personal and unapproachable. So, according to their own logic, the Hindu and Christian beliefs about ultimate reality cannot both be true. Other than go mad, what can Indy do? Or more importantly, what can we common folk—that is, we who are not action heroes with side-gigs as tenured professors—do when we encounter competing facts and warring truths?

Three Ways Out

Indy has at least three ways out of his predicament. He can remain agnostic, pick a faith, or find a way to live with the logical inconsistencies that he discovers on nearly every adventure.

His first path is to remain agnostic. Perhaps, respect for the truth demands that he should keep searching for the deciding fact, or an overarching explanation that can unify the many contradictory histories he uncovers. In a way, this is what Indy, the constant explorer, does. Even though he validates one myth after another and achieves a reasonable basis for belief in every religion, he continues searching for something more, something to break the deadlock of evidence. He lets his decision hang like an open note. He chooses to remain agnostic. For this to work, he must accept living in a state of indecision, a state that might prove unsatisfying, like a story without an ending.

In fact, this seems to be Indy's primary path. In *Crystal Skull*, Indy is finally called out on his agnosticism when Spalko flatly asks him, "Why do you choose not to believe your own eyes?" She seemingly speaks for all of us; because Indy has seen a great many things and has convincing evidence for multiple myths and stories. Spalko says that, given what she has seen, the ancient astronaut thesis is the only way to explain Akator: "Early man couldn't have conceived it, much less built it. It was a city of supreme beings, with technologies and paranormal abilities." But Indy calmly reminds her, "There is always another explanation." If there is always another explanation—another way to understand what one sees or discovers—then how could Indy come to any definitive conclusions about his discoveries?

Alternately, Indy could take a "leap of faith" and commit to a single conception of reality. The person who takes a leap of faith admits that they do not have all the evidence to guarantee truth, but they are willing to risk belief. Based on his many adventures, Indy could have been partial to this path. After all, he took a leap of faith in *Crusade* when he stepped onto the invisible bridge and later drank from what he took to be the "cup of a carpenter." Nonetheless, a leap of faith comes with the possibility of dire consequences. What if you leap and don't like where you land or, worse, don't land at all and fall to your death? Choosing without all the evidence runs the risk of error. Does anybody want to be the person for whom a sad ghost of the Crusades might say, "You have chosen poorly" (after rapidly aging and turning to dust)?

The third approach Indy could take to his predicament would be to treat all stories as true and to ignore the contradictions. Admittedly, this is hard to do, and in most cases, it is probably a bad idea. But Indy could reconcile competing truths by giving priority to the deeper symbolic truth of the story over the factuality of the story. He could find a way past the contradiction by remembering that a story can be *morally true* while *factually untrue*. For example, some Arthurian legends differ as to who found the Grail. Percival finds the Grail in the story of the Fisher King, whereas Galahad finds the Grail in *Le Morte d'Arthur*. If Indy treats these stories as histories, then both cannot be true. But symbolically, they complement rather than contradict each other. Percival's story tells us that only an innocent soul can discover what is most prized, and Galahad's story teaches that only the perfectly pure person can locate the Grail. These "histories" contradict but point to the same truth: that the elusive Grail, representing Christ, is something that humans cannot attain on their own, but only with God's gracious assistance.

Indy comes closest to this symbolic approach to truth in *Crystal Skull* when he explains Akator's not being a city of gold. Noting that the Ugha word for "gold" translates as "treasure," Indy conjectures that knowledge was their treasure. Deft maneuvers like this can't save Jones from all contradictions, though. In his adventures, he still must navigate multiple, conflicting stories that tend to be factually *true* (and not merely reinterpret those that initially seem false). Thus, Indy's world conveys human history rife with incompatible facts. He can accept the stories as symbolically and morally true, but he still must deal with contradictory histories—which will make fine work if he ever hangs up his bullwhip and becomes a philosopher like Professor Tyree.

You and I may not live the life of a globetrotting archaeologist, but our world is like Indy's—with histories vying for legitimacy, cultures competing for dominance, and old stories claiming perennial relevance. When we deal with the meaning of stories, we may prefer to rise above cobwebbed graveyards and questions of history. Concerning such stories, we might be tempted to ask, "Does it matter whether they are historically true as long as the deeper meanings of the stories are true?"

"Fact, not truth," Dr. Jones teaches his class. He's not wrong. But when dealing with interpretation and finding deeper meaning in a story, the search for fact doesn't negate the importance of seeking truth (despite Indy's advice to the contrary).

Seeking a Singular Treasure

For Indiana Jones, adventure lurks around every corner, and every myth turns out to be historically true, rather than just a story. How a person gets along in a world of competing (alleged) facts and truths depends on the individual. Agnosticism can be a path forward, but so can a life of faith for the person who commits to one of many religions. If neither of those paths appeal, a person could choose to live with the logical impossibilities and feed from a cornucopia of multiple symbolic truths, perhaps in the hope of finding deeper meaning.

The *Indiana Jones* franchise offers an extreme version of what many people experience, a world where what seemed true turns out to be false, and things that seemed straightforward are bursting with greater truths than at first appeared. Our world shares with Indy's the potential for conversion—to remake ourselves based on what facts reveal and what truths teach.

All of us, at one time or another, invariably find ourselves in the situation of not knowing what to believe in the face of conflicting evidence. How should we react? Should we take a leap of faith, content in knowing that we've made a choice and a commitment? Should we continue to interpret the various facts to find something symbolically true upon which we can hang our fedoras? Or should we take a lesson from Dr. Jones and continue adventuring until we find the treasure—the fact—that will confirm the true story?

Notes

1 These exploits are conveniently reprinted in *Indiana Jones Omnibus, Volumes 1 and 2* (Milwaukie, OR: Dark Horse Books, 2008).

2 These exploits are recorded in Rob Macgregor, *Indiana Jones and the Dance of the Giants* (New York: Bantam Books, 1991), Rob Macgregor,

Indiana Jones and the Genesis Deluge (New York: Bantam Books, 1992), Max McCoy, *Indiana Jones and the Philosopher's Stone* (New York: Bantam Books, 1995), Max McCoy, *Indiana Jones and the Hollow Earth* (New York: Bantam Books, 1997), Max McCoy, *Indiana Jones and the Secret of the Sphinx* (New York: Bantam Books, 1999), and Stever Perry, *Indiana Jones and the Army of the Dead* (New York: Del Ray Books, 2009).

3 Jacques Derrida, "There is No *One* Narcissism," in Elisabeth Weber ed. and Peggy Kamuf trans., *Points ... Interviews, 1974–1994* (Stanford: Stanford University Press, 1995), 200.

12

The Shadow Realities of *Indiana Jones*

Matthew Crippen and Matthew Dixon

Philosophy begins in wonder, and mysterious voids fuel a sense of wonder. It's a natural connection. Truly, caves have captured the imagination of everyone from the prehistoric Lascaux painters to modern-day spelunkers and moviegoers. It's philosophically fitting, then, that some of the most memorable scenes in the *Indiana Jones* films occur underground. We can remember being on the edge of our seats watching Indy fleeing the rolling boulder in *Raiders of the Lost Ark*, and feeling intrigued by the beam of sunlight pinpointing the Ark's true location in the map room. Who could forget the alarming events in the cave under Pankot Palace in *Temple of Doom*, as Indy navigates psychological and physical labyrinths to come out wiser? We recall Indy choosing wisely again in the cavern near the end of *The Last Crusade*, and escaping his subterranean trials in the *Crystal Skull* with the revelation about the alien spaceship. All these examples are to be expected given that Indy is a comic book archaeologist. But is something deeper going on?

Storywriter George Lucas was a fan of the mythologist Joseph Campbell, who showed that humankind faces primal realities that consequently lurk in collective imagination and hence in cross-cultural mythic archetypes.[1] One of those archetypes is the cave. Exploring this, our chapter focuses on *Crusade* to argue that there is indeed something philosophically deeper to the cave imagery we see in the *Indiana Jones* saga.

Shadows in Plato's Cave

Among the most famous cave stories of all time is Plato's (428–348 BCE) allegory in which the philosopher asks us to imagine prisoners chained and perpetually facing a subterranean wall. A fire burns at

Indiana Jones and Philosophy: Why Did It Have to Be Socrates?, First Edition. Edited by Dean A. Kowalski.

their backs, and between the flames and the prisoners there is a walkway over which people carry sculptures. Because the prisoners only ever see shadows, they take them to be true reality. In fact, though, the shadows are only silhouettes of the sculptures, which in turn imitate true things outside of the cave.

Plato loved geometry, and the allegory is often explained in terms of that subject. Suppose a teacher draws a circle and then asks students to close their eyes to imagine it. The fuzzy image students will picture is a low level of reality—an imitation of the figure on the chalkboard. Yet even the figure on the board is not a real circle, but only an approximation of the true circle "seen" through reason and understanding. This is because the chalkboard circle is never rendered perfectly so as to have a circumference everywhere equidistant from the center. Notice further that the color, specific size, whether it's drawn on slate or plastic, produced with chalk or ink are all irrelevant to its true nature, indicating that the real circle is *ideal* and independent of the material world.

The true circle is real and discoverable in the same way the Pythagorean theorem is. From this standpoint, true form is immaterial, unchanging, and perfect: eternal and god-like. Though the quest for eternity is part of our mythic heritage and a driving force in *Crusade*, it's worth noting—as Friedrich Nietzsche (1844–1900) did—that true form lacks attributes of living beings, which are material, changing, and messy.[2] Above the rest of the world outside the cave, Plato also spoke of a still more transcendent realm, identifying it with the Sun in his allegory. The Sun allows life to flourish and lets us see it, so it is simultaneously the source of reality and our knowledge of it. Plato used the Sun to represent what he called the Good. Many later philosophers equated it to God, here, too, understood as the wellspring of being and knowledge.[3]

Paralleling Plato's allegory, *Crusade* has obvious religious significance in its title and content. Indeed, the movie begins and ends with stand-ins for God in caves, namely, a golden cross and the Holy Grail. The pattern holds elsewhere. Part way through, Indy and Elsa—a Nazi agent pretending to be an ally—navigate catacombs beneath a church that has been converted into a library. Religious iconography is everywhere, including the dead knight's shield and sarcophagus (and Indy is "pretty sure" he sees a drawing of the Ark of the Covenant). However, none of these things are God; they are instead representations of God. So it's fitting that they're inside cavernous enclosures. Indeed, the movie's culmination incorporates decoy chalices, which are imitations of a representation of God, giving them the same status as Plato's shadows. It's also Platonically appropriate that pivotal moments of self-realization and fulfillment of certain values—for example, Indy and Henry Jones Sr. actualizing their roles as father and son at the end of the film—occur near cave entrances within the reach of sunlight.

Crusade sets other self-transformative truths near cave entrances. Most notably, a flashback to a cavern in the American West shows a teenage Indiana confronting an archaeological looter, who is an archetype for the Odysseus-like rogue Indy will become. Odysseus, the hero of *The Odyssey*, was a cunning and daring trickster. The young maverick Indy follows his mythic counterpart in voyaging through underworlds in search of "fortune and glory," as he puts it in *Temple*. After the initial confrontation with the looter, there's a frenzied chase involving knife- and gun-wielding assailants, horses, automobiles, and a train with dangerous circus animals, typifying situations Indy will find himself in as an adult. The scene also explains some of his character traits. It is by falling into a serpent pit on the train that Indy develops his snake phobia. In fending off a lion with a nearby bullwhip, he accidentally strikes his own chin, accounting for the scar and his bullwhip fixation. Jones goes on to adopt elements of the comportment, dress, and even verbal tropes of the rogue, who puts his hat on Indy when he takes the looted crucifix back, gruffly but affectionately remarking: "You lost today, kid, but that doesn't mean you have to like it."

Although Indy never becomes a model archaeologist, he seems to inch from the depths of Plato's cave to its opening, rising to an ideal higher than that of the crass materialist, who plunders for mere gain and without interest in uncovering hidden truths. In *Temple*, Jones ends up more preoccupied with mysteries than physical artifacts, also displaying moral character by giving the remaining Sankara Stone to the desperate villagers. This pattern repeats in *Raiders* and *Crystal Skull*, not incidentally in the context of caverns. Likewise in *Crusade*: Indy does not steal the cross from the looters to keep or sell it, but because "it belongs in a museum," an idealistic observation he makes just within the reach of sunlight near the cave opening. At the movie's culmination, he seeks the Grail to use its healing powers to save Henry Sr. from a mortal gun wound. Ultimately he relinquishes the cup to take his father's hands, and he avoids falling into a dark abyss. This elevation of life and family over treasure is again accented by sunlight flitting through the cavern entrance.

Indy never quite reaches the ideal, though. The opening scene of *Crusade* has him stealing the cross from its legal owners; later, he shatters a beautiful marble floor, smashes through a wall, and callously overturns the ornately carved sarcophagus lid in the library crypt; and he similarly breaches norms of good archaeology on his way to the Holy Grail at the end of the movie, albeit to help his dying father. One might say Indy is a shadow of a good archaeologist, but he's still interested in higher truths and values, in this way clawing closer to the exit of Plato's cave.

New and Old Shadows: Action and Revelation

Roughly 2,500 years after Plato, American transcendentalists and pragmatists built on Greek philosophy to refashion concepts of truth. Specifically, they abandoned static concepts, arguing that we discover things by systematically jostling and changing them, or altering conditions of observation.[4] As William James (1842–1910) put it, "Truth happens to an idea. It *becomes* true, is *made* true."[5] Along similar lines, John Dewey (1859–1952) pointed to art as truth revealing. Poetry is an archetypal example. The word "poetry" has ancient Greek roots that connote "making," "doing," "creating," and "handiwork." Poets are makers in the obvious sense of being creative wordsmiths. They are also revealers, bending language to help us see things that we missed, almost as black light divulges what was previously hidden. Dewey accordingly remarked that poetry "radiates the light that never was on land and sea but that is henceforth an abiding illumination of objects."[6] Summarizing roughly the same idea in squarely mythic terms, the German philosopher Martin Heidegger (1889–1976) discussed *aletheia*, a Greek word for "truth."[7] The term combines the prefix *a-* with the word *lethe*. The prefix means "without," and *lethe* means concealment. (In Greek mythology, Lethe was the name of an underworld river that would obscure a person's memory when they drank from it.) Heidegger accordingly maintained that truth brings things out of hiding; it lifts the veil and reveals.

These newer notions accordingly build on old Greek traditions, and we also see a merging of old and new in *Crusade*. The movie starts with Indigenous singing and percussion, suggesting pre-Columbian times, then flashes to Indy's youth in the American desert where the plunderers have just discovered the crucifix: an Old-World relic in the New World. Newer and older concepts of truth—which are not utterly divergent—are specifically personified by Indy and his father. The elder and younger Joneses exemplify Old- and New-World customs respectively, and are appropriately played by a Scotsman and an American. Their first interaction highlights the contrast. Having just seized the cross from the plunderers, Indy rushes up a pathway that cuts through an unkept yard, leading to a rundown house. Clamoring in, he passes the dog from which he adopted his nickname, "Indiana," and bursts into his father's study, which has a cluttered cave-like appearance, with sunlight streaming through the windows. His father wears professorial garb, including a bowtie that will be his signature up until almost the movie's end. Henry Sr. pores over a medieval manuscript depicting a knight and Christian iconography. Annoyed by Indy's intrusion, he stalls the action by instructing his son to count to 20 in Greek. This early scene effectively depicts a contrast between an older man, who excavates preserved truths through quiet contemplation, and his younger son, who seizes them through energetic action that often entails testing their world-changing mysteries.

The two Joneses nonetheless share a lot, to the point of shadowing one another. Indy hates snakes, his father rats. Indy becomes highly educated like his father, and already shows a command of ancient languages when a teenager. History fascinates both men, who dwell in silhouettes of the past. They are both named Henry, which is why Indy's father calls him Junior. Yet they also have different personas. Henry Sr. relishes academic life, and for much of the film is comically out of place in action-packed scenarios. Although Indy adopts a professorial career too, he seems reluctant. At one point he flees students, absconding into his office that doubles as a boiler room. It is appointed with rustic furniture and wood shelves cradling stone and clay artifacts, giving it a cave-like appearance. Once again sunlight seeps through a window, the one Indy uses to escape his irate students.

As the movie progresses, Henry Sr. gradually comes to shadow Indy's active ways. Shocked when his son kills a group of Nazis, he exclaims "Look what you did!" But the elder Jones soon finds himself manning the turret in a biplane, albeit incompetently. To his credit, Henry Sr. adjusts. After crash landing, and with a German fighter bearing down, he startles a flock of birds with his umbrella; the flock takes flight into the plane, causing it to crash. Here, he fuses his son's active tendencies with his contemplative ones. In a fictitious quote invented for the movie, he chuckles that "I suddenly remembered my Charlemagne: 'Let my armies be the rocks and the trees and the birds in the sky'."

Such patterns repeat. Later, Henry Sr. is captive in the belly of a World War I-style tank, once again with sunlight pouring through viewports and an open hatch, recalling the prisoners in Plato's cave. At one point, he fights a soldier for a pistol, while his endearingly helpless friend Marcus sits idly by. As his enemy gets control over the firearm, Henry Sr. squirts ink from his fountain pen into his attacker's eyes. Although a cartoonish act, it expresses the idea that pens can defeat guns when wielded by those steeped in the art of writing. That said, Henry Sr. decides guns can work too, pulling the trigger on a side cannon, demolishing an approaching truckload of soldiers. Marcus incredulously says, "Look what you did!", shadowing the earlier remark of Indy's father. Even Marcus, who, in fact, pointed out the power of the pen to Indy's father in his soft-spoken way, determines that big sticks can get the job done when he clubs an assailant with a metal pipe.

Indy similarly undergoes a transformation that brings him closer to his father's Old-World thoughtfulness, while simultaneously accentuating his New-World brashness, particularly when he encounters trials that demand elevated contemplation and daring at the same time. This is especially so in the three tests to gain entry to the cavern chamber with the Grail. Each comes with a clue. The first proclaims: "The penitent man is humble before God." Indy figures out that a humble man kneels, taking this position, narrowly avoiding decapitating blades. The second clue declares: "Only in the footsteps of God will he proceed," a statement implying action while referencing the opening of the Gospel of John, with its Platonic overtones. This puzzle is easier because Indy confronts a walkway with rough tiles, each with a letter. Yet passing through requires more knowledge since the word for God is inscribed in Latin. Getting through, of course, demands action, with missteps causing death. As Nietzsche observes, a healthy life is one of *overcoming*. Fittingly, Indy surmounts obstacles through a *growing* appreciation of the wisdom of old books.[8]

The third challenge is the most interesting and connects squarely with concepts of truth as revelation. It presents the following puzzle: "Only in the leap from the lion's head will he prove his worth." Indy here encounters a sculpted lion's head overlooking a chasm, maybe 50 meters across. Indy is hesitant, but the voice of Marcus echoes through the cavern, urging him to get the Grail to resuscitate his wounded father. He steps into the void, only to find sure footing on a walkway perfectly camouflaged with the surrounding rock so as to be invisible. This exactly captures a sentiment that William James expressed when he said that belief is measured by willingness to act; actions can generate, and hence reveal, realities that were initially taken on faith.[9] But insofar as the leap depends on faith in something superseding mere material existence, it also signifies a return to Plato.

Myth and Family in Plato's Cave

Parent–child conflicts are part of the human condition, and central in the history of myth, whether with ancient gods overthrowing their parents, or with children disobeying their heavenly father in Abrahamic traditions, or again with tragic figures such as Agamemnon, Electra, and Medea. Parent–child issues are also prominent in the *Indiana Jones* movies. *Temple* and *Crystal Skull* respectively have Indy as the surrogate and absentee father. *Crusade*, in its turn, has Indy struggling with an emotionally distant father.

Without suggesting sexual hang-ups, father–son conflicts in *Crusade* approach the Oedipal myth at times, with Henry Sr. and Indy romantically involved with the same woman. Partly crafted by renowned playwright Tom Stoppard, the film shows a love scene with Indy and Elsa, but soon after the audience learns about Henry Sr.'s relationship when he explains that her Nazi allegiance was obvious because she talks in her sleep. The two men are next restrained back-to-back in a Nazi lair. Elsa comments to Indy that she "can't forget how wonderful it was." Henry Sr. is facing away from her, so assumes this is directed at him, remarking, "Thank you, it was rather wonderful." Indy later chastises Henry Sr., indicating he's old enough to be her grandfather. The indication is—again, along Oedipal lines—that she's young enough to be Indy's daughter. This is fitting because she is a darker shadow of himself—of what he could have become had he solely fixated on fortune and glory.

The relationship between the Jones men is generally tense. Early on, Henry Sr. mistakes Indy for a Nazi, breaking a vase over his head, showing more concern for the smashed artifact—which turns out to be a forgery—than for his possibly concussed son. A little later, he declares the Grail even more important than his friend Marcus. Indy complains that neither he nor his mother ever understood his father's Grail obsession. Henry Sr. laments that his wife understood only too well, keeping the distraction of an illness from him until all he could do was mourn her death. Aboard a Zeppelin leaving Germany, the two share a drink. Indy remarks that he had a milkshake the last time they had a moment like this, indicating it was decades ago. His father—more interested in his Grail journal—distractedly asks what they discussed. Indy replies: "We never talked." Henry Sr. interjects that he was a great father: he didn't tell Indy what to do and taught him self-reliance. His son rebukes: "What you taught me was that I was less important to you than people who had been dead for 500 years."

Henry Sr. evolves, however, and by the end of *Crusade* Indy has become more important than the Grail. This is, in fact, the elder Jones's path out of Plato's cave. We see this change when Indy is reaching for the Grail, as his father clings to one of his hands to prevent him from tumbling into an abyss, sunlight once again dappling the cavern entrance. Almost exactly echoing what his darker shadow, Elsa, said before she fell to her death trying to grasp the Grail, Indy blurts: "I can almost reach it, Dad." Henry Sr. gets his son's attention by finally calling him by his preferred name, Indiana. His father has relinquished his lifelong quest for the artifact, and calmly urges his son to do the same.

The closeness of the Jones men in this climactic scene is symbolized by the fact Henry Sr. has lost his tweed jacket, and his signature bow tie is undone, along with the top buttons on his now-filthy shirt. This all gives him a rough-and-tumble appearance approaching that of his son. Simultaneously, he retains his high-minded, Platonic thinking. When Indy queries what he got out of the quest, his father answers simply: "Illumination." The Grail as a physical artifact has lost sway over him, but he cherishes the wisdom he has gained. Given that Henry Sr. has moved to the ideal, it's fitting that this exchange occurs outside the cave in full sunlight. Yet the scene crashes down from the ethereal when Henry Sr. asks his son what he gained, unfortunately reverting to the habit of calling him Junior, which annoys Indy, reintroducing a petty conflict and preventing an answer. The return to earth is accentuated by the soft umbers of the desert and the fact that the men—Henry Sr., Indy, Marcus, and Sallah—return to action, riding horses into the sunset.

Truth, Acts, and Shadow Facts

Crusade highlights the risks of overly contemplative life: Henry Sr.'s mode of existence not only damages his relationship with his son, but limits his capacity to discover the Grail. At the same time, the movie depicts the dangers of fervent action without adequate contemplation. As Nazi collaborator Walter Donovan says, his allies "want to write themselves into the Grail legend and take on the world." Marcus warns Donovan that "you're meddling with powers you cannot possibly comprehend," and the latter is indeed killed by mystical forces he does not understand. Henry Sr. similarly laments that "Elsa never really believed in the Grail. She thought she'd found a prize," and she died seeking it.

Additionally, *Crusade* shows that newer, active notions of truth are not diametrically opposed to older, more static ones. Even if it turns out that older notions are false, they retain a role by providing solid ground for truth-revealing action. Indy's development calls to mind ideas advanced by Nietzsche. Simultaneously criticizing and appreciating Greek philosophy, Nietzsche rejected the unchanging "true" ideas of Plato as false yet potentially life-enhancing fictions that can bring out and thus reveal new ways of being.[10] So, for example, the golden cross at the beginning of the film is nothing more than that; it's an empty fiction of sorts, not worth risking one's life over as Indy later does on the ship at sea. Yet the initial fight over the cross generates Indy's self-identity—everything from his hat, chin scar, bullwhip fetish, and fear of snakes to his maverick attitude. Moreover, we must overcome static concepts; tired and conventional thinking traps us. We learn this from Plato's allegory where the shadows might be understood as commonplaces that people unquestionably take to be true.

Crusade offers a cartoonish, colorful, and sentimental spectacle. But it nonetheless deals in sophisticated ways with ideas percolating in the collective culture that Campbell described, including ideas that captivated Plato. The film also flips Plato to reveal other archetypes. Indy prefers action, and says he's interested in facts, not truth. Facts are occurrences, and the Latin root of "facts" means "do" or "make" or "act." In ancient contexts "pure act" is total achievement of ideal form, where the completely *act*ualized thing has full truth and being. To the extent that Indy and his father become more truly who they are, the transitions are in keeping with the general thrust of the allegory of the cave, while simultaneously exemplifying pragmatic, transcendental, and existential trajectories.

Notes

1 See Joseph Campbell, *The Hero with a Thousand Faces* (Princeton: Bollingen Foundation, 1949) and *The Masks of God*, vols. 1–4 (New York: Viking, 1969).

2 Friedrich Nietzsche highlights this in *Twilight of the Idols* [1888], trans. Walter Kaufman, in *The Portable Nietzsche*, ed. Walter Kaufman (New York: Penguin, 1954), 473–486. Plato appeared sensitive to this, indeed defining truth-seeking inquiry as a practice of death. Plato, *Phaedo*, trans. G.M.A. Grube, 64–68, available at http://cscs.res.in/dataarchive/textfiles/textfile.2010-09-15.2713280635/file.

3 See Etienne Gilson, *Being and Some Philosophers* (Toronto: PIMS, 1949), ch. 1.

4 See John Dewey, *The Quest for Certainty* (New York: Minton, Balch & Co., 1929), ch. 4; Ralph Waldo Emerson, *Nature* (Boston: Munroe and Co., 1836), esp. ch. 8.

5 William James, *Pragmatism: A New Name for Some Old Ways of Thinking* (New York: Longman Green and Co., 1907), 77–78.

6 John Dewey, *Experience and Nature* (Chicago: Open Court, 1925), 360.

7 See Martin Heidegger, *Poetry, Language, Thought*, trans. Albert Hofstadter (New York: Harper and Row, 1971), 56–86.

8 Friedrich Nietzsche, *Thus Spoke Zarathustra* [1892], trans. Walter Kaufman, in *The Portable Nietzsche*, ed. Walter Kaufman (New York: Penguin, 1954), 225–228.

9 For example, William James, "Rationality, Activity and Faith," *Princeton Review* vol. 2 (1882): 58–86.

10 For example, Friedrich Nietzsche, *Gay Science* [1887], trans. Walter Kaufmann (New York: Vintage Books, 1974), §110; Nietzsche, *Twilight*, 473–479.

13

Pride and Prudence in the Pursuit of Knowledge: Indiana Jones, René Belloq, and Irina Spalko

Alexander Hooke and Dean A. Kowalski

Perched high on a rock face, Indiana Jones points a stolen bazooka at a squad of marching Nazi soldiers. He shouts, "I'm going to blow up the Ark, René." René Belloq, Indy's nemesis, replies, "Your persistence surprises even me." Nazi commander Colonel Dietrich is also surprised by Indy's resolve: "Dr. Jones, surely you don't think you can escape from this island?" Still peering through the sighting mechanism, Indy retorts, "That depends on how reasonable we're all willing to be; all I want is the girl." Marion Ravenwood beams. Dietrich looks back at Belloq, who shakes his head, and then inquires, "And if we refuse?" "Then your Fuehrer has no prize," Indy mutters. Belloq calls Indy's bluff: "Okay, Jones, you win. Blow it up. Blow it back to God." Belloq pauses a moment and then continues, "All your life has been spent in pursuit of archaeological relics. Inside the Ark are treasures beyond your wildest aspirations. You want to see it open as well as I. Indiana, we are simply passing through history. This [pointing at the Ark] … This *is* history. Do as you will." Indy closes his eyes, swallows hard, and lowers his weapon.

Indy is stuck between a rock and a hard place. The rock is behind him—literally—but putting that observation aside, how does he choose between one of the most prized archaeological artifacts of all time and the love of his life, especially when blowing up the former does not guarantee the safety of the latter? Further, Belloq is not wrong: The Ark represents everything Indy got into archaeology for in the first place. The temptation to see it opened—to learn its secrets—is all but irresistible. Indeed, as we'll see, most philosophers believe that it's only

Indiana Jones and Philosophy: Why Did It Have to Be Socrates?, First Edition. Edited by Dean A. Kowalski.

natural for humans to seek out what we do not know, but some scholars caution that some pursuits of knowledge are more advisable than others. In this chapter, we'll explore how Indiana Jones serves as an important guide to seeking the truth, especially by contrasting him with his two ill-fated antagonists René Belloq and Irina Spalko.

"If It's Truth You're After ..."

Aristotle (384–322 BCE) writes: "All men by nature desire to have knowledge. An indication of this is the delight we take in the senses ... and above all others the sense of sight ... The reason is that this, most of all the senses makes us know, and brings to light many differences between things."[1] Of course, the other senses are also effective sources of knowledge, but so is the careful use of our reason.

Regardless of how we pursue knowledge, Socrates (469–399 BCE) believes that we *ought* to seek unknown truths. Plato recounts Socrates's words:

> I would contend at all costs both in word and deed as far as I could that we will be better men, braver and less idle, if we believe that one must search for things one does not know, rather than if we believe that it is not possible to find out what we do not know and that we must not look for it.[2]

The *Indiana Jones* films offer many vivid examples of people seeking unknown truths. Indy has spent his entire life exploring past civilizations, first with his father in *The Young Indiana Jones Chronicles*, and then on his own as an archaeology professor. His goal is to enhance our understanding of human history by discovering artifacts and by placing them in public museums for future study. His father pursued clues about the Holy Grail his entire adult life, which might have influenced Indy to become an expert on the occult. Thus, Indy's pursuit of knowledge was not limited to well-established scientific principles—even if his commitment to science makes him doubt the supernatural powers associated with the artifacts he seeks. Dr. Colonel Irina Spalko—Order of Lenin recipient, Hero of Socialist Labor medal-winner, and Stalin's favorite scientist of psychic research—pursued the occult with gusto, especially when it might have paranormal military applications. She scoffs at Indy's entrenched skepticism about the supernatural and asks him, "Why do you choose not to believe your own eyes?"

Socrates never shied away from a difficult path in pursuit of truth. Plato recounts Socrates's famous words: "It is the greatest good for a man to discuss virtue every day and those other things about which you hear me conversing and testing myself and others, for the unexamined life is not worth living."[3] Socrates inquired into the nature of human excellence, which led him to explore universal truths about what is right and good. By utilizing our natural tendencies to seek knowledge, Socrates believed that we gain important insights into the best kind of human life.

Contemporary scholar Gilbert Meilaender cautions that our natural inclinations toward curiosity can lead us to good or bad results. Meilaender agrees with Aristotle that "our desire for knowledge is natural and praiseworthy as it is in itself," but reminds us that knowledge "is only the raw material out of which we construct character, develop virtues and vices."[4] Socrates stresses that knowledge ought to lead to virtue and human excellence, but Meilaender is more concerned about those who fail to put knowledge to good use.

Meilaender seems sympathetic to the common view that curiosity leads us astray when we seek useless knowledge, but his primary worry is when our quest to know is driven by power and control. When it becomes a thirst that must be quenched and is not limited by ethical considerations, including a proper appreciation of one's appropriate place in the order of things, then curiosity becomes a vice. As Meilaender sums up: "Our search for knowledge must accept limits or become an empty destructive urge to possess … It becomes vice … when we can never find reasons why we *ought* not gratify our desire to see and know, when we regard no secrets as closed to our inquiring minds, when curiosity is bounded neither by respect for others nor reverence for God."[5]

In the *Indiana Jones* films, we find two vivid examples of Meilaender's prescriptions about pursuing knowledge. The first is Belloq's irreverence toward God. The second is Spalko's extreme attempts to overcome the Soviet Union's rivals. Both characters are driven by hubris—extreme pride—in their attempts to gain knowledge.

"Do You Know What the Ark Is?"

Major Eaton and Colonel Musgrove inform Indy and Marcus Brody that they have intercepted a German communiqué: The Nazis have found the lost city of Tanis and now seek the Staff of Ra headpiece. Additionally, the Nazis believe Indy's mentor Abner Ravenwood has the headpiece medallion, but he's gone missing. Indy doesn't know where Abner is, but he suspects that the Nazis are looking for the Lost Ark of the Covenant, because Tanis is one of its presumed resting places. After Indy and Marcus provide the government agents some background on the Ark, Eaton says, "I'm beginning to understand Hitler's interest in this." Brody concurs: "Oh, yes. The Bible speaks of the Ark leveling mountains and laying waste to entire regions. An army that carries the Ark before it ... is invincible."

Once the government agents grasp the potential ramifications of Hitler possessing the Ark, they authorize Indy to search for it. As Brody explains, "They want you to get ahold of the Ark before the Nazis do. And they're prepared to pay handsomely for it." Indy is much more interested in the Ark's historical significance: "The museum gets the Ark when we're finished?" When Marcus assures him it will, the two celebrate with a glass of champagne. As they toast, Indy reminds his friend, "The Ark of the Covenant ... That thing represents everything we got into archaeology for in the first place." Still, Marcus advises caution: "For nearly 3,000 years, man has been searching for the Lost Ark. Not something to be taken lightly. No one knows its secrets." Indy thinks Marcus is overreacting, as he states, "I'm going after a find of incredible historical significance; you're talking about the bogeyman." Indy may not fully appreciate all the religious mystery traditionally associated with the Ark, but he does not seek it for monetary gain—and he has no interest in its alleged powers. He seeks the Ark for the prospects of studying it and learning about history.

René Belloq's motivations regarding the Ark are more personal than professional. Rather than using his archaeological skills to prevent the Nazis from finding the Ark, as does Indy, he works with them. But Belloq's alliance with the Nazis is murky, as he informs Marion, "At this particular time and place, to do my work, they are necessary evils. They're not my friends." And the Nazis soon become suspicious of Belloq. When Belloq objects to throwing Marion into the Well of Souls (wearing the white dress Belloq gave her the night before), Dietrich reminds him, "Only our mission for the Fuehrer matters. I wonder sometimes, monsieur, if you have that clearly in mind."

Belloq's primary goal is securing the Ark. Believing Marion is dead, Belloq and Indy meet in a Cairo tavern. Indy is crestfallen and well into his bottle of whiskey. Belloq pontificates: "You and I are very much alike. Archaeology is our religion, yet we have both fallen from the purer faith. Our methods have not differed as much as you pretend. I am a shadowy reflection of you. It would take only a nudge to make you like me." Belloq undoubtedly projects himself onto Indy here and not entirely convincingly, but he then turns the conversation to the Ark, as he tells Indy it is "priceless" and "men will kill for it. Men like you and me." Not taking the bait, Indy scoffs, "What about your boss, *der*

Fuehrer? I thought he was waiting to take possession." "All in good time. When *I* am finished with it," replies Belloq.

Belloq's primary motivation becomes clearer: he wants the Ark for himself. His eyes widen and he explains to Indy, "Jones, do you realize what the Ark is? It's a transmitter! It's a radio for speaking to God, and it's within my reach!" Belloq believes the Ark will give him an audience with the Almighty Himself! Indy finally turns to look his adversary in the eye, and states, "You want to talk to God? Let's go see him together," and as he reaches for his gun, he continues, "I've got nothing better to do." At that moment, Sallah's many children unexpectedly enter the tavern and rescue Indy from Belloq's armed henchmen. Belloq remarks, "Next time, Indiana Jones, it will take more than children to save you."

When Belloq and the Nazis resecure the Ark from the hold of the *Bantu Wind*, Belloq convinces Dietrich to open the Ark before presenting it to Hitler. Despite Dietrich's discomfort with the pending Jewish ritual, Belloq muses: "Let me ask you this: Would you be more comfortable opening the Ark in Berlin, for your Fuehrer? Finding out only then if the sacred pieces of the Covenant are still inside? Knowing only then whether you have accomplished your mission, and obtained the one true Ark?" Belloq's questions are, of course, rhetorical. Dietrich cannot risk failure. But Belloq doesn't care about Dietrich, or Hitler, for that matter. He cares only about knowing what happens when the Ark is opened—the secrets revealed to him via his personal audience with God.

Dressed as a Hebrew High Priest, Belloq conducts a Jewish ritual before opening the Ark. With such attention to detail, he must be aware of the biblical prohibitions about looking upon the face of God. Perhaps Belloq believes that if the ritual is conducted carefully enough, God will favor him.[6] With the ritual complete, Nazi soldiers remove the lid. Indy, chained to a pole with Marion in the distance, smirks when Belloq realizes the Ark contains not the stone tablets of the Ten Commandments, but only sand. Belloq grimaces in frustration. But then Belloq notices bright light and eerie movement within the Ark; angelic beings soon emanate from it. Belloq shouts, "It is beautiful," but the spirits quickly become gruesome, frightening the crowd. A flame rises above the Ark and spreads to the Nazi soldiers, killing them and melting Dietrich's and Major Toht's faces. Belloq can only stare at the horrors that beset him. Consumed by the flames, he attempts to protect himself by placing his hands over his face, but to no avail. Screaming, his head explodes. Belloq's insatiable curiosity about the divine was his doom.

Belloq believed that God would reveal to him the secrets of the Ark on Belloq's terms. Hubris led to his demise. Indiana Jones was also curious about the Ark and its secrets, which accounted for (in part) his reluctance to "blow it back to God," but he was much more prudent. Having expressed his doubts about the Ark's power to Marcus—derisively referring to the legends as "a bunch of superstitious hocus pocus"—Indy nevertheless tells Marion, "Don't look at it, no matter what happens." Indy chooses not to see the Ark's secrets. It's not that he does not wish to study and learn about the Ark, but he has qualms with the way in which Belloq releases its secrets and the motivations that drive his methods. Indy's choice suggests that there are appropriate and inappropriate ways to gain knowledge of sacred objects, especially those that represent God's presence on earth. In this, Meilaender would agree.

Tell Me Everything You Know—I Want It All!

Irina Spalko is even more driven in her personal pursuits than is Belloq. She orders her troops to kill the American soldiers manning the guard posts of the Hangar 51 military installation. After giving a similar order concerning the Ugha warriors who guard the Akator temple, she simply walks by dead warriors strewn about riddled with gunshot wounds. Spalko kidnaps Harold Oxley and Indy for their knowledge of Akator and its crystal skulls, and also kidnaps Marion and Mutt Williams to ensure Indy's compliance in her quest to learn Akator's secrets. Belloq was party to the Nazi's kidnapping Marion for information, but he never had anyone killed in his quest for the Ark.

After kidnapping Indy again, Spalko shares her intentions regarding the crystal skull with him. She believes that it will provide the Soviet Union the upper hand in the Cold War. The crystal skull is "a mind weapon. A new frontier of psychic warfare; that was Stalin's dream." The crystal skull that drove Oxley mad belongs to a race of extraterrestrial beings (and as Ox later informs us, they are "interdimensional beings, in point of fact"). The skull was stolen from Akator in the fifteenth century. Spalko states, "Whoever returns it ..." and then Indy finishes her sentence, "to the city's temple will gain control over its power." But then Indy's skepticism kicks in: "I've heard that bedtime story before; it's a legend." Spalko disagrees, claiming that Harold Oxley—currently her prisoner—has found Akator and Indy will help him find his way back.

Spalko connects electrodes to Indy's temples and places the Akator skull in front of him. She informs him, "The skull's crystal stimulates an undeveloped part of the human brain, opening a psychic channel." Indy retorts, "I got a better idea; you look at it." Spalko implies that she already has, but the skull did not connect with her the way it did with Oxley and hopefully Indy. She muses, "Surely you're not afraid, Dr.

Jones. You've spent your entire life looking for answers. Think of the truth behind those eyes [placing her hands on the skull]." She continues, "There may be hundreds of these skulls at Akator. Whoever finds them will control the greatest natural force the world has ever known … Power over the mind of man." Unimpressed, Indy cautions, "Careful, you might get exactly what you wish for." Equally unimpressed, Spalko retorts, "I usually do," and then begins monitoring Indy's reaction to the skull.

When it becomes clear that the skull opens a channel to Indy's mind, a wide-eyed Spalko stares at her test subject and whispers:

> Imagine. To peer across the world and know the enemy's secrets. To place our thoughts into the minds of your leaders. Make your teachers teach the true version of history, your soldiers attack on our command. We'll be everywhere at once, more powerful than a whisper, invading your dreams, thinking your thoughts for you while you sleep. We will change you, Dr. Jones, all of you, from the inside. We will turn you into us. And the best part? You won't even know it's happening.

Spalko's nefarious goal is clear: She wishes to harness the psychic powers of the Akator crystal skulls to develop the ultimate Cold War weapon, thereby securing the Soviet Union's victory over the United States. Controlling American minds—politicians, teachers, and soldiers—will make Americans mere puppets on invisible strings. All of this will occur without struggle. American citizens (and those of any country who dare oppose the Soviets) will not know any of this is happening. Everyone will be blissfully ignorant of the Soviet Union's secret for world domination.

The power Spalko seeks by unlocking the secrets of Akator and its crystal skulls is immoral. It is the epitome of failing to respect persons, as the intention is to reduce people to mindless slaves, which is tantamount to treating them as mere things.[7] Meilaender would point out that Spalko's pursuit of ultimate power is not constrained by examining reasons why she ought not to seek such knowledge. Such an examination never occurs to her. The goal of global domination completely overshadows all moral considerations.

Meilaender's concerns with Spalko's pursuit of knowledge wouldn't end there. After a tussle with the fiercest ants on the planet, Indy, Ox, Marion, and Mutt believe they have escaped their Soviet captors, only to unwittingly lead Spalko and her troops to the Akator temple. As if stepping on hallowed ground, Spalko enters the temple, takes the skull from Ox, and, walking toward the headless skeleton, murmurs, "Imagine what they could tell us." Indy warily replies, "I can't imagine. Neither could the humans that built this temple, and neither can you."

Not heeding him, she continues toward the headless skeleton and states, "Belief, Dr. Jones, is a gift you have yet to receive. My apologies."

The crystal skull flies out of Spalko's hands and reattaches itself to the skeleton. The group takes a few cautionary steps back, except Ox, who now approaches the restored interdimensional being. Ox begins speaking Mayan, channeling the restored being's thoughts. Indy translates: "It wants to give us a gift. A big gift." This is the moment Spalko has yearned for. She again approaches and beseeches the being, "Tell me everything you know. I want to know everything. I want to know." As the being directly acknowledges Spalko's presence, Indy mutters, "I got a bad feeling about this." (Those words are eerily familiar from Harrison Ford.) The eyes of the interdimensional beings glow, and wisps of smoke surround their skulls. The temple begins to shake and crumble. The remnants of the wall soon begin to rotate around its base. Indy looks up and states, "I don't think we want to go that way," and he pushes Marion and Ox through an opening in a temple wall. Indy and Mutt jump through another opening, leaving Spalko and her troops behind.

Spalko remains motionless, uttering, "I want to know. Tell me. I'm ready. I want to know." The interdimensional beings bestow their "big gift," as mystical waves of smoke emanate from their eyes into Spalko's. She is in awe: "I can see. I can see." But soon she becomes overwhelmed, crying out, "No more … Enough. Enough." As one of the beings menacingly peers down at Spalko, her eyes begin to glow ominously. She, like Belloq, attempts to protect herself by covering her face with her hands, but to no avail. Her eyes burst into flames, which then consume her entire body. Her glowing remains are taken up into the interdimensional portal.

The hubris driving Spalko's curiosity leads to her demise. Although she wished to curry favor by achieving Stalin's dream and ending the Cold War, her aspirations of gaining knowledge for her own edification were unquenchable. Perhaps because of this, the interdimensional beings satisfied her deepest wish, and it consumed her, literally—making Indy's warning about getting what one wishes prophetic. Recalling Aristotle, the desire to know is natural and the eyes are wondrous instruments for gaining knowledge, but the film suggests that Spalko overstepped and her eyes were her undoing. Indy, however, was prudent and showed advisable restraint. He, in effect, closed his eyes to Spalko's reckless pursuit by leaving the temple before the interdimensional beings bestowed their "big gift." Indy thereby suggests that some forms of knowledge must be sought carefully; striving to learn too much can be dangerous.

"Knowledge Was Their Treasure"

The interdimensional beings exit dramatically. Although Indy is unsure of how they can travel into "the space between spaces" (as Ox claims), he's more confident answering Mutt's question about the legend of El Dorado—that is, Akator—being a "city of gold." Indy explains: The Ugha word for gold translates as treasure. But the treasure wasn't gold, it was knowledge. Knowledge was their treasure." The vast and advanced knowledge of the interdimensional beings would explain why Akator's "technology would not be seen again [on Earth] for five thousand years," as Indy claims, and why Spalko believes that "early man could not have conceived it, much less built it."[8]

Let's forgive the film for propagating (debunked) ancient astronaut pseudoscience, because its philosophical message is important: Not only is knowledge a treasure, knowledge also must be *treasured*. We ought to seek truths about past civilizations to better understand ourselves, rather than simply assuming such knowledge is unattainable. What's more, we should explore difficult abstract issues about human nature, including ideals about right and wrong and what kind of life is best for human beings. Socrates is correct that such explorations are conducive to leading the good life. Yet there are better and worse ways to be knowledge seekers. We must be careful not to lose ourselves—or our moral sensibilities—in the search. When attempting to unlock the secrets of the universe, sometimes pride should give way to prudence.

Notes

1 Aristotle, *Metaphysics*, trans. W.D. Ross (Oxford: Oxford University Press, 1925), 980a. Aristotle's point pertains to men and women—all humankind.

2 Plato, *Plato's Meno*, trans. G.M.A. Grube (Indianapolis: Hackett, 1980), 86b–c. Socrates' points, like Aristotle's, pertain to all humankind.

3 Plato, *The Trial and Death of Socrates*, trans. G.M.A. Grube (Indianapolis: Hackett, 1975), 38a.

4 Gilbert Meilaender, *The Theory and Practice of Virtue* (Notre Dame: University of Notre Dame Press, 1984), 144.

5 Meilaender, 149–150.

6 Intriguingly, Belloq recited a traditional Jewish prayer associated with opening the Ark. See J.W. Rinzler, *The Complete Making of Indiana Jones: The Definitive Story Behind All Four Films* (New York: Del Ray Books, 2008), 83.

7 For more on the ethical significance of human persons, see Chapter 4 by Wood in this volume.

8 Here the filmmakers incorporate ancient astronaut pseudoscience, popularized by Erick Von Däniken's *The Chariot of the Gods*, which was originally published in 1968. For a touted critique, see Kenneth Feder, *Frauds, Myths, and Mysteries: Science and Pseudoscience in Archaeology*, originally published in 1990 (but currently in its 10th edition).

Part IV

"YOU WILL BECOME A TRUE BELIEVER": RELIGION AND THEOLOGY

14

Raiders of the Lost Ark and the Numinous Presence of God

Matthew Brake

Everyone remembers the climactic scene in *Raiders of the Lost Ark*. After multiple valiant attempts to obtain the legendary Ark of the Covenant, Indiana Jones and his love interest Marion are captured (again) by the Nazis and taken to a remote island. There Dr. René Belloq, dressed as an Israelite High Priest, performs a ceremony in preparation for opening the Ark. He wishes to gaze upon the contents inside, contents that the Nazis believe will grant them supernatural power. The Germans seemingly believe as does Marcus Brody that "An army which carries the Ark before it is invincible."[1] This, of course, is why Indy was sent to obtain it in the first place.

One wonders how much of the Hebrew Bible (what Christians call the "Old Testament") Belloq recalls. Prescriptions against being in the presence of the Ark are explicit. In Leviticus 16:2, God informs Moses, "Tell your brother [and High Priest] Aaron that he cannot come whenever he wants into the holy area inside the inner curtain, to the front of the cover that is on the chest, or else he will die, because I am present in the cloud above the cover."[2] Even among God's own people and the best among them, encountering the Ark could be dangerous. Belloq and the Nazis should tread carefully indeed.

Undaunted, Belloq opens the Ark. Initially he finds only sand, but then, ghostly, angelic images appear. We know what happens next. Belloq peers longingly at the spectral figures claiming, "they are beautiful," but their visages turn ghastly and Belloq is consumed by fire. The heads of Colonel Dietrich and Major Toht gruesomely melt away, and the rest of the soldiers are killed by "lightning … fire … the Power of God, or something" (as Indy would put it), emanating from the Ark. But Indy and Marion survive, because they wisely

Indiana Jones and Philosophy: Why Did It Have to Be Socrates?, First Edition. Edited by Dean A. Kowalski.

chose not to look upon the Ark. Had they chosen poorly along with Belloq and the Nazis, they would have perished. Truly, Indy and Marion were also in mortal danger, despite their superior morality and heroic standing.

This realization suggests an arbitrariness about the supernatural presence attached to the Ark. It holds the stone tablets inscribed with the Ten Commandments, but the Ark's divine presence doesn't seem concerned with morality. If the divine presence isn't "moral," then how should we describe it?

In this chapter, we will explore the ambiguity and arbitrariness of the divine presence—the "sacred" or "holy"—in *Raiders of the Lost Ark* through the lens of German theologian Rudolf Otto (1869–1937). As we'll see, Otto defines the holy as a nonrational feeling where the so-called "wrath" of God as portrayed in *Raiders* should be understood in nonmoral terms. As we'll also see, Otto's ideas about religion provide novel insights about the Ark as depicted in *Raiders*, including its famous closing scene.

The Holy

In *The Idea of the Holy*, Otto argued that too often "the holy" and "the moral" are confused. The "real innermost core of religion" is the holy, not the moral.[3] Otto describes the initial feeling of the holy or "the numinous" as real and existing apart from one's self; it is accompanied by a second experience that he calls "creature-feeling" or the feeling of being overwhelmed and submerged in something overpowering and mighty. As contemporary philosopher Merold Westphal puts it, these feelings "are based on a sense of the presence of something that is more real than I myself and the world of my immediate experience."[4]

Engaging with the numinous produces a religious experience. For example, in 2 Chronicles 5, King Solomon and the Israelite priests bring the Ark to the newly constructed Jerusalem Temple for the first time. Verses 13–14 describe a cloud (representing the divine presence) filling the temple, the experience of which was so powerful that the priests were not able to stand up. They feel submerged, overpowered by the numinous presence. In their experience we glimpse the true nature of the holy.

Raiders illustrates Otto's views about the holy at the beginning of the film. When Indiana and Marcus are speaking with the army intelligence agents, Jones opens his old Bible to show the men an image that depicts terrified Hebrews looking away in horror from the Ark and its awesome power. One of the men gasps, "Good God!" To which Marcus wryly replies, "Yes, that's just what the Hebrews thought." Marcus highlights how the Hebrews must have *felt* in the presence of the Ark. In effect, he questions whether the Hebrew God can be understood in ethical terms. Otto would approve.

The Rational and the Nonrational

Otto believes that religion has been overly rationalized. People think God must be a certain way because believing otherwise doesn't make sense to them. But actually our ideas about God initially result from felt experience (more on the felt nature of that experience later). Religion arises out of this original experience, Otto claims. The rules, rites, and beliefs that make up a religious tradition are ultimately derived from a religious experience, the feeling of which can be hard to put into words. Because of this, religious language and action can seem incoherent to those who do not share a faith.

Consider the group of Sufi Muslims called whirling dervishes who spin in repetitive circles. Outsiders may consider this an odd religious practice, but whirling dervishes claim to experience the felt sense of Allah's presence, as though from outside of themselves, leading them to engage in these movements. The outsider who observes the movement is not privy to the inner experience of the worshiper.

In the world of Indiana Jones, Judaism, via the religion of the ancient Hebrews, has its inception in the experience of something that exceeds rational explanation. Why might the Hebrews have constructed elaborate purity rituals, such as the many bodily washings they performed in order to remain ritually "clean," as well as a complicated religious system, which included, but was not limited to, meticulous guidance on the construction of their Temple and holy instruments to be used for Temple sacrifices? Without the original numinous experience, it might not make any sense, but if they were trying to contain a presence that they feared would "break out" and destroy them, then the construction of the Ark makes sense, as do the various purity rituals, which Otto points out also derive from the original experience of the numinous. Religion and the holy are not "exhausted" by rational ideas. Rather, they are rooted in numinous experiences that give rise to various feelings, including joy, rapture, and terrifying wrath!

Divine Wrath and the Ambiguity of the Sacred

Indy's warning to Marion—"don't look at it, no matter what happens"—takes on greater significance in light of the biblical injunction that none may see God and live. In Exodus 33:18–20, when Moses asks to see God's glory, God shows Moses his backside and tells him, "you cannot see my face because no one can see me and live." God's presence is a terrifying and, at times, seemingly arbitrary force. In a famous passage from 2 Samuel 6:1–11, King David is bringing the Ark of the Covenant to Jerusalem in a cart. At one point, the cart begins to shake and a man named Uzzah tries to steady it. God is incensed by this violation of his holiness and strikes Uzzah dead (just like Belloq). This act against Uzzah may seem morally arbitrary to our modern consciences, but it communicates that the presence and holiness of God is a fearsome phenomenon.

Some people prefer to think of God as merely a loving, gentle presence, but Otto argues that such conceptions omit key elements of numinous experience. As he describes it, "The daunting and the fascinating, now combine in a strange harmony of contrasts, and the resultant dual character of the numinous consciousness ... The daemonic-divine object may appear to the mind an object of horror and dread, but at the same time it is no less something that allures with a potent charm."[5] Otto's words remind us of the ghostly images that emerge from the Ark in *Raiders*. Indeed, Dietrich, Toht, and especially Belloq are initially captivated by the beauty of the spectral images, but that fascination turns to horror, including Toht's unforgettable scream. That horror is transferred to the viewers as we watch Dietrich's and Toht's faces melt and Belloq's head explode. Thus, *Raiders* follows Otto by portraying God biblically in ways that may make some modern-day believers uncomfortable.

Otto speaks of the dual nature of numinous experience with the language of "ambiguity" to capture how the divine presence is simultaneously pleasing and repulsive. Although humans find comfort in feeling the welcoming and loving side of numinous experience, there is more to it. Numinous experience also consists of more daunting elements, including "unapproachability" and "absolute overpoweringness," resulting in a "submergence, of being but 'dust and ashes' and nothingness"—notions that the Nazis in *Raiders* suffered quite literally.[6]

Numinous experience also has an "urgency" or "energy" that is characteristic of the divine. As Otto explains, there is "vitality, passion, emotional temper, will, force, movement, excitement, activity, impetus" to the divine presence. This keeps religion "from being 'rationalized' away"—there is something alive within![7] Otto likens numinous experiences to capricious energy discharges, as he writes: "There is something very baffling in the way it 'is kindled' and manifested. It is ... 'like a hidden force of nature', like stored-up electricity, discharging itself upon anyone who comes too near. It is 'incalculable' and 'arbitrary'."[8] It's tempting to recall Brody's wry observation at the beginning of *Raiders* and interpret such expressions of power with divine wrath.

The language of "arbitrary discharge" and "electricity" has scriptural basis. In Exodus 19:16–19 and 21–22, we read about an encounter between God and the Israelites:

> When morning dawned on the third day, there was thunder, lightning, and a thick cloud on the mountain, and a very loud blast of a horn. All the people in the camp shook with fear. Moses brought the people out of the camp to meet God, and they took their place at the foot of the mountain. Mount Sinai was all in smoke because the Lord had come down on it with lightning. The smoke went up like the smoke of a hot furnace, while the whole mountain shook violently. The blasts of the horn grew louder and louder. Moses would speak, and God would answer him with thunder ... The Lord said to Moses, "Go down and warn the people not to break through to try to see the Lord, or many of them will fall dead. Even the priests who come near to the Lord must keep themselves holy, or the Lord will break loose against them."

Here, lightning signifies God's presence, and the Israelites are warned that approaching Sinai could cause God to "break loose" against the people, almost as a reflex or uncontrollable response.

Raiders captures the terrifying nature of the Ark's presence by using a lot of the imagery that we see in Exodus, particularly the lightning. As Belloq opens the Ark and the presence within is unleashed, not only are Belloq and Toht killed, but the soldiers in attendance are also killed. While clouds, thunder, and wind accompany the supernatural presence, it "breaks loose" against the Nazis, as the entire company is struck by bolts of lightning and electrical discharges. The numinous is on full display as the Nazis and Belloq suffer God's wrath.

Yet in *Raiders*, and in the Bible, God's numinous wrath isn't dependent on moral status. Indiana Jones would have died right along with the Nazis if he had opened his eyes. Moses himself is warned against looking at God's face, again, because God's wrath, like a reflex, could consume him! This wrath doesn't result from a sin one has committed or as a response to one's moral status generally. It is simply part of the numinous. Otto explains:

> This is conceived as fundamentally independent of *moral* elevation or righteousness, and as indifferent toward good or evil action. It is rather a "ferocity", a "fiery wrath" about something unknown; or, better still, not about anything at all, but Wrath on its own account and without reference to any object.[9]

Otto is clear that the holy is not equivalent to the moral. In fact, the numinous contains its own irreducible quality. An offense to God's holiness is not the same as a violation of a moral command calling for divine punishment.

An Indy fan might think the Ark singles out the Nazis for moral condemnation. When the Ark is being held in Katanga's ship, it burns away the Nazi symbol on its crate without damaging the rest of the box. This might be interpreted as God distancing himself from Nazi atrocities and the beliefs that motivated them. Indeed, those familiar with the biblical texts might recall the story from 1 Samuel 4–5, where the Philistines, famous enemies of Israel, steal the Ark and place it in the temple of their god Dagon. The next morning, the Philistines discovered that the statue of Dagon had been knocked over and disfigured. As worshippers of Dagon, the Philistines were in clear violation of the "moral" commandment to have "no other gods," and this story can be read as a rebuff of their idolatry. Is this what is happening in *Raiders?*

Not so fast! We must also recall the ominous lightning storm that inexplicably develops as Indy and Sallah attempt to open the Well of Souls (the first rumbles occur when the old scholar translates the medallion). The storm can be interpreted as an indication of God's displeasure or perhaps a not-so-subtle warning not to disturb the Ark. (Remember Sallah's earlier worry that if the Ark "is there at Tanis, then it is something that man was not meant to disturb. Death has always surrounded it.")

It seems natural to assume that God would prefer for our hero to find the Ark, because the Nazis are evil and represent "the scum of humanity" (as Indy's father would later say). But this assumption requires that the holy and the moral are synonymous. Not so. God punished Dagon, but he also killed Uzzah, one of the Israelites who was trying to "help God" by keeping the Ark from falling. Even Aaron—an actual Israelite high priest—must take great care when approaching the Ark, lest he share Belloq's fate (a non-actual Israelite high priest acting impiously).

So does morality play *any* role in Otto's understanding of the numinous? Yes, but to understand how, one must examine the natural progression of how encounters with the numinous are incorporated in the history of religion, a point to which we now turn. Doing so will explain how the depiction of the numinous in *Raiders* may miss the mark and give the wrong impression.

Daemonic Dread, Horror, and the Numinous

Otto believes that humanity has become gradually aware of the numinous over time, and our ability to properly discern it has matured through stages in our history as a species. For Otto, religious dread originates in what he calls "daemonic dread," which equates with the fear of ghosts. He says, "It first begins to stir in the feeling of 'something uncanny', 'eerie', or 'weird'. It is this feeling which, emerging in the mind of primeval man, forms the starting-point for the entire religious development of history."[10]

The human awareness of the numinous goes through stages, beginning with magic and developing with the worship of the dead and the belief in souls, spirits, and specters. For Otto, the numinous is present in all religions, but uniquely and supremely so in Christianity. Otto thus epitomizes a problem with the field of Religious Studies—in spite of its claim to objectivity, the field still has an inherently Christian bias.

The religion of the ancient Israelites is also given prominence in Otto's account. Hebraic religion, Otto believes, is not a perfected form of the numinous, but it's on the right track. He writes:

> The lower stage of numinous consciousness, viz. daemonic dread, has already been long superseded by the time we reach the Prophets and Psalmists. But there are not wanting occasional echoes of it, found especially in the earlier narrative literature ... The story in Exodus. iv. 24, of how Yahweh ... met Moses by the way "and sought to kill him", still bears this "daemonic" character strongly, and the tale leaves us almost with the suggestion of a ghostly apparition.[11]

So, for Otto, while the religion of ancient Israel is more developed and farther along than the earlier belief in the worship of the dead and fear of ghosts, it still retains some of those elements.

Otto believes, though, that the ancient Israelites moved passed daemonic dread. So, as much as *Raiders'* depiction of the numinous aligns with Otto, and even though daemonic dread is in some ways the start of religious development that culminates later in Christianity, the spectral depictions of the beings in the Ark are too much like the fear of ghosts that was a part of a much more primitive stage of religious development. There is something almost fiendish about the apparitions. Though much of the Ark's display of power seems genuinely numinous, the images of ghosts, for Otto, would indicate a less than biblical, and even deficient, offshoot of genuine representation of the numinous.

Understanding the proper development of numinous consciousness is important for Otto. There is something distinct about the Hebraic religion that sets it apart for him: "The venerable religion of Moses marks the beginning of a process which from that point onward proceeds with ever increasing momentum, by which the numinous is throughout rationalized and moralized, i.e., charged with ethical import."[12] Otto would see *Raiders* as misrepresenting the numinous within this "religion of Moses" by associating it too much with an earlier stage of religious development. He sees the religion of the Israelites as being an important stepping stone to the numinous as found within Christianity, a religion for a "civilized humanity" as he calls it, one that does not ignore the "rational" content of religion (ideas, beliefs, and morals), but understands the meaning and significance of the "nonrational" content (feelings and experiences).

So while religion doesn't start as either a belief system or a code of ritual, Otto thinks the development of religion has a trajectory, which sees it increasingly coupled with moral content. This content could be compared to something like the petals of a blossoming flower. Moral content, the petals, are a part of the mature version of religion, but the seed or the roots of religion, the innermost core, is an experienced feeling, "the numinous," which lays the groundwork for religion in its more mature forms and from which religion draws its truest sustenance.

The Ark and Its "Top Men"

Raiders and Otto invite us to consider what it would be like to encounter the divine presence. Such experiences are difficult to articulate clearly, but they seem to point to—or be in response to—a power beyond all our concepts, plans, and ideas, one that has a mind of its own, one that could fascinate us ... or frighten us. Or both. The film and the theologian also invite us to reexamine our common assumptions about God as they pertain to morality. Indy is the hero and the Nazis are the bad guys, but none of that seems to matter as each confronts the holy.

Finally, Otto offers us the opportunity to reexamine the ending of the film, to see it in a different light. As you know, the Ark is crated up (again) and left in a huge warehouse, lost among thousands of other crates, and not seen again until Indy visits two decades later. Some audience members might believe that locking the Ark away is misguided. Indy and Marcus certainly do. Marcus exclaims, "The Ark is a source of unspeakable power and it has to be researched!" Indy concurs, "Bureaucratic fools. They don't know what they've got there." Just think of all the research that Indy and Marcus could do—what a wasted opportunity. But maybe it's better that it is hidden away, somewhere safe, and Otto can help us understand why. The "top men" who would study it—regardless of their upstanding moral character or the extreme reverential care they put into their work—may find themselves overwhelmed by a power beyond their capacity to conceptualize ... or even survive.

Notes

1 Marcus might be paraphrasing such biblical passages as Numbers 10:35–36 and Joshua 6:1–27.
2 All biblical passages quoted from the Common English Bible.
3 Rudolf Otto, *The Idea of the Holy*, trans. John W. Harvey (New York: Oxford University Press, 1958), 6–7.
4 Merold Westphal, *God, Guilt, and Death: An Existential Phenomenology of Religion* (Bloomington, IN: Indiana University Press, 1984), 27.
5 Otto, *Idea of the Holy*, 31.
6 Otto, *Idea of the Holy*, 20.
7 Otto, *Idea of the Holy*, 23.
8 Otto, *Idea of the Holy*, 18.
9 Otto, *Idea of the Holy*, 107.
10 Otto, *Idea of the Holy*, 14.
11 Otto, *Idea of the Holy*, 72.
12 Otto, *Idea of the Holy*, 75.

15

Indiana Jones and the Leap of Faith

Tait Szabo

Indiana Jones, our favorite hero, faces an impossible task. To save his father's life, he must obtain the Holy Grail. To do that, he must survive three challenges of "lethal cunning." Having barely survived the first two, even after careful use of his wit, he emerges from a narrow tunnel at the lion's head, just as his father's diary predicted. He peers into a bottomless abyss. It's the third test! Indy rereads the diary clue: "The Path of God. Only in the leap from the lion's head will he prove his worth." The other side of the chasm is at least 100 feet away. "Impossible. Nobody can jump this," Indy mutters. Then it dawns on him: "It's a leap of faith. Oh, geez." Indy's breathing and pulse quicken. His father, as if to steady him, whispers, "You must believe, boy. You must believe." Indy puts his hand over his heart, closes his eyes, takes a deep breath, steps out over the ledge ... and lands on an invisible bridge, expertly camouflaged by the opposing rock face. He inches his way across, that much closer to the Grail.

When watching (or rewatching) this tense scene in *The Last Crusade*, perhaps you said, "Hey, isn't a 'leap of faith' a philosophy thing?" Indeed, it is. In this chapter, we'll explore the leap of faith through Søren Kierkegaard's (1813–1855) *Fear and Trembling*, particularly as it relates to the biblical figure of Abraham. As we'll see, even if Indy's seeming leap of faith is not exactly what Kierkegaard had in mind, *Crusade* and its characters provide an intriguing opportunity to revisit what it means to have faith in God and what kind of faith is most valuable.

The Example of Abraham

Four characters in *Crusade* provide examples of religious belief: Henry (Indy's father), Marcus, Kazim of the Brotherhood of the Cruciform Sword, and the Grail Knight. Recall Henry, while copying the

Indiana Jones and Philosophy: Why Did It Have to Be Socrates?, First Edition. Edited by Dean A. Kowalski.

stained-glass window that becomes important later in the film, murmurs, "May he who illuminated this, illuminate me"; he also slaps Indy for his blasphemous reference to Jesus Christ. Marcus tells Indy that "the search for the Cup of Christ is the search for the divine in all of us," which, at his age, he is comfortable taking on faith; when a dying Henry drinks from the Cup of Christ, Marcus crosses himself at the sight of the miraculous cure. Kazim and the Grail Knight—albeit in different ways—have dedicated their lives to serving God.

Kierkegaard was fascinated by distinctive elements of religious faith. Writing under the ironic pseudonym Johannes de silentio ("Silent John"), in *Fear and Trembling* Kierkegaard carefully explores the story of Abraham and the binding of Isaac from the Book of Genesis.[1] For Kierkegaard, Abraham is an exemplar of faith because of his unwavering trust in God. Indeed, Abraham's actions are done in silence or concealment, but also joy, even in the face of hardship. (There is also an important ethical component we will discuss later.)

At Genesis 12:1–3, God promises to make a great, blessed nation of Abraham's descendants if Abraham emigrates from the land of his fathers and follows God's commands. But Abraham and his wife Sarah were childless and already approaching their hundredth birthdays. Despite the absurdity of thinking that God's promise could be fulfilled, Abraham believes. His patience is rewarded when Sarah gives birth to Isaac. But at Genesis 22:2, God then commands Abraham to sacrifice him: "Take your only and beloved son Isaac and go to the land of Moriah. Offer him there as a burnt sacrifice." If Isaac is to be killed, then it seems absurd to believe that God's promise will be fulfilled. But Abraham, despite his intention to follow God's command, persists by expecting the impossible.

Abraham never attempts to explain himself to others. Even when Isaac asks where the lamb for the sacrifice is, Abraham deflects by answering that God will provide the lamb for the burnt offering. Abraham responds indirectly, concealing the most direct and honest answer. He does not, for example, say, "You, my son, are the sacrifice." If he did so, Isaac would likely resist. To communicate is to give reasons, but Abraham is acting in ways that defy human reasoning. His actions cannot be justified to others; he must remain silent.[2]

According to Kierkegaard, there is no indication that Abraham experiences any sorrow throughout his ordeal. Genuine faith, as displayed by Abraham, involves an ability to persist even in the midst of "fear and trembling" in the face of circumstances that would ordinarily cause sorrow. Perhaps some other father could kill his child without sorrow if so commanded by looking forward to an eternal life in which he and the child are reunited. But that is not the case with Abraham. Faith that is only "for a future life" is not genuine faith. According to Kierkegaard, it is, "only the remotest possibility of faith, which faintly spies its object at the edge of the horizon yet is separated from it by a yawning abyss within which despair plays its tricks."[3] Abraham takes God at his word and expects God's promise to be fulfilled. He expects the impossible, the absurd, the miraculous: he expects to kill Isaac and expects Isaac to live.

The Paradox of Genuine Faith and Unethical Behavior

Abraham's example of genuine faith is also anchored in his willingness to do something completely unethical. This serves as an important challenge to Kierkegaard's account. How can Abraham be *praised* for his unwavering intention to willfully kill his son?

According to Kierkegaard, fully understanding the story of Abraham should make you sleepless with anxiety. To see why, consider a hypothetical sermon in which the priest or pastor shares the story of the binding of Isaac. Afterward, an acquaintance says to you, "Wow! I was moved by that sermon! In fact, while I listened, God spoke to me. He told me that, like Abraham, to show that I love and fear God, I should sacrifice my children to him." Kierkegaard expects that you, like him, would be horrified. Nonetheless, Abraham, for his willingness to kill his child at the command of God, is held up as the father of faith. This, Kierkegaard says, is the central contradiction of faith: "The ethical expression for what Abraham did is that he intended to murder Isaac; the religious expression is that he intended to sacrifice Isaac."[4] Abraham is a faith exemplar, but consider how many other people have been denounced for their willingness to justify violence on the grounds that "God told me to do it."

Kazim can serve as an example of Kierkegaard's point here. Kazim is willing to kill Indy—by burning him alive—and he does not hesitate when dropping the lit match into the petroleum-infused catacomb waters. Indy has done nothing to deserve this fate. (*Could* anyone deserve that fate?) But Kazim does not see himself as a murderer. Rather, he sees himself as God's faithful servant. Later, after Indy and Elsa narrowly escape the catacombs, only to find themselves pursued by the Brotherhood in speedboats, Indy asks, "Why are you trying to kill us?" Kazim responds, "Because you are looking for the Holy Grail." When Kazim admits that he knows of Indy's father, Indy threatens to end Kazim's life if he does not divulge Henry's whereabouts. Unmoved, Kazim says: "If you don't let go, Dr. Jones, we'll both die … My soul is prepared. How is yours?" Indy relents, but repeats: "And why were you trying to kill me?" Kazim explains, "The secret of the Grail has been safe for 1,000 years. And for all that time the Brotherhood of the Cruciform Sword has been prepared to do anything to keep it safe." Should he be praised for his willingness to go to any lengths to serve God, or condemned as a murderer?

Regardless of your answer about Kazim, Kierkegaard believes that Abraham's case is truly paradoxical. The key to resolving it is found in the ability to act in ways that are contrary to reason. Consider a variation in which Isaac is killed. Even in that case, Abraham would continue to believe, because by virtue of his ability to embrace the absurd, he would expect a miracle where God gives him a new Isaac or calls the sacrificed one back to life. Still, the person hearing the hypothetical sermon would not become great if he claimed "It's okay! After I sacrifice my children, God will resurrect them." This person's ability to believe something contrary to reason as a justification for his act will not change our reaction. The same is true of anyone else we condemn for justifying violence in the name of God (including, perhaps, Kazim). There is something importantly different about Abraham's actions.

The "Teleological Suspension of the Ethical"

Kierkegaard remains stuck at the "prodigious paradox" of faith, "a paradox that is capable of making a murder into a holy act well pleasing to God, a paradox that gives Isaac back again to Abraham, which no thought can lay hold of because faith begins precisely where thinking leaves off."[5] Kierkegaard (plausibly) believes that ethics applies to everyone, at every moment, without exception, and is the highest end. And to put one's own (selfish) ends above what ethics demands is thereby unethical. When we claim that it is wrong to kill your child, we mean that it is wrong for anyone to do it, at any time, for any reason. So, like any one of us, Abraham has an ethical obligation not to kill his child. As Kierkegaard states, "Abraham's relation to Isaac, ethically speaking, is quite simply this, that the father must love the son more than himself."[6] Ethically, Abraham cannot be praised for his willingness to kill Isaac.

Possibly, there is a higher ethical duty that justifies Abraham's willingness to kill his child. Perhaps Abraham is an example of a tragic hero, who violates one ethical duty for the sake of another competing ethical duty. Tragic heroes find themselves in an ethical dilemma, where acting according to one duty requires violating another. However, the central contradiction of faith cannot be resolved by regarding Abraham as another tragic hero. If Abraham is a tragic hero, then he is no more special, no more praiseworthy, no higher example of faith than other tragic heroes. Understanding Abraham as a tragic hero fails to understand him as the father of faith.

Indeed, Abraham does not think ethically about what to do. In his willingness to kill Isaac he shows a willingness to violate an ethical duty, but not for the sake of a competing ethical duty. Rather, Abraham is willing to kill Isaac for the sake of his private, personal relationship with God. In this way, genuine faith involves the "teleological suspension of the ethical," or a willingness to suspend ethics for the sake of something greater, namely one's relationship with God; it involves putting one's personal, private relationship with God above ethics. The teleological suspension of the ethical, however, is not the total abandonment of the ethical. It takes the demands of ethics seriously. It makes an exception to the demands of ethics for a separate but higher end. The paradox of faith is that there is one end, namely one's relationship with God, that is higher than that which, according to reason, nothing can be higher than, namely ethics. The only way to resolve the central contradiction of genuine faith is to take the demands of ethics seriously, to condemn those who violate them, and yet, if necessary, violate them ourselves in service of God—without losing sight of ethical demands as having the utmost importance.

How, then, does Abraham differ from the person moved to kill his children as a result of hearing the hypothetical sermon? In at least one important way: The person makes the mistake of explaining his intention to us. Of course, we will condemn him and fail to understand him. What he intends to do is absurd. It is contrary to reason and ethics. He should not have tried to explain himself to us. He should have acted in accordance with God's command for the sake of his relationship with God and nothing more. We might interpret Kazim similarly; perhaps he should not have attempted to explain himself to Indy.

Genuine faith, then, is a paradox in which there is a relationship with God that is direct, private, or personal; unmediated, or non-communicable; and transcends our understanding of ethics. It is a rationally unjustifiable, private relationship with God that outweighs human reasoning about ethics without undercutting its importance. This is the "leap" that Abraham accomplishes. Steeped in his faith, he lives for God and is willing to give up anything for God without hesitation, but also without retreating from or giving up earthly concerns. This account of Abraham is difficult, if not impossible, to understand. It is also frightening. But any other interpretation cheapens Abraham's example and renders his faith shallow.

Kierkegaard's Two Knights

Kierkegaard believes that some people might be able to act like Abraham, while still lacking genuine faith. He calls them Knights of Infinite Resignation. Such people take something like Abraham's "leap of faith," but they do so in resignation—hence the name. Knights of

Infinite Resignation can do what God commands, but only because they have given up earthly, finite concerns; they renounce the here and now and look instead to the eternal. Kierkegaard imagines that if God commanded him to sacrifice his child, he could, but not like Abraham. He would not maintain joy in life. He would feel sorrow. He could do it only by resigning himself to giving up everything in this world, including his child, for God in the hope that they would be reunited in the next life.

Abraham is no mere Knight of Infinite Resignation. Abraham's sacrifice is great insofar as he loves Isaac. The sacrifice of a child one loves and wants to keep is greater than the sacrifice of a child that one is resigned to losing. A person whose daily life, hopes, and dreams revolve around their child has a more difficult task when commanded to sacrifice their child, and their sacrifice is thereby greater. Abraham has no expectation of giving up Isaac until he receives God's command. In fact, everything he has done in life since making the original covenant with God depends on Isaac growing up and having children of his own. God's promise was for this life, not some future life. God thus commands Abraham to make the greatest of all possible sacrifices.

Knights of Faith—unlike Knights of Infinite Resignation who live only by giving everything up to God—are not easy to recognize. Their external appearance is plain, ordinary. They will neither reveal themselves to you, nor justify themselves to you. Abraham is a shepherd, belonging to this world. Nothing in his appearance or in how he lives his daily life suggests he has resigned everything of the here and now for the sake of an eternal, future life. The Knight of Faith both gives up *and* holds onto the finite. Abraham is willing to kill Isaac, but also expects to keep Isaac. "He therefore acknowledges the impossibility and at the same moment believes the absurd."[7] If Abraham had acted with the thought that "It's just a test, and God will not let me kill Isaac," then the sacrifice would not have been as great, tarnishing Abraham's example. Without sorrow or remorse, he acts with the expectations that Isaac will die by his hand *and* the impossible miracle that Isaac will be returned to him. Abraham is the epitome of the Knight of Faith.

What can we say about the four *Crusade* characters who demonstrate religious faith? Are any Kierkegaardian Knights of Resignation or Faith? Marcus's character is not very well fleshed out, so it is difficult to determine whether he rises to the level of either. Henry's character receives more treatment. Henry possesses a healthy sense of right and wrong. He calls the Nazis the "scum of humanity," and warns Indy that the Grail quest "is a race against evil"; if the Nazis capture the Grail, then the "armies of darkness will march over the face of the earth" at everyone's peril. Henry was willing to risk his own life to ensure that the Nazi's Grail quest failed, but it is unclear whether Henry is willing to make all sacrifices for his faith. He pleaded with Indy to let the Grail go rather than allow him to risk his life in its recovery. Unlike Abraham, he would not part with his son. Further, because Grail lore was his lifelong obsession, it seems that Henry is not resigned from this world. Indeed, it might be that pursuing the Grail is his way of justifying his faith. In this way, it might be some sort of "prize," even if not exactly the way Elsa prized it.[8] Thus, it seems that Henry, although devout, is not a good candidate for being either a Knight of Faith or Resignation.

Kazim seems to be a Knight of Infinite Resignation. Not only is he willing to kill others in God's name, he's also willing and ready to die, to give up everything else he may value in this world, all in service of God in his quest to keep the Grail safe. However, it's less clear if Kazim is a Knight of Faith. On the one hand, he possesses strong ethical sensibilities. When Indy informs him that he is interested in finding his father and not the Cup of Christ, Kazim wishes him well and tells Indy where Henry is being held. Further, Kazim lives an ordinary life. Apart from his Brotherhood chest tattoo, which he invariably keeps hidden, nothing about him stands out. He seems just as comfortable on the streets and jetties of Venice as he does as a member of the Hatay Sultan's royal court. On the other hand, Kazim is somewhat prone to explaining himself, again recalling the speedboat scene with Indy. He also explains to Donovan that he is "a messenger from God" and forewarns the Nazi conspirator, "For the unrighteous, the Cup of Life holds everlasting damnation." Further, it is not clear whether Kazim expects to receive everything back. Recall that the power of the Knight of Faith is not merely in the ability to give up everything for God, but rather to hold onto *everything*, even if contrary to reason. We do not know whether Kazim expects a miracle when he takes a life or gives up his own.

The Grail Knight, at first glance, appears to be the *Crusade* character that comes closest to being a Knight of Faith. It is his honor to guard the Grail and thus he is not filled with sorrow about his fate. To protect the Grail, he has sacrificed everything for God, including ordinary human life. Even his immortality, which requires living a solitary life in a dusty old cave, forever bound by the Temple Seal, appears sacrificial. Further, it might be that his duty to God involves absurdity. After all, he remains tranquil as the Temple implodes; his wave to Henry harkens back to Abraham's calming response to Issac: God will provide for his continued service, even if this requires the miraculous recovery of the Grail and his not perishing in the crumbling Temple. Perhaps this falls short of proving the Grail Knight expects the miraculous; nevertheless, a worrisome issue remains: A Knight of Faith, like Abraham, lives in the ordinary world, and not locked away in a remote stone temple that can be reached only after passing three challenges of "lethal cunning."

The great value of genuine faith is found in what it can provide a person in his or her ordinary life. Thus, the Grail Knight is not a perfect candidate for being a Knight of Faith.

Indy at the Lion's Head

And what of our intrepid hero? Does Indy take a leap of faith when he steps off the ledge? In a way, yes. Genuine faith, according to Kierkegaard's Johannes, comes after reason, but is contrary to reason. Indy does not blindly act without thought or purpose. Nor does he act in accordance with his reasoning. Reason tells him the jump is impossible. But he doesn't turn back. He takes the step anyway. Importantly, belief alone is not enough (despite Henry's passionate pleas). The leap of faith is not a leap of reason or (mere) belief. It is an action. The hero moment requires one to act, and Indy (not surprisingly) plays the part.

Although Indy does not fall into the abyss, he falls short of being either a Knight of Resignation or Faith. Consider that both Abraham and Indy, despite their commendable moral sensibilities, risk behaving unethically with their respective decisions. Abraham is willing to kill his son. Indy risks providing the Nazis with an immortal army. Abraham is willing to do what is otherwise immoral for the sake of his personal, private relationship with God. However, Indy takes moral risk for the sake of another moral duty, namely the duty to save his father's life. In this respect, Indy is more like the tragic hero, faced with a hard choice between competing ethical duties. Whereas Abraham is willing to give up his son's life for God, Indy is willing to give up his own life for his father and accepts that even if he succeeds it would allow for the armies of darkness to march over the face of the earth.

Although Indy, in taking the leap of faith, acts contrary to reason, and performs a heroic action, he does not act out of love for God, resigned to give up everything else he values for God. Remember Indy had no interest in seeking or attaining the Cup of Christ. He accepted Donovan's invitation because he wished to find and rescue his father. He pursues the Grail now because it is the only way to cure his father's mortal gunshot wound. A Knight of Infinite Resignation would step off the ledge, but not for any other earthly reward. Furthermore, Indy's step off the ledge is nothing like the anonymous Grail Knight, who, in Henry's diary, is depicted in a confident stride over the abyss, holding the Grail high and confident as he proceeds to the other side. Indy appears relieved and surprised not to have fallen to his death. Despite fear and trembling, the Knight of Faith has unwavering trust in God, and thus would not be surprised at all by the miracle of walking on air to the other side.

That Indy is neither a Knight of Resignation nor Faith is subtly confirmed in *Crusade*. Recall when Indy first encounters the Grail Knight. The Knight, admitting that he cannot defeat Indy because his strength has left him, offers the mantle to Indy, regardless of the fact that he is "strangely dressed for a knight." Indy shrugs, and replies, "I'm not exactly a knight. What do you mean?" The Grail Knight explains: "I was chosen because I was the bravest and the most worthy. The honor was mine until another came to challenge me to single combat. I pass it to you who vanquished me." Indy has absolutely no interest in becoming the next Grail Knight, as he gulps and says, "Listen, I don't have time to explain, but …" He is interrupted by Elsa and Donovan, but given everything we know about Indiana Jones, it is incredibly unlikely that he would be chosen by God for this task, even if Indy did "believe in that sort of thing," which he (probably) doesn't, at least not fully.

Riding Off into the Sunset

Sometimes examples from popular culture that seem philosophical fall short of their intended goal, but do so in interesting and instructive ways. This is the case with Indy's leap from the lion's head. He calls it a "leap of faith" and in some ways it is. Because we recognize that phrase as philosophical, it invites us to learn more about Kierkegaard, the philosopher most associated with it. Accepting that invitation, we now know that Kierkegaard would complain that Indy's leap is not genuine because he lacks genuine faith.

Not surprisingly, Kierkegaard prizes faith in the biblical world over faith of the modern world. People today claim to have faith, but their faith is dirt cheap like commercial objects at a clearance sale. Cheap faith is easy and lacks value. In the biblical world, faith was not a sometimes sort of thing; it was a lifelong and arduous task. As the example of Abraham shows, genuine faith is difficult, rare, and valuable. According to Kierkegaard, although genuine faith causes much fear and trembling, without it, "how empty and hopeless life would be!"[9]

The best movies, like *Crusade*, invite you to think long after the heroes have ridden off into the sunset. Although Indy's "leap of faith" is not genuine, on Kierkegaard's (via Johannes) terms, it does invite us to consider Kierkegaard's ideas about Abraham and genuine faith more carefully. Is he correct that Abraham should be praised as a faith exemplar? Is he correct that modern day expressions of faith pale in comparison to genuine faith from the biblical world? If so, why? Only we can decide, and this is exactly how Kierkegaard—often considered the father of existentialism—would have it.

Notes

1 There is much scholarly debate about the significance of Kierkegaard's tendency to use pseudonyms. It is difficult to know whether Kierkegaard believes everything Johannes writes, but for convenience, and despite his advice that we not do so, the discussion that follows refers to Kierkegaard as the author of *Fear and Trembling*.

2 The silence of genuine faith contrasts with the faith of philosophers like G.W.F. Hegel (1770–1813) or René Descartes (1596–1650), who begin with faith, then go further, providing reasons for, or attempting to justify, their faith. The faith they describe and justify is not the faith of Abraham.

3 Søren Kierkegaard, *Fear and Trembling*, ed. C. Stephen Evans and Sylvia Walsh (New York: Cambridge University Press, 2006), 17.

4 Kierkegaard, *Fear and Trembling*, 24.

5 Kierkegaard, *Fear and Trembling*, 46.

6 Kierkegaard, *Fear and Trembling*, 49.

7 Kierkegaard, *Fear and Trembling*, 40.

8 Arguably, the "illumination" Henry finds as a result of the Grail quest is not overtly religious and further separates him from Elsa. For more on this interpretation see Chapter 7 by Tilsley in this volume.

9 Kierkegaard, *Fear and Trembling*, 12.

16

Sacred Objects and Cosmic Justice in *Indiana Jones*

Christopher Helali

> *Archaeology is our religion, yet we have both fallen from the pure faith … I am a shadowy reflection of you. It would take only a nudge to make you like me, to push you out of the light.*
>
> —René Belloq to Indiana Jones in *Raiders of the Lost Ark*[1]

In my youth, I was captivated by the sacred objects from the first three *Indiana Jones* movies: the Ark, the Sankara Stones, and the Grail. In the movies, when a character treats a sacred object with respect, the object functions in beneficial or appropriate ways. By contrast, when a character attempts to use a sacred object for evil or selfish purposes the character is punished. Reflecting on the effects of the objects, especially in conjunction with the distinction between the sacred and profane, teaches us something about the nature of good and evil. As we'll see, the fictional world of *Indiana Jones* reminds us that universal ethical truth, including the value of respect, is part of the fabric of our real world.

The Sacred and Profane

French philosopher and sociologist Emile Durkheim (1858–1917) defines religion as "a unified system of beliefs and practices relative to sacred things, that is to say, things set apart and forbidden."[2] For Durkheim, there is a categorical difference between the sacred and the profane. In his words, "The sacred thing is par excellence, that which the profane must not and cannot touch with impunity … Sacred things are things protected and isolated by prohibitions; profane things are those things to which the prohibitions are applied and that must keep

Indiana Jones and Philosophy: Why Did It Have to Be Socrates?, First Edition. Edited by Dean A. Kowalski.

at a distance from what is sacred."[3] The sacred is associated with religion, that which is deserving of reverence as most important, and the profane is that which is *not* sacred—the common, mundane, and everyday aspects of our existence.

Philosopher and theologian Paul Tillich (1886–1965) stresses the role that symbols play in representing the sacred, claiming, "Man's ultimate concern must be expressed symbolically, because symbolic language alone is able to express the ultimate ... The fundamental symbol of our ultimate concern is God."[4] The sacred transcends the words we use to describe our mundane world. The sacred is expressed symbolically—the cross, star, crescent moon, chanted "Om"—and these mediate our rituals, rites, and religious beliefs, including the proper interactions between a person, the sacred, and the profane. Some behaviors are required, others taboo. As Durkheim notes, "Religious beliefs are those representations that express the nature of the sacred things and the relations they have with other sacred things or with profane things."[5]

Not surprisingly, the sacred–profane distinction has been foundational to the religious faith and observances of peoples throughout history. For example, the Book of Leviticus is replete with rites, rules, and taboos for the Israelites. At Leviticus 10:10, Yahweh instructs Aaron that he and future priests are to distinguish "between the holy and the profane, and between the unclean and the clean." Regulations extend to all aspects of life, from what food can and cannot be consumed, to proper sexual relations. As stated by Yahweh at Leviticus 21:9, punishment for transgressing these regulations was severe, and in many cases was punishable by death: "They shall keep my charge, so that they may not incur guilt and die in the sanctuary for having profaned it."

The Ark of the Covenant

In *Raiders of the Lost Ark*, the quest for the Ark of the Covenant becomes a mission to thwart Nazi supremacy. Representing American interests, Major Eaton and Colonel Musgrove tell Indy and his colleague Marcus Brody that they've intercepted a German communique stating that the Nazis found the city of Tanis. Indy replies, "Tanis is one of the possible resting places of the Lost Ark." Marcus ominously describes how Tanis was "consumed by the desert in a sandstorm which lasted a whole year ... wiped clean by the wrath of God."

Indy shows Musgrove and Eaton an illustration of the Ark, and the government men are awestruck. "Good God," murmurs Eaton. Marcus wryly replies, "Yes, that's just what the Hebrews thought." Musgrove points at the illustration and asks about the things emanating from it.

Indy shrugs and replies, "Lightning, fire, power of God, or something," Marcus continues, "The Bible speaks of the Ark leveling mountains and laying waste to entire regions. An army which carries the Ark before it is invincible."

Indy is keen to find the Ark before the Nazis do, but Marcus warns him, "For nearly 3,000 years man has been searching for the Lost Ark. It's not something to be taken lightly. No one knows its secrets. It's like nothing you've ever gone after before." In Cairo, Indy's friend Sallah echoes Marcus's foreboding words, "If it is there, at Tanis, then it is something that man was not meant to disturb. Death has always surrounded it. It is not of this earth." Indy ignores this warning (and all the other not-so-subtle signs and wonders we see in the film).

Despite Indy's best efforts, the Nazis take the Ark to a secluded Mediterranean island. René Belloq, the archaeologist hired by the Nazis to help them find the Ark (and one of Indy's chief professional rivals), prepares to open the Ark. German Commander Dietrich confides in him, "I am uncomfortable with the thought of this Jewish ritual. Are you sure it is necessary?" Belloq slyly plays on Dietrich's insecurities, responding, "Would you feel more comfortable opening the Ark in Berlin for your Führer? Finding out, only then, if the sacred pieces of the Covenant are inside? Knowing only then whether you have accomplished your mission, and obtained the one, *true* Ark?" Clearly, Belloq's motives are just as selfish as Dietrich's, to say nothing of Hitler's.

The Nazis prepare an altar and bring the Ark to Belloq. Dressed as a Jewish high priest, Belloq carries out a Jewish ritual that includes reciting a prayer from the Torah, presumably to curry God's favor. With the brief ritual complete and the Ark open, Dietrich reaches in and finds only sand; he is furious. The Nazi interrogator Major Toht laughs hysterically. Belloq, perplexed and crestfallen, reaches for the sand falling from Dietrich's hand.

But soon the illustration from Indy's Bible comes to life. Mechanical equipment begins to short circuit. Lightning and fire—"the power of God or something"—rip through Nazi soldiers. Dietrich and Toht scream as their faces melt off their skulls. Belloq's head explodes. The sky above opens frighteningly. All evidence of the Nazis is taken up into the heavens never to return, while the Ark lid falls back into its proper place atop the Ark. The small island is again dark and empty, except for Indy, Marion, and, of course, the Ark.

The Ark of the Covenant is a highly sacred religious object for Jews, containing the Ten Commandments given to Moses. As Indy would remind us, "Yes. The *actual* Ten Commandments. The original stone tablets Moses brought down from Mount Horeb and smashed—if you believe in that sort of thing. Didn't … you guys ever go to Sunday school?" It symbolizes the active presence of God made manifest in his covenant with the Israelites. There are multiple passages in the Hebrew Bible (or *Tanakh*) where people are told they risk death if they look at the face and power of God. When Moses asks to see God's glory in Exodus 33:18–23, God tells him that he "cannot see my face, because no one can see me and live." Indy must have gone to Sunday school. He understands what the Ark symbolizes and takes such prescriptions seriously. He tells Marion not to gaze upon the opened Ark and the destructive powers emanating from it—"no matter what happens." Neither Indy nor Marion is Jewish, but their show of respect for the Ark keeps the sacred "set apart and forbidden," as Durkheim would say. Their behavior conforms to the prescribed rules governing interactions with the Ark.

The Nazis and Belloq have no intention of keeping the sacred Ark separate from the profane world, and in this way, disrespect its value and importance for their selfish purposes. The Nazis see the Ark as little more than a military super-weapon. They intend to use it for world domination. Belloq isn't interested in world domination, but his interest is still selfish. He tells Indy, "Jones, do you realize what the Ark is? It's a transmitter! It's a radio for speaking to God, and it's within my reach!" Belloq's intentions violate the sacred–profane distinction in a different way. Rather than bringing the Ark to dominate the profane world, Belloq brazenly wishes to bring himself to the sacred.[6] He does not respect the sacred object, and he pays the price.

The Sankara Stones

In *The Temple of Doom*, Indy, Short Round, and Willie Scott (fantastically) survive a plane crash and meet the Shaman of Mayapore Village in India. The Shaman leads them to the village, which is eerily destitute, and explains how their sacred Shivalinga stone was stolen by a re-emerging evil acting like a "monsoon ... [that] moves darkness over all country."

Shiva is one of the most important deities in Hinduism and part of the *trimurti* or "triple form" that consists of the creator, Brahma; the sustainer, Vishnu; and the destroyer, Shiva.[7] Shiva can be portrayed symbolically as a *linga*, or a phallus-shaped stone, emphasizing fertility and erotic energy.[8] Mayapore's Shivalinga is a smooth stone with a *tripundra*, "three marks (lines)," carved into it. Indy is familiar with the stone and describes it as "very smooth like a rock from a sacred river with three lines across it representing the three levels of the universe." The Shaman implores Indy to return the stone to Mayapore, and of course Indy takes on the challenge (even if his initial motivations are mixed, at best).

While traveling from Mayapore to Pankot Palace, the source of the re-emerging evil, Indy shows Willie a manuscript fragment depicting the legend of the holy man Sankara meeting Shiva. Jones recounts how Shiva gave Sankara five sacred stones possessing magical properties and "told him to go forth and combat evil." Indy remains skeptical of the legend, earlier calling the missing stone Mayapore's "good luck rock," but he treats the Sankara Stones with respect.

In the ceremonial caves under Pankot, Indy witnesses Mola Ram, the leader of the Thuggee, perform a ritual to remove a person's beating heart in sacrifice to Kali Ma. Also known as "Mother Kali," Kali Ma is a Hindu goddess who is Shiva's consort. Kali is often terrifyingly portrayed standing atop Shiva's lifeless body wielding weapons and wearing a necklace of severed heads. This portrayal is symbolic "of her protective role as the destroyer of evil, with her sword being used to cut the ties of bondage and so offer liberation."[9] Kali and Shiva are intimately related, not through a dialectic of good and evil, but through a unified force for good and the destruction of evil.

Mola Ram seeks all five Sankara Stones, not to combat evil as Shiva intended, but for world domination. As he maniacally explains to Indy:

> The British in India will be slaughtered, then we will overrun the Muslims. Then the Hebrew God will fall. And then the Christian God will be cast down and forgotten. Soon, Kali Ma will rule the world ... Soon, we will have all the five Sankara Stones, and the Thuggees will be all powerful.

Mola Ram intends to use the stones for his nefarious purposes. Recall the Shaman's warning, "Again the [Pankot] palace has the power of the Dark Light. It is that place kill my people." He calls it "evil" and likens it to a monsoon moving darkness over all the country. Mola Ram is the personification of evil, and his followers—under the influence of the black sleep of Kali Ma—spread his "dark light" throughout the world.

During the climactic scene, Mola Ram and Indy struggle for control of the stones on a damaged rope bridge, as hungry alligators await in the river below if either slips. Mola Ram shouts, "The stones are mine!" as he begins the mystic ritual to remove Indy's beating heart. Indy pries Ram's hand away from his chest and exclaims, "You betrayed Shiva!" Jones begins a ritual of his own, causing the Sankara Stones to glow red-hot. Two stones burn through Indy's satchel. Mola Ram momentarily clutches the third—the Mayapore stone—but its extreme heat causes him to slip from the bridge. Indy catches the stone, now cool, as Mola Ram plummets to his death.

Although Indy is not a Hindu, the ritual he performs is successful because he understands and respects Shiva's intended goal for the

Sankara Stones. Jones does not intend to use the Sankara Stones for selfish gain, which explains why he succeeded whereas Belloq did not with the Ark. Mola Ram meets his demise because he violates the sanctity of the Sankara Stones, much as the Nazis did with the Ark.

In the end, Indy returns the remaining Sankara stone, and the Shaman will use it to sustain and protect his village. Durkheim would remind us that the Mayapore Sankara Stone belongs in its designated area—a prominent place in an altar in the village square. Although it is in the village, the altar sets it apart from the profane and creates a sacred space for the stone. As a result, it serves its proper function of warding off evil, allowing the village to prosper.

The Holy Grail

In *The Last Crusade*, Indy is on a quest to find the Holy Grail and his missing father, Professor Henry Jones. As his quest begins to take shape, Indy asks, "Do you believe, Marcus? Do you believe the Grail actually exists?" Marcus responds, "The search for the Cup of Christ is the search for the divine in all of us. But if you want facts, Indy, I've none to give you. At my age, I'm prepared to take a few things on faith." Later, Kazim, a member of the Brotherhood of the Cruciform Sword, reaffirms the Grail's religious significance when he asks Indy, "Why do you seek the Cup of Christ? Is it for His glory, or for yours?"

Indy rescues his father, but loses Henry's Grail diary to the Nazis. Because the diary is the best source for securing the Grail, Henry demands they retrieve it. Indy thinks it's crazy to go to Berlin for the diary, especially when Marcus is being held hostage elsewhere. "What about Marcus?" Indy asks his father. Henry replies, "Marcus would agree with me." Exasperated, Indy mutters, "Two selfless martyrs, Jesus Christ." His father slaps him and explains, "That's for blasphemy! The quest for the Grail is not archaeology; it's a race against evil! If it is captured by the Nazis, the armies of darkness will march all over the face of the Earth!" Once again, world domination explains the Nazis' interest in the sacred.

Antiquities collector Walter Donovan conspires with the Nazis on their Grail quest, and they arrive at the Grail Temple before Indy and his companions. When Indy confronts Donovan, calling him a Nazi stooge, Donovan replies,

> The Nazis? Is that the limit of your vision? The Nazis want to write themselves into the Grail legend, take on the world. Well, they're welcome to it. But I want the Grail itself, the cup that gives everlasting life. Hitler can have the world, but he can't take it with him. I'm going to be drinking my own health after he's gone the way of the dodo.

Like Belloq in *Raiders*, Donovan pursues the sacred for his selfish gain and is willing to conspire with the Nazis.

To make Indy complicit in his quest for everlasting life, Donovan shoots Henry in the stomach and declares, "The healing power of the Grail is the only thing that can save your father now. It's time to ask yourself what you believe." Indy uses his father's Grail diary to pass three tests, meanwhile Donovan and his Nazi collaborator, Dr. Elsa Schneider, follow behind. When they discover that there are many grails in the antechamber, Donovan asks, "Which one is it?" The Grail Knight responds, "You must choose, but choose wisely. For as the true Grail will bring you life, the false grail will take it from you." Here, the Grail Knight echoes Kazim's earlier warning that, "For the unrighteous, the Cup of Life holds everlasting damnation."

Donovan allows Elsa to choose for him. She dupes him, selecting the most extravagant and ornate cup. Captivated by its beauty, Donovan says, "This certainly is the cup of the King of Kings." He fills it with water and drinks heartily. As a result, he ages rapidly until he becomes a skeleton and finally melts into dust, only his Nazi party badge remaining. "He chose poorly," the Knight confirms. Elsa and Indy quickly go to work selecting the true Grail. Elsa asserts, "It would not be made of gold." Indy examines the alternatives and says, "That looks like the cup of a carpenter." Indy fills it, pauses, and drinks. The Knight says, "You have chosen wisely." Indy quickly makes his way back to his father to heal his gunshot wound. Jesus was not an earthly king, so it stands to reason that the Grail would be the humblest and least ornate cup. Donovan neither understood nor respected the significance of the sacred object he sought, which led to his downfall. Indy is not a practicing Christian, but because he understood and respected the Grail and its significance, he succeeded where Donovan failed.

Before Indy and Elsa leave the antechamber, the Grail Knight warns, "The Grail cannot pass beyond the Great Seal. That is the boundary and the price of immortality." The Knight confirms the Grail's symbolic significance for Christianity: it represents salvation and everlasting life with God. The Grail Knight's words also resonate with Durkheim's views about keeping the sacred separate from the profane: The Grail must remain in the Grail Temple. Still, Elsa, who heard the Knight's words and witnessed the Grail heal Henry, grasps the cup and walks toward the Temple entrance. As she crosses the Great Seal, the Temple begins to collapse on itself and its floor splits open. Indy rushes to grab one of her hands. With the other, she reaches for the Grail on a nearby ledge, which leads to her demise as she falls into an abyss.

Donovan and Elsa meet their doom because they fail to respect the Grail as a sacred object. Donovan desired to take the Grail with him into *his* world so he could live forever, and Elsa thought "she had found a prize." She, too, wished to bring the Grail into *her* world. Both, in effect, failed to heed the point of Kazim's question: They pursued the Grail for *their* glory and not God's.

A Moral Universe

How do we make sense of the fact that the "Indyverse" has three sacred objects from three different religious traditions and *each* of them serves as a vivid indicator of what is right and wrong, good and evil? It might be that three different divine beings have agreed that things should be that way. Each divine being, of their own accord and discretion, has decreed that the relevant sacred object behaves the way that it does. This interpretation aligns with the philosophical view known as divine command theory, which has roots going back at least as far as Plato's *Euthyphro*.[10]

Most philosophers (including Plato) disagree with divine command theory as a way to determine right and wrong, good and evil. For example, one might ask: But *why* do these three divine beings agree? Is it a coincidence, or is there something deeper? Perhaps the divine beings agree because the relevant sort of behavior is *already* right or good. In other words, maybe ethical truth goes deeper than divine will.[11] Indeed, there may be universally binding moral principles, such as respect, that exist apart from divine commands. Consider that the statements "$2 + 2 = 4$" and "$a^2 + b^2 = c^2$" are true even without some grand mathematician (or God) to decree them true. They are true simply because they must be. Likewise, perhaps moral imperatives such as "Show proper respect" and "Do not act with selfish motives" are binding simply because they follow from fundamental and axiomatic moral truths.

In each of the films of the original trilogy, cosmic justice is meted out according to how one (mis)uses a sacred object, including whether one violates the sacred–profane separation for personal gain. All of this holds regardless of the characters' personal religious beliefs. The Indyverse is thus a moral universe, even if it's one with religious trappings. Our universe may not have the same level of cosmic drama as the Indyverse, but when we reflect on the movies, we are reminded that our world has its own unyielding moral truths, regardless of one's particular religious beliefs.

Notes

1 *Indiana Jones and the Raiders of the Lost Ark*, 1981, Steven Spielberg Lucasfilm Ltd.
2 Emile Durkheim, *The Elementary Forms of Religious Life* (New York: The Free Press, 1995), 44.
3 Durkheim, *Elementary Forms*, 38.
4 Paul Tillich, *Dynamics of Faith* (New York: Harper and Brothers, 1957), 41 and 45.
5 Durkheim, *Elementary Forms*, 38.
6 For a different perspective on the Ark and its connection to common ethical beliefs, see Chapter 14 in this volume by Brake.
7 This is distinct from the Trinity in Christianity. Freda Matchett, "The Puranas," in Gavin Flood ed., *The Blackwell Companion to Hinduism* (Malden, MA: Blackwell Publishing, 2003), 139.
8 Travis L. Smith, "Siva," in Denise Cush, Catherine Robinson, and Michael York eds., *The Encyclopedia of Hinduism* (New York: Routledge, 2008), 800.
9 Paul Reid-Bowen, "Kali and Candi," *Encyclopedia of Hinduism*, 399.
10 Harold North Fowler, trans., *Plato: Euthyphro, Apology, Crito, Phaedo, Phaedrus* (Cambridge, MA: Harvard University Press, 2005), 35.
11 For an accessible account of ethical objectivism, see Dean A. Kowalski, *Moral Theory at the Movies: An Introduction to Ethics* (New York: Rowman & Littlefield, 2012), 118–134.

Part V

"YOU CALL THIS ARCHAEOLOGY?": ARCHAEOLOGY AND POLITICS

17

On My "Colleague" Dr. Jones and His "Publications"

Aren M. Maeir

I am a professional archaeologist, specializing in the Bronze and Iron Age cultures of the ancient Near East. No, really. I've had the honor to direct a large-scale archaeological project in Israel, the Tell es-Safi/Gath. I've excavated, researched, published, lectured, and presented on archaeology to scholarly and general audiences alike.

After nearly 40 years of practicing archaeology, I believe I am (finally) in the proper position to accurately and fairly assess the work of my esteemed "colleague," the well-known archaeologist and adventurer, Dr. Henry Walton (Indiana) Jones, Jr., of Marshall and Barnett Colleges, USA. (I have yet to ascertain why he left Marshall for Barnett only to return to Marshall again—or why Marcus Brody was always present throughout.[1])

In this chapter, I will summarize and assess Dr. Jones's contributions to our joint professional field, and do so by revisiting some of your favorite moments from the *Indiana Jones* films. Although Indy's archaeological techniques leave something to be desired, to say the least, I still think archaeologists owe him a debt of gratitude for popularizing our profession.

Living in the Present, Remembering the Past

When I started my archaeological career in the early 1980s, and would introduce myself as an archaeologist, I received such exclamations as, "Now that's a cool job!" My newly met acquaintances would often inquire whether what I do is at all similar to Dr. Jones's exploits. In fact, and often to my embarrassment, my own university's (Bar-Ilan University, in Ramat-Gan, Israel) public relations department more than once introduced me, as "our Indiana Jones." It seemed I had a lot to live up to. I didn't even own a bullwhip, let alone know how to use one.

Indiana Jones and Philosophy: Why Did It Have to Be Socrates?, First Edition. Edited by Dean A. Kowalski.

Archaeologists attempt to unlock secrets about our past. That we seek such secrets in exotic locations only adds to the fascination. Journalists inform me that whenever they write about archaeology, their readership jumps substantially. But my job is not just cool or fascinating. It's culturally vital. Archaeology enables peoples and societies to form cultural memories of who they are and where they come from.

Exploring our past impacts how we remember it, but memory is not perfect. In fact, it seems prone to revision with later experiences.[2] The memories that we, as humans, create and recreate, change and even distort, are an important part of the human condition. Our dynamic social and cultural memories play a crucial role in how we understand the societies in which we live, including their importance to who we are.[3]

Yet there are also multiple examples of so-called quests to "understand" the past that are actually attempts to (re)invent the past for the ideological needs of various groups in various times and contexts.[4] It's not just the *Indiana Jones* Nazis who wish to "write themselves into" various "legends" of the past.

How Not to Be an Archaeologist

As fascinating as archaeology is in itself, this chapter is primarily concerned with one particular archaeologist. Dr. Henry Jones, Jr. is incredibly popular—in fact, almost *everyone* refers to him as "Indy," which is short for his self-chosen nickname of "Indiana." How many people have a nickname for a nickname? Still, his work is not above criticism.[5] His exploits are well-documented in his "publications"—four major motion pictures, with a fifth on the way, and various television, comic book, and novel spin-offs. Here we'll focus on his four most well-known "publications."

Unfortunately, Dr. Jones's archaeological research techniques, both in the field and back in the lab, often fail to meet expected professional standards. In fact, his exploits often border on grave robbing. True, he tersely cautions his students in his first major publication *Raiders of the Lost Ark* not to confuse site excavation with grave robbing. But just days before his words about "not removing the contents of a barrow," Indy absconds with the Chachapoyan Fertility Golden Idol from Peru, fleeing from a giant rolling boulder. Decades later, in his fourth major publication *Kingdom of the Crystal Skull*, he reassures Mutt that they won't be shot because they are not grave robbers. But only minutes later it certainly *seemed* that he intended to steal a golden dagger from Orellana's Cradle. When Mutt clears his throat to subtly inquire about Indy's intentions, he mutters, "I can't always borrow yours … I was going to put it back." Mutt—and the rest of us—are not so sure. It looked like it was headed for his jacket pocket.

Dr. Jones regularly fails to document the contextual background of his finds. For example, instead of taking the time to understand the cultural and environmental context of the Golden Idol, he simply grabs it, runs, and causes the entire context in which it was placed to implode—literally. (What were the odds of his simply "eyeballing" its weight with a bag of sand? What kind of scientific method is that?)

Dr. Jones seems overly preoccupied with attractive looking finds—so-called "museum pieces"—such as the Ark of the Covenant and all but ignores more "boring" objects. To be fair, he reminds Marcus that his *other* finds in South America are "good pieces," but it's clear they are consolation prizes for the museum. In practice, archaeologists strive for a complete array of finds from an archaeological site, from the mundane to the unique, man-made and environmental. Doing so provides the most interesting details about ancient peoples and cultures. We must study not only the objects themselves, be they museum quality pieces or "boring" plain pieces of pottery, but also how they relate to the contexts in which they were found, and how the combination of all this tells us about the people who lived in the sites and cultures that we study. Without a robust context to place archaeological finds, our knowledge of the relevant culture remains incomplete.

Dr. Jones is famous for his noble dictum "it belongs in a museum," but it's also controversial. Many objects should go to museums (and not be hidden in a secret US military warehouse), because unearthed artifacts are fundamental to a society's identity, character, and understanding of itself. As such, they should be accessible to the public! Often, objects of deep meaning in very specific cultural contexts should be exhibited in local museums. After all, large international museums, such as the Met in New York or the Louvre in Paris, already have plenty of objects. Of course, local museums must be accessible to the general public and must be able to protect and conserve their pieces. Still, in some cases, an object is best left where it is. Dr. Jones seems to be aware of this distinction, as he claims that the Mayapore Sankara Stone "would've just been another rock collecting dust." So, by his own admission, sometimes objects don't belong in a museum. I wish he would have elaborated. Alas.

There are times when Dr. Jones's choices not only go unexplained but are also quite dubious. Here I refer to his search for Nurhachi's remains in his second major publication *The Temple of Doom*. Rather than work to place the urn in a museum, Indy contracted with a private collector—a Chinese crime boss by the name of Lao Che. It certainly seems like a black-market deal: Lao Che receives the remains of an early Chinese emperor for his personal collection and Indy receives a large diamond he covets (for some unknown reason). Clearly, working with criminal elements in search of artifacts is not to be condoned, and if clear proof of this were to be brought to Dr. Jones's employers, he would almost certainly lose his position at Marshall! (Maybe *this* explains why he left for Barnett?)

One wonders how Professor Jones conducts any research. Here I am not merely referring to how much time he spends trapsing the globe on his many adventures. I'm making a practical point about his very limited excavation toolkit.[6] The bullwhip, pistol, and fedora are iconic, but where are his trowel, buckets, sieve, camera, measuring equipment, or notebooks? Well, we do see him consult his notebook in the Tanis map room, and his father's Grail diary is prominently displayed in his third major publication *The Last Crusade*, but neither is used to document and contextualize his finds.

Indy's "do it alone" approach to archaeology doesn't fit with the collaborative nature and interdisciplinary, if not multidisciplinary, character of modern archaeological research. Most of Indy's compatriots seem to have little if any archaeological training. In fact, some have yet to reach high school. Short Round successfully drives Indy's getaway car through crowded Shanghai streets (with wooden blocks strapped to his feet), but I wonder about his contributions on a complicated dig. Even the characters with formal training are suspect. Professor Harold "Ox" Oxley, who also studied under Abner Ravenwood at Chicago University, spent his career searching for one object, only to become obsessed and driven mad as a result (although he seemed to regain his senses having finally returned the crystal skull). Sallah, "the best digger in Egypt," connects Indy with a learned scholar to translate the markings on the Staff of Ra headpiece. Still, he excavates in a very uncareful fashion, preferring a crowbar to a trowel.

Dr. Jones's major publications are well known, and usually enthusiastically received by the public, but they are not subject to any sort of rigorous scientific peer review. His initial publications were never updated or revised. Since no one is perfect, any self-respecting scholar would have put out updated, revised, and expanded versions of their publications. If only Indy would have explained his choice to leave behind the Sankara Stone when risking his life at sea to obtain the Cross of Coronado from the gentleman in the Panama hat! But Dr. Jones's publications seem to be serialized, almost snapshots in time, with little reference to previous events. Indeed, it almost seems that he lives in an imaginary world, a world where he can do whatever he wants, whenever he wants to, without considering his colleagues' views and accepted research paradigms! (All archaeologists should be so lucky—or maybe not, as there is great value in interacting with one's professional community.)

Okay, I'll just be honest. Dr. Jones's archaeological field and laboratory techniques—including his theoretical and methodological underpinnings—are atrocious. Most, if not all, of what goes on in these movies has just about nothing to do with what archaeology really is (and should be). As a long-time teacher of archaeology in academic settings, I would not want my students to emulate Dr. Jones in how they set their research goals; how they carry out their field projects; how they interpret the finds; and, of course, how they publish the results of their research. Ideally, I want cutting-edge, multidisciplinary research that challenges previous assumptions—not the dramatic exploits of someone traveling the globe, cracking his whip, and seeking only attractive museum objects!

Indy as Emissary

My criticisms are admittedly scathing. If I offend, I apologize. Perhaps it's unfair to hold Dr. Jones to the same standards as other archaeologists. He does live in his own world, after all, and his publications are like none other. Further, and with all due respect to Lara Croft, he is undoubtedly the best-known archaeologist, and his is one of the first images that comes to mind when one hears about archaeology.

This is no small accomplishment. I often meet youngsters who express a desire to pursue a career in archaeology, inspired by their initial exposure to Dr. Jones's publications. The same is true for many students I've encountered over the years; Indiana Jones and his exploits are among the reasons why they joined the profession.

So, despite his professional failings, Dr. Jones makes a distinctive and unique contribution to the modern profession of archaeology because of his unparalleled popularity. This contribution began almost immediately after his first major publication. To be clear, this contribution was *not* leading a bunch of stuffy academics to buy fedoras and bullwhips, "obtain" South American fertility idols, get into bar fights in Nepal (while looking up an old flame), hitch a ride on a moving submarine, or threaten to blow up one of the most important religious artifacts in the history of the world with a bazooka. Trust me. Rather, it was his bringing the very term "archaeology" to the public's awareness—across the globe and in numerous cultures and contexts.

If I show a picture of Dr. Jones during one of my public lectures, it catches everyone's attention. He is immediately recognized. Indeed, Indiana Jones has created a deep and sustained interest in my field. For this, I am thankful. Modern archaeology is an expensive endeavor, for both the work and analyses in the field, but also for all the various analyses (Carbon 14, ancient DNA, Isotope analyses, Physical Anthropology, etc.) that go on during and after the excavation. Pleading for a plane ticket to Marrakesh to chase the likes of Belloq is one thing. Properly funding quality archaeological research is something else entirely. And since, as you know, most funding for scientific research comes from the public, if the public is interested in archaeology, it's more likely that archaeologists will get some of this funding! If not, we won't be able to go out there and study the past to help us better understand who we are and how we got here.

Dr. Jones serves as one of our most important ambassadors. He bridges many types of fans, from the very young who enjoy his exploits on Blu-ray (or streaming) to the not-so-young who recall watching him on VCR machines. Archaeologists like myself should take the interest Dr. Jones sparks and utilize it to propagate our work—what we do and how we do it, the scientific reasoning behind it, and the importance of archaeological research. This message should be aimed to the general public—from grade school children to the educated adult lay public in the hope of better securing archaeology's future.

Professional archaeologists should of course stress how the archaeology that we practice differs from what is presented in Dr. Jones's well-known publications—even at the risk of putting a damper on fun and adventure. As Dr. Jones himself explained to his students in his third publication, archaeology can be meticulous and complex work that involves long hours and much research. Recall his advice to his students: "Forget any ideas you've got about lost cities, exotic travel, and digging up the world. You do not follow maps to buried treasure and 'X' never, ever, marks the spot ... Seventy percent of all archaeology is done in the library. Research. Reading." Well, there is some travel to exotic lands and we do quite a bit of digging—Indy overstated his case there (and he seemed to forget about the tattered map he used to find the Golden Idol)—but he is correct about not skipping the library.[7] Archaeology can be fun and rewarding, too, but not (always) in the vivid ways portrayed in his publications—even if some days one wishes one could bash a hole in the library floor!

Come for the Fun, Stay for the Truth!

Apart from spectacular life in the public eye, Indiana Jones serves as an example of a highly motivated individual who is willing to take risks. This is an important lesson for those who strive for a profession in archaeology. Archaeology is intellectually challenging, but it is also physically demanding. You often have to travel to very distant and not always clean, safe, and hospitable locations. Often, you must wake up at very early hours, sleep in not so comfortable beds (if at all), work long hours in very hot (or frigid) conditions. But, as with most professions, putting in this kind of effort accounts for how rewarding—and fun—archaeology can be.

As the contemporary archaeologist Kent Flannery once (infamously) said: "Hell, I don't break the soil periodically to 'reaffirm my status.' I do it because archaeology is still the most fun you can have with your pants on."[8] Despite all the hard work it involves, there are very few things in the world that are as fun as archaeology! In fact, as anybody who has excavated with me knows, I always say: "There is no reason to do archaeology—unless it's fun!" It is physically demanding, but you work in really cool places, find new and interesting things every day (often with every turn of the trowel), and spend time with other fun-loving characters! I wouldn't trade it for anything—not even the Cross of Coronado!

Although I have discussed Dr. Jones's methodological shortcomings, he does suggest important insights into archaeological epistemology. Consider this claim from his third publication: "Archaeology is the search for fact, not truth. If it's truth you're interested in, Dr. Tyree's philosophy class is right down the hall." As I interpret him, Indy is warning us of the dangers associated with seeking "the truth." Too often—in archaeology and other fields—the present state of research and scholarly interpretation is viewed as the ultimate truth. But scientific and historical knowledge remains fluid. Archaeologists ought to strive to interpret the archaeological objects we discover in the best way available at a given time, clearly aware that theoretical and methodological developments in the future may alter our current understanding of the past![9]

Simply put, what we do today will probably look old fashioned and perhaps even ridiculous to future generations. Today's tools, methods, and assumptions may yet be proven completely mistaken, and our interpretations of the past quite off the mark. That is how science advances! We do the best we can now, and hope things will develop further in the future. And Indy's famous quote provides us with the proper perspective. What we know now is what we know *now* based on available theory and method. Nevertheless, research constantly develops, and much (if not all of) what we currently know will eventually be shown to be outdated—or plain mistaken—by future generations. Let us not think that we find "the truth" in our research; what we find are data and objects—facts—that then require interpretation and contextualization, utilizing currently available analytic techniques. Nothing more, and nothing less.

Aspiring archaeologists should not emulate Dr. Jones for his fieldwork or methodology, but nonetheless Indy provides an important service to the field of archaeology by vividly reminding everyone that archaeologists are still here. Like Indy, we have to continuously keep channels open to the public. It is not enough to do excellent research and publish it in stodgy books or high-end peer-reviewed journals.[10]

In a way, then, professional archaeologists should look to produce Indy-inspired "publications" by doing accessible outreach for general audiences. These publications may not be as pronounced as major motion pictures directed by Steven Spielberg, but they are necessary for the future of the profession. Putting a twist on an old saying, if we do not "publish" this way, we will "perish" from the public eye! With the current crisis in academia and science in general, and in the humanities and social sciences in particular, and the anti-science mentality of many, it is important to bring archaeology to the public's notice—including the cool, cutting-edge, and exciting research that we conduct. Otherwise, we may be become a marginalized academic endeavor, with less and less funding, and fewer jobs, thus diminishing our ability to hone the collective knowledge of humankind's past.

What Indy Taught Me (Including About Office Hours ...)

Although Indiana Jones is a fictional tenured professor of archaeology, actual professional archaeologists owe him a debt of gratitude. We honor him by following his lead in making archaeology a viable, worthwhile, and enjoyable endeavor. By producing our own "publications" for mass appeal, we continue his message for generations to come.

Now please do excuse me. I've just received a mysterious postal delivery from an exotic foreign land, leading me to set out on another exciting adventure! There is treasure to find, and hopefully "X" will mark the spot! No, *not* really, but I'm not sure I'm up for grading stacks of papers and endless student conferences today. I think I'll crawl out my office window. Thankfully, like Indy's, my office in on the ground floor! (Okay, so maybe he influenced my behavior a little bit.)

Notes

1 Brody was the Dean of Students at Marshall from 1939 to 1944, but Jones was at Barnett during that time. Brody was a curator at the National Museum prior to becoming Dean of Students.

2 See Marcel Proust, *À la recherche du temps perdu* (Paris: Bernard Grasset, 1913–1927).

3 See Maurice Halbwachs, *The Collective Memory* (New York: Harper & Row, 1980).

4 See Aren M. Maeir, "Keys to the Past? Archaeological Correlates of Social and Cultural Memory from the Ancient Levant," in Cynthia Shafer-Elliott, Kristin Joachimsen, Ehud Ben Zvi, and Pauline A. Viviano eds., *The*

Hunt for Ancient Israel: Essays in Honour of Diana V. Edelman (Sheffield: Equinox, 2021).

5 For example, Kevin McGeough, "Heroes, Mummies, and Treasure: Near Eastern Archaeology in the Movies," *Near Eastern Archaeology* vol. 69 (2006), 174–185; Neil Asher Silberman, "Raiders of the Lost Art: Real Archaeologists Don't Wear Fedoras," *Washington Post*, May 25, 2008, available online at: https://www.washingtonpost.com/wp-dyn/content/article/2008/05/23/AR2008052302453.html.

6 I do admire his proclivity to punch Nazis, although the high regard that I have towards this specific field technique is due to reasons unrelated to archaeology.

7 For a careful analysis of Indy's iconic "fact not truth" lecture, see Chapter 24 by Brown in this volume.

8 Kent V. Flannery, "The Golden Marshalltown: A Parable for the Archeology of the 1980s," *American Anthropologist* vol. 84 (1982), 278. I suspect that if Flannery said this today, even with his iconic standing in the profession of archaeology, he would be accused of inappropriate language.

9 See Michael Shanks and Chris Tilley, *Re-Constructing Archaeology: Theory and Practice*, 2nd ed. (London: Routledge, 1992) and Guy Gibbon, *Explanation in Archaeology* (Oxford: Basil Blackwell, 1989).

10 For an example of other professional colleagues with similar views, see Karen A. Pyburn, "Public Archaeology, Indiana Jones, and Honesty," *Archaeologies* vol. 4 (2008), 201–204.

18

"Sharing Your Adventures Has Been an Interesting Experience": Indiana Jones and Professional Archaeology

Louise A. Hitchcock

Mutt Williams's mother and a long-time family friend, Dr. Harold Oxley, are missing, maybe kidnapped. Something about a fabled South American crystal skull. Mutt explains, "Ox said he hid that skull someplace, and if my mom doesn't come up with it, they're gonna kill them both." Emphatically planting his pointer finger in a malt shop table, he continues, "Now, she said you'd help me. She said if anybody could find the skull, it's you. Like you're some type of … grave robber or something." Dr. Henry Jones, Jr. stares back at his new young acquaintance and calmly corrects him, "I'm a tenured professor of archaeology." Unimpressed, Mutt sarcastically quips, "Oh, you're a teacher. Well, *that's* gonna be a big help."

I've been there. As a tenured professor of archaeology myself, informing people of my profession doesn't always impress. Okay. Mutt is *probably* correct that being a tenured professor of archaeology isn't incredibly useful when attempting to rescue a graduate school friend from a battalion of KGB soldiers dedicated to unearthing artifacts believed to possess paranormal military applications. But Indy's also correct that archaeologists are not grave robbers. In this chapter, I'll share some of the ways that Indiana Jones's activities compare to what actual tenured professors of archaeology tend to do. As we'll see, there are some intriguing similarities, but also some glaring differences.

Indiana Jones and Philosophy: Why Did It Have to Be Socrates?, First Edition. Edited by Dean A. Kowalski.

"If I Walk It Through Mayan First ..."

Archaeologists do teach, of course. Mutt's right about that. I've taught such courses as Greek Art and Archaeology, Sea Peoples and the Fall of Troy, New Kingdom Egypt, and Archaeology of Cult among others, including research methods courses for archaeology students.

In the movies we *occasionally* see Indy in the classroom, which might explain his quip to Mutt about being a "part-time" teacher. He lectures on famed ancient sites such as Skara Brea and includes material on the differences between migration and the Exodus in *Kingdom of the Crystal Skull.* He cautions his students about mythology, enigmatically distinguishes between fact and truth, and includes material on Egyptology in *The Last Crusade.* He defines "Neolithic" (even if stumbling over its spelling), lectures on Turkdean Barrow (even if it wasn't excavated until 1980—go figure), and tersely explains how archaeology is not to be confused with grave robbing (!) in *Raiders of the Last Ark.* Indy further uses the Turkdean site to impress upon his students "one of the great dangers of archaeology—not to life and limb, although that does sometimes take place—I'm talking about folklore. In this case, local tradition held that there was a golden coffin buried at the site and this accounts for the holes dug all over the barrow and the generally poor condition of the find." You would learn about such topics in an archaeology classroom, and Indy is correct about his last point. Local legends often motivate the public to dig for buried treasure, which damages the site and hampers any further attempts at proper archaeological investigation.

Yet I have never heard tell of an undergrad inscribing her right eyelid with "love" and her left eyelid with "you" in preparation for a classroom lecture on ancient British burial sites. Maybe because I am female and such behavior today might invite a sexual harassment suit Or at least, no colleague has been willing to admit this ever happening. It's almost as uncommon for a student to leave an apple on her professor's desk as he hurriedly leaves the room after a lecture. I suppose it is possible that Professor Jones uses the same Michaelson textbook for 20 years (although I would hope it went through a few updates or new editions), but it is simply beyond me how Indy gets away with crawling out of his office window to avoid holding office hours, especially given my office is on the sixth floor!.

It's also incredibly uncommon for a professional archaeologist to possess near-omniscient knowledge of every language and culture he or she encounters. The vastness of Indy's expertise is simply not possible. He lectures about the history of the Ark of the Covenant, including obscure details about Tanis and the Staff of Ra, with no preparation, and similarly schools Mutt about crystal skulls and South American history over a cup of coffee with a jukebox blaring "Wake Up Little Susie" in the background. Further, per *Temple of Doom*, he is sufficiently fluent in Hindi to translate the shaman's troubling words as he speaks them. He also has an impressive command of German, Latin, and Quechua (remember that one's a local Incan dialect). But his ability to decipher Ox's riddle by recognizing it as Koihoma (it was the diagonal stresses on the ideograms of course!) and interpreting it by walking it through Mayan first—all while sitting at on his living room couch—really takes the cake. Mutt is again thoroughly unimpressed, rather commenting that "for an old man" Indy "ain't bad in a fight." Alas.

Typically, archaeologists specialize in a region, a time period, and a type of material culture such as architecture, pottery, or animal bones. The reason for such specialization is that it is simply impossible to develop expertise in all the world's cultures, regions, and time periods. My own specialty is architecture of the Late Bronze Age Mediterranean (ca. 1700–1200 BCE), with fieldwork specialties in drawing and photography.

Professional archaeologists require specialization, not just in a time period or a region, but usually in a sub-specialty as well. The sub-specialty might require a scientific background in human or animal anatomy for studying human remains or the leftovers of an ancient meal, botany for studying plant remains, or in a particular artifact type such as ceramics, sculpture, stone tools, metallurgy, ancient inscriptions, or underwater exploration. Ideally, archaeologists know a little about enough different things to be able to knowledgeably consult with different specialized experts and ask the right questions.

Although we sometimes draw on the expertise of scientists trained in materials analysis or even physics, most archaeologists are not scientists. In fact, many of us received our education in classics, biblical studies, art history, history, or anthropology. Still, we pride ourselves on being trained in scientific methods of observation and record keeping for purposes of the careful documentation of what we see through accurate descriptions, measurements, drawings, and photographs. What unites us is the interest in what the material remains (garbage) of the past can tell us about how people lived. In ancient times, writing typically represented the elite male stratum of society. Thus, archaeological remains provide us with information about everyone else: women, children, slaves, the humble Roman soldier, and even pirates.

Such specialization and attention to detail not only make us better teachers but also improves our fieldwork. *Raiders* suggests that archaeology is done by excavating large amounts of sand and earth that is hauled away in railway cars. But as Belloq himself points out, those methods are "far too primitive" and are akin to using "a bulldozer to find a china cup." Excavation sites are typically laid out in a strict grid of squares, often 5 × 5 meters with a 1-meter balk of soil surrounding each square, which is left untouched. This preserves the vertical and chronological record of what we excavate through as we go to deeper and deeper levels. After all, archaeology is a destructive activity—when we remove something from the ground or excavate more deeply to find the remains of an earlier period, what we uncover is forever removed from its context. The ability of future generations to explore the same things that we are studying depends on the completeness and accuracy of our written records, and on wider dissemination through academic and popular publications. Anything less—especially fleeing from a giant rolling boulder as the antechamber closes in on itself—and our work uncomfortably begins to resemble that of grave robbers.

"Good Thing We're Not Grave Robbers"

The term "grave robber" often serves as a type of shorthand among archaeologists to refer to a looter. Although some looters are very knowledgeable about finding and excavating archaeological sites, a looter excavates for personal enrichment and profit through selling finds on the international antiquities market, not to learn about the past. Looters do not record architectural features or establish a chronology for what they dig up. Fedora's Utah crew obviously fits this definition. Admittedly, Indy's exploits sometimes border on looting, recalling the Golden Idol fiasco. Really, would it have killed Indy to investigate the boobytraps? Think of what might be learned from studying that technology! In any case, this was not Indy's only close encounter with looting. If Chattar Lal is to be believed, Indy is no longer welcome in Honduras or Madagascar, being accused of grave robbing in both countries.

Looting can be a dangerous activity, with a spade in one hand and machine gun for protection in the other. However, unrobbed graves—like Orellana's cradle, with its gold coins and (ahem) bejeweled daggers—are often the most desirable sources of valuable finds for looters. This is because many archaeological sites in the form of ancient cities or villages might have been abandoned, destroyed, rebuilt, or conquered in ancient times leaving mainly broken items behind. In contrast, an unrobbed grave might contain not only gold, but many fine objects in the form of complete pots, metal tools, jewelry, inscriptions, weapons, and pieces of sculpture placed there for the deceased to make use of in the afterlife.

Hollywood depictions aside, my colleague Dr. Hanan Charaf once excavated an unlooted Byzantine (Eastern Christian Orthodox Period) tomb at a site where she worked in Lebanon. Hanan and her small team were threatened by the landowner and local villagers (known to loot nearby tombs). So, Hanan and her team worked under police protection and went several days without sleep to properly document the tomb and its contents. Hanan withstood accusations of being a spy and a looter herself just to undertake the responsible and professional role of recording the tomb architecture, the coffins, the human remains, and the finds, before getting them safely to a museum for further cleaning and more detailed study. This tomb contained several untouched sarcophagi (carved stone coffins) of the deceased along with a rich array of jewelry in precious materials, numerous coins, and many terracotta lamps.

While a grave robber might shove the bones aside, grab the most valuable finds, run, and seek fortune from selling them on the illegal antiquities market, Hanan and her colleagues had to document the excavation through mapping in the "find spots" of all of the objects including the human remains, making a thorough record of the tomb architecture, drawing and photographing each layer of finds before removal, and carefully giving them multiple labels to ensure that the information about the finds wasn't lost. The purpose of these activities is to be able to recreate a picture of how the tomb looked when discovered as accurately as possible. In this way, all the information about the grave becomes accessible to future researchers.

Similar to Indy's point about the Turkdean site, we should note that any time objects made from precious metals and stones are found, elements of danger and difficulty are introduced into the project. Even a find of the tiniest fragment of a broken gold earring can set off exaggerated rumors throughout the surrounding area that there is a treasure trove, resulting in the potential destruction of a site by treasure hunters. For this reason, I always joke to students that, we're not looking for gold, we're looking for dung (the proper archaeological term is coprolite). In fact, I am only half joking, as I am trying to communicate to students that a humble piece of dung, pottery fragment, or stone tool may give us more information than the piece of gold because we can learn about diet, husbandry, and even the wealth of the owner of the animal that left the dung.

The careful and sometimes dangerous work done by professional archaeologists like Hanan allows us to see Belloq's point about the gold pocket watch in a different light. Holding up the watch, Belloq explains to a dejected Indiana Jones: "Look at this. It's worthless. Ten dollars from a vendor in the street. But I take it, I bury it in the sand for 1,000 years, it becomes priceless!" Yes, but have you ever asked why, exactly, it becomes priceless? From where I sit, its value derives not from what it's made of, but from its value as a source of knowledge of the human past, something known as the "rubbish theory of value."[1] Archaeologists strive to gain an understanding of what the daily life of people in the past was like. Archaeology is uniquely suited to answer these questions because, as noted earlier, it can give us the history of groups of society that did not write their own history. This is the reason why it's good that archaeologists are not grave robbers and any inclination to keep the smallest and most insignificant fragment of an object is punished with banishment from the field.

"I'm Going Home to Missouri ..."

Rarely is *Temple* anyone's favorite *Indiana Jones* movie. Some complain its tone is too dark in that it contains human sacrifice and child slavery. Others criticize its rather shallow and stereotypical portrayal of the Willie Scott character. It's true that Willie is little more than the ditzy-blond, love interest for Indy. She is continually disgusted by the dirt, strange food, lack of sanitation, and creepy-crawlies.

Kate Capshaw's portrayal of Willie Scott contrasts sharply with Karen Allen's Marion Ravenwood in *Raiders*. Marion is a hard-drinking heroine and is not afraid to out-drink male counterparts, be they a rotund Nepalese or a snobbish Frenchman serving up his "family label," whatever that is. You might be surprised to know that Marion captures some aspects of the lifestyle in field archaeology, often typified by hard drinking and casual sex. (You're probably not surprised to learn that contemporary archaeologists are striving to tone down this aspect of life on a dig.[2])

An important part of the plot in *Raiders* is that Indy was trained by Marion's father at the University of Chicago. But it's also the case that Abner Ravenwood dragged Marion with him as he searched the globe for his "little bits of junk." While Marion punches Indy in the jaw because he abruptly walked out on her a decade ago, in the real world she might be upset for a different reason as well. Genealogical connections between prominent archaeologists and their offspring play a bigger role in real archaeology than most people realize, with even rights to publish excavated materials being passed on as if they were personal property. So, it might be that Indy "ruined her life" not by being "the most gifted bum" Abner ever trained, but because he connivingly took Marion's place as his successor! (Of course, Indy ruined any chance he had at this by jilting his daughter.)

It's no secret that the *Indiana Jones* movies have very few strong female characters.[3] Yet if you look closely at Indy's two classroom scenes, you can't help but notice that most of his students are women. This, in turn, always reminds me of another feature of professional archaeology: the bulk of Ph.D.s in archaeology and in its related discipline of art history go to women, but the majority of prestigious university positions are held by men.

Still, *Temple* remains my favorite *Indiana Jones* movie for two reasons. One is the emphasis on finding the unglamorous Sankara Stone, which is then returned to the village as a cultural treasure. Sometimes the value of returning artifacts—not placing them in a museum—is overlooked. The second reason that I like *Temple* is, in fact, Willie Scott. Apart from the stereotype she conveys, the Willie Scott character behaves like many typical excavation volunteers regardless of their gender. As it turns out, and viewed in the right way, she *is* just a little bit more than merely Indy's love interest.

Volunteers who remind me of Willie are often away from home for the first time—be it Missouri or elsewhere. They are expected to physically exert themselves, for example, climb a hill at dawn each day. They must suffer through extreme weather, stomach strange food, and endure challenges for maintaining hygiene—all while also experiencing culture shock because they are so far from home in a strange land. Kate Capshaw's character has normal reactions: she complains about burnt fingers and cracked nails; revels in apples and oranges due to refraining from eating strange, unfamiliar foods (although snakes stuffed with live eels is something I've never seen); and she simply wants nothing more than to go home. Yet, by the end of the film, Willie becomes more than just the ditzy-blonde. She overcomes (most of) her fears and develops the resilience to do her part in saving her friends. I've been on digs with people like Willie Scott, and we're both better for it.

"Fortune and Glory, Kid. Fortune and Glory"

Marion is with Indy when the Nazis open the Ark, and Willie is with him when he activates the Sankara Stones against Mola Ram. These are important archaeological moments for our brave adventurer. I'm happy to report that "Indiana Jones moments" do happen in real archaeology, even if they are not quite as frequent as the movies would lead us to believe.

For the professional archaeologist, there are different kinds of such moments: The feeling of surprise one experiences with an unexpected archaeological find, the excitement one feels in encountering an archaeological site that was surprising, or the satisfaction of success or accomplishment one feels in overcoming an obstacle or perceived danger. In short, an Indiana Jones moment involves a spontaneous experience of the unexpected that leads to a great story to tell afterwards.

One vivid kind of "Indiana Jones" moment is a solar event. Remember when Indy finds just the right spot for the Staff of Ra in the map room and waits impatiently for the sun to shine through the off-center crystal in the medallion? And remember the look on Indy's face when the laser-beam light uncovered the location of the Well of the Souls and the Ark? That was Indy reveling in his own solar event. In reality, though, solar events typically manifest themselves on special days such as an equinox or solstice. I was lucky to have such an experience once during a summer solstice; we got up before dawn to watch the sun illuminate the doorway of a Mycenaean Greek tholos tomb.[4] The only thing that could have made it better was John Williams's orchestra!

To be honest, how welcome Indiana Jones moments are depends on the circumstances. Sometimes the moments depend on the archaeologist's resilience, bravery, and dedication. Sometimes they depend on the intensity of the experience or the archaeologist's desire for extraordinary experiences. Such experiences can range from the tame to the downright dangerous.

On the tame side of archaeological adventure, I once took a nap in a valley on the banks of the Euphrates and was awoken by a flock of sheep. Another time, I tried to sell a colleague to a tribe of Bedouin in exchange for a souvenir camel saddle (all in fun, of course). More surreal and sublime, I once jogged around a deserted Roman city alone at sunrise. (I don't know what I would have done if a Capuchin monkey gave me the Heil Hitler sign as I ran past!)

In a slightly riskier move, I dropped into a monumental tomb through its roof in a heavily forested area of Turkey. To be honest—and although I hesitate to admit it—I felt a bit like being dropped into the Well of Souls by Sallah (without the Nazis, of course). And in an experience that was downright cinematic I once pretended to be a rich American tourist in Syria, looking to buy antiquities to trick villagers into selling me Byzantine mosaics they had uncovered in their fields. However, I was acting on behalf of the local authorities trying to retrieve the mosaics and display them in the provincial museum. Going undercover like this was probably my most unusual archaeological experience, and it allowed me to feel like Indiana Jones, Sherlock Holmes, and James Bond all rolled into one!

On the more dangerous side, I have excavated in Israel while 2,500 enemy rockets were being fired into the country, with some being exploded by Israel's Iron Dome missile interception system within clear view. While this was enough to cause some of our volunteers to pack it up and go home, others ignored the warnings and even avoided shelter to better "enjoy" the "fireworks."

When practicing archaeology threatens "life and limb" for the sake of experiencing some Indiana Jones moment like this one in Israel, male archaeologists sometimes use the term, "archaeo-macho"—or archaeo-facho if you're female! Archaeo-macho is a means of asserting one's willingness to attain "fortune and glory" through overt displays of strength, bravery, and toughness. Along these lines, I've often walked to sites through waist high thorn bushes while wearing shorts and dined on shots of still-made alcohol and grilled goat testicles. Although nearly all modern archaeologists make it home from a dig, tropical illnesses including dysentery and malaria remain a common hazard in some regions. And a routine condition such as appendicitis can represent a terrifying confrontation with mortality in regions where the medical care may not be up to the standards found in urban areas.

One need not go to an exotic foreign location to exercise one's archaeo-facho/-macho. I spent one summer working on a survey in my home state of California.[5] My survey adventures included an encounter with a rattle snake—I, for one, am not paralyzed with fear of snakes—and shimmying across a river on a log. Once when driving to the day's starting point, we stopped for a colony of around 1,000 tarantulas crossing the road. Although Satipo would have been scared silly, we picked a few up and petted their soft fur. One even went to sleep on my shoulder!

Archaeological sites are typically littered with hazards not encountered in the typical office, from creepy-crawlies, some benign and some poisonous, to uneven and unstable surfaces. I know of at least two instances where excavation directors have died by falling into their archaeological site, a case of misfortune and glory!

So, what of fortune and glory for the professional archaeologist? While the early history of archaeology was peopled with rich eccentrics, those of us lucky enough to have a job in archaeology today derive our glory from our discoveries, experiences, stories, and publications rather than from our bank balances. Our fortunes (and our promotions) come from earning the esteem of our colleagues, through our ability to skillfully pass on our knowledge to the next generation of academics, in teaching our students, and in communicating the value and excitement of studying the past to the public. So, for archaeologists not named Indiana Jones, the fortune and glory we seek is ultimately extending humankind's knowledge about the past. That we get to experience "Indiana Jones moments" along the way is an added plus!

"You and I Are Very Much Alike"

You don't need to be "a tenured professor of archaeology" to begin learning field archaeology. Many excavations seek eager volunteers, who have the chance to learn field skills in exchange for their labor.[6] Indeed, most professional archaeologists receive their first taste of archaeology through volunteering or academic programs run by a university. Howard Carter, who is famous for discovering the tomb of King Tutankhamun, originally traveled to Egypt as a 17-year-old apprentice artist to help document Egyptian tomb paintings by making copies of them. He later developed expertise as an archaeologist during his life in Egypt.

What's more, many people encounter archaeological artifacts in their daily life. We often hear stories from people who find cultural objects such as stone tools on nature hikes or camping trips. When this happens, please do not pick up the object and keep it. Instead try to make a record of the location where you found it, document it through a description, drawing, and a photograph, and then turn over this information to a forest ranger, local museum, or local university. In this way, you can further our understanding of humankind's past, and you don't need to learn Koihoma—or any dead language—to do so.

Notes

1 John Carman, "Commodities, Rubbish and Value: Valuing Archaeological Objects," *Archaeological Review from Cambridge* vol. 9 (1990), 195–207.

2 Allison Miller, "In Some Disciplines, Heavy Drinking is Part of the Culture. That Can be a Problem," *Science*, December 6, 2018, available at: https://www.sciencemag.org/careers/2018/12/some-disciplines-heavy-drinking-part-culture-can-be-problem.

3 For more on feminist themes in the Indiana Jones films, see Chapter 5 in this volume by Schmidt.

4 Brent E. Davis, Anne P. Chapin, Louise A. Hitchcock, and Emilia Banou, "Like Dolmen, Like Dromos: Contextualizing the Solar Orientations of Some Mycenaean Tholoi," in Michael Fotiadis, Robert Laffineur, Yiannis G. Lolos, and Andreas Vlachopoulos, eds., *HESPEROS: The Aegean Seen From the West, the 16th International Aegean Conference, Ioannina, 18–21 May 2016 Aegaeum* 41 (2017), 525–532.

5 A survey is where archaeologists walk over a defined area looking for and making note of evidence for the existence of archaeological sites.

6 The Archaeological Institute of America publishes a yearly Fieldwork Opportunities Bulletin, which advertises field schools and projects seeking volunteers the world over, available at: https://www.archaeological.org/programs/professionals/fieldwork/afob. Fieldwork opportunities in the biblical world are advertised through the Biblical Archaeology Society, available at: https://www.biblicalarchaeology.org/digs.

19

Meddling with (Almost) Incomprehensible Powers

Robert Seddon

On their way to the Valley of the Crescent Moon in *The Last Crusade*, Donovan pompously declares, "Well, Marcus, we are on the brink of the recovery of the greatest artifact in the history of mankind." Of course, he's referring to the Holy Grail. Marcus, who is much less impressed with Donovan, replies, "You're meddling with powers you cannot possibly comprehend." The *Indiana Jones* films are replete with mysterious objects imbued with incomprehensible power, but we sometimes overlook the fact that Indy must navigate various political powers during his adventures—including the US government. These powers, themselves often difficult to fully grasp, determine (in part) what Indy, or any archaeologist—including actual ones—ought to do.

Archaeological ethics is a relatively new area of philosophy. Clearly, Indiana Jones didn't always follow the code of ethics—or wouldn't have, assuming it existed before he retired. Archaeological ethics isn't only about how archaeologists handle bones and artifacts but also what politics would like to do with archaeology. Occult powers might not be real, but archaeology really can become drawn into political power plays. In this chapter, I'll share some insights about archaeological ethics, how it impacts and is impacted by politics, and make some observations about the interconnections between Indy's world and our own. As we'll see, for good or for ill, Indiana Jones has left his indelible mark on how we view archaeology and how archaeologists view themselves.

Ever-Present Politics

Politics was the one trap Indy never could evade. Indy's adventures entangle him with the Nazis, Soviets, and Mola Ram pursuing artifacts as part of their territorial ambitions. And when he bests them, there's his own

Indiana Jones and Philosophy: Why Did It Have to Be Socrates?, First Edition. Edited by Dean A. Kowalski.

government, which uses him to pursue its strategic interests but sequesters the Ark in a warehouse instead of displaying it in Brody's museum.

This is where the *Indiana Jones* franchise comes nearest to a realistic portrayal of archaeology, which was and is frequently politicized. Archaeologists who scrupulously don't politicize their research may find it's been done for them. For example, in the Holy Land, interpreting the physical evidence of who settled where in ancient times fuels a proxy battle in the Israeli–Palestinian conflict. And in Belize, disputes over land and logging rights catalyzed a contest over whose ancestors lived there first.[1]

In addition to sending an archaeologist looking for the Holy Grail, Nazi Germany plundered treasures from occupied nations for a planned Führermuseum.[2] (This was not new; Napoleon's armies were tasked with a similar goal.) What's more, Dark Horse Comics' *Indiana Jones and the Spear of Destiny* takes its cue from the Nazis' real capture of relics from Vienna, including a lance that was supposedly involved with the Crucifixion. In this case, Hitler's actual interest in the objects was not about harnessing occult powers. Rather, he wished to rally support for bringing Austria into the new German Empire.

In the 1920s, in what was then the French Protectorate of Cambodia, archaeologists backed by Paris removed numerous artifacts from the temple complex of Angkor Wat. When a young adventurer was caught trying to do something similar, he contested the charge of trafficking, convinced that any Frenchman could lawfully take antiquities from an "abandoned" site.[3] He lost, though without reputational harm: he later became France's Minister of Cultural Affairs. *That* he lost gives us a clue about Indy's position in the world.

Despite Indy's stints in or working with the military, he is excluded from the "top men" of the government machine. Unlike Mola Ram, and despite the Thuggee High Priest's ambitions toward world domination, Indy has no intention to upend the colonial system. Then again, Indy shows little interest in respecting the status quo. If he did, then we would see him negotiating with foreign powers for permission to excavate on their property, as did the Nazis with the Sultan of Hatay, gifting the Sultan his first Phantom 2 Rolls Royce, in *Crusade*. So, Indy gets frowned at from two directions. Our era may see him as "Mister Colonial Adventurist," but by the standards of his own heyday, what's problematic about him is that he's much more an adventurer than a representative of the powers that be.

Stewardship

The Society for American Archaeology only started creating a code of professional ethics in the 1990s. The code consists of official standards and ideals archaeologists are supposed to follow. By comparison, consider that medical professionals are supposed to follow standards and ideals of medical ethics, for example, toward patient autonomy and away from paternalism.

According to Alison Wylie, a philosopher who was involved in the process of constructing the code of ethics for archaeology, stewardship emerged as the central theme.[4] Putting a price on the priceless had frustrated everybody, from Indigenous peoples seeking redress after theft, to museum curators trying to insure their collections. Making stewardship the underlying principle of archaeological ethics was supposed to shift the focus to archaeologists' responsibilities as caretakers of the world's entire archaeological record, including the parts that are still out there somewhere in the ground. The goal was to preserve and maintain archaeological knowledge for the betterment of humankind.

Of course, the archaeological record crucially includes artifacts. It's tempting to be cynical about archaeologists being stewards for the artifacts they collect. After all, high-minded claims about stewardship can be a convenient cover for one's selfish desire to hold onto prestigious artifacts—regardless of complaints from those who want them returned to their lands. This seems uncomfortably close to the "foxes setting themselves up to guard the chicken coop."

Even if there is no malicious intent on the part of the archaeologist, some might simply not be up to the task. Yes, they should be, but what if they are not? Indy's no paragon of modern archaeological stewardship, and the franchise knows it: LucasArts' tie-in computer game *Indiana Jones and the Fate of Atlantis* opens with Indy searching haphazardly for a statuette in the archives of his own college, and eventually finding it in a locker in the boiler room.

At the very least, then, Indy should leave the curating—and the bulk of the stewardship of collected artifacts—to those like Marcus (or other curators who *don't* get lost in their own museums). After all, Indy's strength is field work, as unconventional as it sometimes is. Recall the 26-year unyielding quest to obtain the Cross of Coronado in which Indy is less a pilfering fox and more a single-minded foxhound in hot pursuit. In this, he receives an implicit endorsement from the Grail Knight, who might be the ultimate steward after guarding a relic for centuries. Still, Indy simply isn't the man to curate the museum, or to explain why the remaining "good pieces" from a jaunt in Peru belong in a museum in America.

Loot(ing): Yesterday and Today

The opening scene of *Raiders of the Lost Ark* is iconic. Apart from its place in cinematic history, it thematically pays homage to a tradition of pulp stories about adventures in darkest foreign land. Its setting could be any territory where you could imagine meeting disgruntled, brown-skinned people wielding pre-modern weaponry. The historical details about the Hovitos—and the Peruvian lands they inhabit(ed)—don't seem to be important.

Thinking about *national* heritage as an interest of *national* politics is a tendency that really got into gear in the decades of postwar decolonization. If the Ark of the Covenant were found in Egypt today, the likely upshot would be immediately escalating tensions between Egypt and Israel, with contested ownership threatening to reignite the Arab–Israeli wars. Tel Shilo, a place that really is associated with the Ark, is in the occupied West Bank, and Israel's promotion of it as a Jewish historical site led to an embroiled legal contest over site management.[5]

Of course, as an American, Indy belongs to a country with a strong national identity and national government. In Indy's world of 1935, he was thwarting Mola Ram's plans for British India. In our world, the US Congress was then passing its Historic Sites Act to preserve places with significance in American history. Indy would certainly have understood the notion of national heritage. However, the international legal order wasn't built around it as it is today.

The only thing close to the Historic Sites Act in Indy's world of 1936 is the so-called International Treaty for the Protection of Antiquities. Indy laments losing the Golden Idol to Belloq, and asks Marcus, "Do you want to hear about it?" Marcus, staring at the pieces Indy did bring home, mindlessly replies, "Not at all. I'm sure everything you do for the museum conforms to the International Treaty for the Protection of Antiquities." The standards of proper archaeological behavior for this treaty are never shared with the audience, but it (ironically) might be that Donovan is better at following them than Indy. In any case, it's pretty clear that Marcus knows Indy doesn't always follow the treaty and he doesn't want to be burdened with knowledge of anything Indy might have done to violate it.

In the real world, the first large-scale attempt to regulate international traffic in antiquities was formulated in the UNESCO Convention of 1970. It firmly established that nation-states have a claim on "cultural property" within their territories, and that other signatories must help them recover illegally exported items. Laundering antiquities and getting them into the legitimate market involves more today than going to Marrakesh. If a museum does buy objects "no questions asked," there are journalists and detectives who may question the museum, so your antiquities-smuggling operation will need to be as ready for them as for the dart traps. You'll be as busy fabricating acquisition histories for the objects as you will fleeing from boulders.

By today's standards, Indy often plays the part of a looter. But looting isn't just a question of ownership. When local peoples dig their own ancestors' objects out of their own traditional soils, in order to make money from unauthorized trade in antiquities, that's also looting because the historical record is destroyed. Only painstakingly documented excavation, the sort of careful science that Indy is presumably capable of when people aren't trying to kill him, preserves the information archaeologists can get by examining the sites where objects are found. So-called "loot and scoot" archaeology—the sort that Indy often unfortunately resorts to—destroys information about the past, which means *everybody* loses it. Ironically, in *Raiders*, Indy lectures about "robbing, in which case we mean the removal of the contents of a barrow," and how such treasure-hunting accounts for "the holes dug all over the barrow and the generally poor condition of the find." So, Indy is aware of the importance of good stewardship, even if he doesn't practice it, presumably due to all the bullets flying about his head and the snakes slithering at his feet. Still, he could do a better job of practicing what he preaches.

The point of clamping down on antiquities trafficking is that it makes illicit digging unprofitable. The positive result is that objects will more often be left in the ground until scientific archaeology reaches them. Who rightly owns them is a secondary concern. If antiquities are ruined forever when excavated improperly, then it's not clear what should be done with them after that. You won't want to hang onto a meaningless object even if you are its rightful caretaker, but sending it to a museum that does want it for exhibition, or putting it up for auction, might continue to encourage black marketeers. Maybe the "top men" with their undisclosed warehouse were on to something after all.

Museums

Archaeologists must navigate political power because politicians create the laws that control archaeological finds. In Egypt, the archaeologist Zahi Hawass used to be Minister of Antiquities. "Egypt's Indiana Jones," claimed *Scientific American*.[6] "But in reverse," added *The National*.[7] Partly it's the hat, but mostly it's his pursuit of famous antiquities. Hawass believes that historic Egyptian objects belong in Egyptian museums. Who rightly owns them is *not* a secondary concern.

Although Indy wavers on the importance of putting antiquities in museums, he expresses no special interest in *national* museums. Peru has had a national museum since the nineteenth century. Not only is it *much* closer than Brody's but its curators have more expertise in Peruvian history. But there's no suggestion that Indy even considered offering the Chachapoyan Golden Idol to Peru's national museum. Indy, as symbolized by the red line advancing across the world map, doesn't have any special interest in national borders either. Nowadays he might be called cosmopolitan.

Today there's a fair amount of friction between cosmopolitanism and nationalism—between "the heritage of mankind" and national patrimony—and Hawass is what a driven archaeologist looks like when he comes down hard for the nationalist team. Archaeological science for him reinforces a sense that relics have roots; ethical stewardship in such lines of thought means undoing everything colonial-era Indiana Joneses did to redistribute objects around the globe. Political battles are still fought over the past, and Indy's era has become part of the past they're fought over.

In some ways Hawass is what Indy aspired to be: an archaeological superstar with such fortune and glory that at one point there was a Hawass-branded range of apparel.[8] But Indy's no politician. Recall his lament to Marion, "Fools. Bureaucratic fools. They don't know what they've got there." *Raiders* ends with Indy the scientist being rebuffed by his government. The way Indy is interrogated by the CIA in *Crystal Skull* is evidence that things did not improve, regardless of how many medals were pinned on his chest. In our world, Hawass was one of the top men *in* government, until looting of archaeological sites in the 2011 Egyptian Revolution forced him out. That's something else we learned from Indy: how archaeology gets dragged into politics *and* political violence and war.

The age of Indiana Jones may be over, but museums like Brody's carry on. Many museum pieces and monuments got where they now are in ways that look murky to modern eyes. Victorious armies and occupiers used to take "spoils of war," a practice that goes back to ancient times. This (in part) explains why the world's largest collection of obelisks is housed in Rome, not Egypt.

By the time Indy was born in 1899, the idea that pillage should be a war crime had at least started to take root, but that restrained soldiers more than scientists. (And not all soldiers: Rome acquired another obelisk in 1937 after Mussolini's army looted it from Ethiopia; it was returned in 2008.) An anthropologist could wander a battlefield after the fighters had left, collecting objects and even body parts for study. However, the reality of handling human remains has never been as glamorous as trading an emperor's ashes for a diamond in a nightclub. The result is that museums today can sometimes be embarrassed by what's in their storerooms; after all, they see themselves as institutions that serve a noble purpose for public benefit.

Objects like the Cross of Coronado may indeed belong in a museum, but there are different kinds of museums with different kinds of missions. So-called "encyclopedic" or "universal" museums, of which Brody's seems to be an example, aim to display the development of the world's various cultures side-by-side. Such museums have a particular problem with a position like Hawass's hard-line nationalism. The punchiest defender of encyclopedic museums is James Cuno, President of the Getty Trust. In Cuno's view, archaeologists have made a devil's bargain with nationalist governments that are just out to shore up their own position, using antiquities as convenient national symbols. Governments, he thinks, may prove false friends for scientists in search of facts, and for curators telling you about art and the interplay of cultures. What governments want from archaeology and museums are stories about a glorious national past, so that they can position themselves as the proper successors to historic rulers.

Indy might sympathize, having retrieved the Ark from Nazis who wanted it as a weapon, only for it to disappear into his own government's custody. Nowhere do the political players leave him with the impression that they appreciate "a find of incredible historical significance" for science's sake, or for God's, or even for the earthly sake of fortune and glory. And yet the army may have done the one thing it could do to *stop* the Ark becoming a political symbol once again. Had Brody's museum got it, Indy the scientist might have been as disappointed by America's religious lobbies as he was by its military.

Raiding the Dead

In *Temple* Indy successfully called upon the Hindu deity Shiva, and in *Raiders* and *Crusade* he witnessed the power of the God of Abraham. So what happens to you after death in Indy's world is anyone's guess. Maybe you reincarnate as Hindus believe; maybe you don't, as Jews and Christians believe. In any case, your typical Western filmgoer, and your typical Western archaeologist, probably expects either to stop existing or to pass over to another "place." If you were brought up in a Christian culture—and we know Indy remembers what he learned in Sunday School—you have a background understanding that you can't take wealth with you, and spiritual treasures in heaven are what will matter when you're dead *and* gone. So you might naturally conclude that dead people won't miss what they left behind.

Of course, even Christian cultures have more than that to say about the treatment of dead people. The "departed" are supposed to be laid to rest in peace, and laws that make exceptions for archaeological research don't always give archaeologists the luxury of time before the law demands reburial.[9] The concern is chiefly about treatment of human remains: Does what used to be a person still deserve privacy, for example? But there's a wider ethics of respectful memory, which underlies the sense that defacing war memorials, say, is worse than routine vandalism. Philosophers have wondered whether the living can harm or wrong the dead. For example, if you promise to carry out someone's dying wish, then break the promise, isn't there a posthumous victim?

Or, because the person you made the promise to no longer exists, are you not blameworthy for breaking it?

Individual persons can own property, but what about cultures? What obligations do we have to a culture that has died out? The obligations owed to cultures might explain why Indy returns the Sankara Stone to the Mayapore village in *Temple*, but in *Raiders*, which comes next in the cinematic timeline, he strives to acquire the Golden Idol against the apparent wishes of the local people. After all, it looks as though he's plundering from a dead civilization: he's somewhere ancient, ruined, and seemingly deserted with no existing community in sight. When living locals, led by Belloq, intercept Indy there's little opportunity for debate about afterlives and ancestors. But what stands out compared to today's disputes over "cultural property" is the absence of any clear suggestion that the Golden Idol belongs to the Hovitos' culture, or even the Peruvian nation (established as an independent republic over a century before).

Property and Value

In terms of the ethics of cultural heritage, there are two common approaches. The first starts with cultural property law and aims to develop the legal philosophies underpinning it. This approach is backward-looking in that you want to know whether the current owner of some item is the legitimate owner. So you go back to the object's earliest known origins, check the chain of transactions that brought it to its current owner, and decide whether those changes in ownership were above board. This approach applies to individuals *and* cultures. Panama Hat's claim to the Cross is not any stronger in 1938 than it was in 1912. Assuming a culture can own property, similar considerations apply, even if finding the proper paperwork for artifacts like the Ark or the Golden Idol might prove a bit difficult.

A second approach stresses the present and possible futures. What would happen if the object now changed hands? Who would gain, who would lose, and would the gains outweigh the losses? Questions about who most values the object, and in what ways, crop up a lot, and can end up feeling like a sadistic exam question:

> Local people where a golden fertility idol was found want it returned as a relic of their ancestors. This might help strengthen their near-extinct community and preserve at least this aspect of their unique culture. Scientists want to continue studying it to learn about ancient art and religion. Concerning its ritual significance for modern locals, they note that it was kept in a spider-infested ruin where nobody even unhooked a corpse from its spike trap. Discuss.

Would Indy's students still write "Love You" on their eyelids if he put *that* question on the final exam?

Although young Indy claimed that the Cross belongs to Coronado, and not Fedora, and despite Fedora's reminder that Coronado—and all of his grandchildren—are dead, Indy seems more sympathetic to the second approach. The Cross of Coronado belongs in a museum, where archaeologists can study it and visitors can admire and learn about it. It belongs *in* a museum; therefore it should belong *to* a museum instead of disappearing as private wealth. (The possibility that a crucifix might best belong in a *church* never seems to come up.) On balance, it also seems better that the Golden Idol be relocated to Brody's museum. On the other hand, Indy believes a museum would reduce the Sankara Stone to "another rock collecting dust." His scientific colleagues wouldn't properly understand or appreciate its power, to say nothing of the general public, so he returns it to the people who do, and happily enough those are the very people it was stolen from.

Apart from foundational ethical questions about rights-based approaches versus value-centric ones, recall that these aren't just regular old property claims but claims on *cultural* property. Claims that objects belong to someone's *cultural* heritage. Culture is a pain merely to define—there are many competing attempts. Even if we could agree on what a culture is, we would still be left with the question of whether a culture can possess property.

The questions don't stop there. Does the Chachapoyan idol belong to (what's left of) the local Hovitos' culture especially, or to Andean Indigenous culture generally, or to Peruvian national culture? Does it matter that the historical Chachapoyas were eventually incorporated into the Inca Empire, which stretched across a sizeable chunk of pre-Columbian South America? If so, does it matter that they were none too happy about that? When we see the Hovitos bowing before the idol in some kind of holy dread, does that imply they practice a continuation of Chachapoyan religion, or have they been duped by Belloq's revisionist history, spoken to them in their own tongue? (If only *we* spoke Hovitos!)

What's more, cultures don't have rigid borders, and they don't stay exactly the same for every generation. People with mixed or ambiguous ethnicity may prefer to identify themselves with whichever heritage is most socially advantageous. Others may try to stop them in order to avoid having to share the advantages. And objects can have mixed or ambiguous ethnicity as well. Does the Ark of the Covenant belong to Egypt, to Israel, to Palestine, to all religiously observant Jews of the diaspora, to all ethnic Jews, or to all the Abrahamic faiths? (The mainly Muslim Egypt of modern times might actually have a better claim to it than the Egypt of the Pharaohs ever did.) Religious relics can be particularly tricky because they invite questions about who counts as a true believer.[10]

What makes an artifact culturally significant enough to be worth fighting over is often the kind of complex history that makes returning it to its rightful owner turn out to be complicated—and not all claims are property claims in the first place. The Grail Knight and the Brotherhood of the Cruciform Sword don't keep the Holy Grail hidden away because they regard it as their private and exclusive *property*. They understand themselves to be its guardians. And that's often true of claims on archaeological finds in real life. People seeking to get back their "cultural property" often think of themselves more as custodians of their cultural heritage. Alongside arguments about what was "stolen" under colonial regimes, or "looted" in violation of modern laws against antiquities trafficking, we also see assertions that sending an artifact back where it came from is just putting it in its culturally appropriate place, where it can be cared for by the culturally appropriate people. This begins to explain why archaeologists place importance on stewardship; they, too, can do their part.

The Fedora Casts a Big Shadow

When Indiana Jones made his triumphant return to the big screen after an 18-year hiatus, it was his shadow on the stolen army jeep that made us smile. The brown fedora rested on hair that was more salt than pepper, but Indy was back! For a generation (or two) of archaeologists, though, he never left, and he doesn't seem to be going anywhere fast.

Somewhere in the Netherlands, the art detective Arthur Brand, the so-called "Indiana Jones of the art world," is tracking down another stolen cultural treasure.[11] Like the knights who previously sought the Grail in the Arthurian romances, Indiana Jones is our cultural heritage now: a cultural archetype we can glimpse in figures as diverse as Zahi Hawass and Arthur Brand, just to name two. Indy, possessing symbolic power of his own, has inspired many scholar-adventurers who in one way or another identify with the famous "Professor of Archaeology, expert on the occult and, how does one say it … obtainer of rare antiquities." May they learn from his (not always perfect) example.

Notes

1 Richard R. Wilk, "Whose Forest? Whose Land? Whose Ruins? Ethics and Conservation," *Science and Engineering Ethics* 5 (1999), 367–374.

2 John Preston, "The Original Indiana Jones: Otto Rahn and the Temple of Doom," *Telegraph*, May 22, 2008, at https://www.telegraph.co.uk/

culture/film/starsandstories/3673575/The-original-Indiana-Jones-Otto-Rahn-and-the-temple-of-doom.html.

3 Lindsay French, "Hierarchies of Value at Angkor Wat," *Ethnos* vol. 64 (1999): 170–191, at https://www.academia.edu/1247202/Hierarchies_of_value_at_Angkor_Wat.

4 Alison Wylie, "The Promise and Perils of an Ethic of Stewardship," in Lynn Meskell and Peter Pels eds., *Embedding Ethics: Shifting Boundaries of the Anthropological Profession* (Oxford: Berg, 2005), at https://web.williams.edu/AnthSoc/IJCP/wennergren03.pdf.

5 Jerusalem Post Staff, "High Court to Rule Tuesday on Management of Tel Shiloh Archaeological Site," *Jerusalem Post*, June 11, 2019, at https://www.jpost.com/arab-israeli-conflict/high-court-to-rule-tuesday-on-management-of-tel-shiloh-archaeological-site-592103.

6 Jeffrey Bartholet, "Zahi Hawass, Egypt's Indiana Jones and One-Time Mubarak Ally, Tries to Cozy Up to Pro-Democracy Activists," *Scientific American*, July 13, 2011, at https://web.archive.org/web/20111012125239/http://www.scientificamerican.com/article.cfm?id=guardian-of-the-pharoahs.

7 Matt Bradley, "Indiana Jones, but in Reverse," *The National*, December 19, 2009, at https://www.thenational.ae/world/africa/indiana-jones-but-in-reverse-1.538230.

8 Barbara Eldredge, "Hawass Criticized for Use of King Tut Chair in Fashion Commercial," *Museummonger*, April 19, 2011, at https://museummonger.wordpress.com/2011/04/19/hawass-criticized-for-use-of-king-tut-chair-in-fashion-commercial.

9 Ian Sample, "Legislation Forces Archaeologists to Rebury Finds," *Guardian*, February 4, 2011, at https://www.theguardian.com/science/2011/feb/04/archaeologists-forced-to-rebury-finds.

10 This doesn't mean secular objects are not problematic. For example, see Sam Jones, "£254m Battle of the Black Swan," *Guardian*, March 24, 2008, at https://www.theguardian.com/world/2008/mar/24/usa.spain.

11 BBC, "Ethiopian 18th Century Crown Returns Home from Netherlands," *BBC News*, February 20, 2020, at https://www.bbc.co.uk/news/world-africa-51571409.

Part VI

"IF IT'S TRUTH YOU'RE INTERESTED IN …": MORE FROM DR. TYREE'S CLASSROOM

20

Timeless Artifacts and Aging Humans: Indiana Jones and the Philosophy of Time

Siobhan Lyons

> What, then, is time? If no one asks me, I know. If I wish to explain it to one that asketh, I know not.
>
> —St. Augustine of Hippo, *Confessions, Bk XI*[1]

The notion of time and how it operates is vital to the success of the *Indiana Jones* films. While each film has a specific, ageless artifact at its center, the actors (and characters) themselves inevitably age, highlighting the significance of time between "timeless" objects and aging humans. The entire franchise therefore acts as a commentary on the influence of time and the divergent processes of aging for humans and artifacts. The importance of aging is addressed in the first film when Indiana is injured, prompting Marion Ravenwood to reflect: "You're not the man I knew 10 years ago." To which Indiana responds, "It's not the years, honey, it's the mileage." But sometimes it is about the years. Indeed, as we will see, the years take a significant toll on both Indiana Jones and Harrison Ford, which has inevitably influenced the way in which Indy functions as an icon of popular culture in a specific time period.

Indy Rides Again

In 2020 it was announced that the fifth *Indiana Jones* film is scheduled for release on July 29, 2022, 16 days after Harrison Ford's 80th birthday, and 41 years after the first film, *Raiders of the Lost Ark*, was released. Seeing an older Harrison Ford in the role of Indiana

Indiana Jones and Philosophy: Why Did It Have to Be Socrates?, First Edition. Edited by Dean A. Kowalski.

Jones—epitomized by a much younger Ford—has been the subject of much discussion that throws into contention what it means to age in an industry obsessed with youth and vitality. In the films, Indiana Jones seeks various historical artifacts, but Indy himself has become somewhat of a fossil. In *The Last Crusade*, the Man in the Panama Hat quips that *Indy* belongs in a museum.

Back in 2008, George Lucas defended Ford's aged appearance in the fourth film, *The Kingdom of the Crystal Skull*, saying, "It's not like he's an old man. He's incredibly agile; he looks even better than he did 20 years ago, if you ask me."[2] This sentiment, however, was not widely shared among fans of the franchise. Various critics have since cast doubt on Ford's ability to return as the titular character for a fifth installment. Keith Harris of *Forbes* wrote that the fourth film only exacerbated the uncertainty about Ford's ability to play Indiana for a fifth time. Among the critic's complaints was Shia LeBeouf and the poor script, but he noted: "The most frequent complaint? Harrison Ford is too old for the role."[3]

Twitter was flooded with jokes, many of them "mean and witless," as Harris writes, while others were more humorous and included suggestions for titles of the new film, including *Indiana Jones and the ... Wait, What Was I Looking For?* and *Raiders of the Lost AARP*. Michael Idato of the *Sydney Morning Herald* wondered, "Will he have to wield his whip in one hand and a walking stick in the other?"[4]

Crystal Skull attempted to deal with Ford's aged appearance by directly engaging with it. At the beginning of the film, Indiana remarks that dealing with Russians is "not as easy as it used to be." When Mac, his double-agent sidekick, notes that they encountered a worse situation in Flensburg, with twice as many opponents, Indiana says: "We were younger then." Mac isn't satisfied with this view, responding, "I'm still young," as if the film is attempting to defend itself. Throughout the film, Indiana's son Mutt repeatedly refers to Indiana as either "old man" or "gramps," directly engaging with the fact that Indiana has noticeably aged. In one scene, he tells Indiana: "You know, for an old man, you ain't bad in a fight. What are you like 80?" Indy all but ignores him. Still, for an audience who saw Indy riding triumphantly off into the sunset in *Last Crusade*, his aged appearance is difficult to overlook.

Aristotle and Aging

Aristotle (384–322 BCE) wouldn't have endorsed Harrison Ford's return to the film franchise, as his comments on "elderly men" in *Rhetoric* attest:

> They are cynical; that is, they tend to put the worse construction on everything ... They are small-minded, because they have been humbled by life. ... They are not generous, because money is one of the things they must have, and ... their experience has taught them how hard it is to get and how easy to lose. They are cowardly, and are always anticipating danger; unlike that of the young, who are warm-blooded, their temperament is chilly; old age has paved the way for cowardice.[5]

Aristotle's views are not surprising, considering his well-known focus on the "golden mean" between two extremes. For Aristotle, the prime of life between youth and old age is the ideal mean and the best stage of our lives. Middle age is the most virtuous because it balances the vigor of youth with the wisdom that comes with maturity. The young, while adored and envied in Western culture, have an abundance of reckless energy that makes them less virtuous than those who are middle-aged. The elderly, in contrast, have a noticeable lack of energy that robs them of their virtue.

Aristotle's views on the elderly may be blatantly ageist and altogether inaccurate when looking at the way Ford and Jones as actor and character push themselves into dangerous territory, but the philosopher's views nevertheless resonate in our age-obsessed culture. Even in the first film, when Harrison Ford was already 39 years old, Indy is shown to be somewhat past his prime. The issue of aging is again addressed in *Last Crusade*, when Indiana teams up with his supposedly much older father, despite the age gap between Ford and Sean Connery being only 12 years. Indiana admonishes his father for sleeping with the much younger Dr. Elsa Schneider: "You're old enough to be her grandfather." (Here Indy overlooks his illicit tryst with a 16-year-old Marion.)

While allusions were made to Indiana's physique and apparent loss of vitality in the original trilogy, in Hollywood years (which operate very differently than human years) Ford's career was just beginning. By the mid-1990s, Ford arguably entered middle age. By 2008, he was decidedly approaching late middle age, leaving Aristotle's ideal prime of life.

The criticisms around Ford's aged appearance operate in contrast to the prevailing leniency for aging men in Hollywood. As Kirsty Fairclough-Isaacs notes, "Preoccupation in the media with the ageing faces and bodies of celebrities has concentrated on women ... [and] it is clear that the mass media is profoundly ageist in its attitudes to women. Older men by contrast can often maintain long and successful careers, ageing without the negative treatment of the media."[6] While men are not completely immune from ageist scrutiny, there is the expectation that an actor's career depends largely on ability to *conceal* the aging process, with women more often scrutinized for failing to hide signs of aging. In contrast, "silver foxes" like George Clooney and Brad Pitt are celebrated for being "distinguished," while Sean Connery is notable for being voted "Sexiest Man Alive" at 59, and "Sexiest Man of the Century" at 69.

Alas, Harrison Ford's so-called "silver fox" years have come and gone. And while many long-time actors successfully transition into more mature roles, the significance of the *Indiana Jones* franchise depends on a ruggedly handsome intrepid adventurer and virile womanizer. In his late thirties and early forties, the grueling acts of running from a large boulder, cutting and subsequently climbing up a rickety bridge, and evading Nazis while being thrown about on a moving tank were tough but doable tasks. In *Crystal Skull*, Indiana is still able to run from the enemy, but he is notably slower. In his seventies, such acts are bound to look problematic in contrast to the young Jones who was immortalized in the 1980s. While our own era is markedly different from Ancient Greece, it seems that Aristotle's views on the elderly are lamentably resonant in the twenty-first century, especially when considering the ways in which Harrison Ford's age has constantly been taken into consideration.

In the *Indiana Jones* films, youth is valorized and revered, whereas older individuals are often mocked. Aristotelian views on the limited capabilities of older people are evident in *Crusade*. When Indy and Marcus Brody find that Henry Jones Sr. has disappeared, Brody quips, "What has the old fool got himself into now?" (Ironically, Brody seems more of an old fool, as Indy laments that he "gets lost in his own museum.") Indiana, meanwhile, calls the search for the Grail "an old man's dream." By the time we get to *Crystal Skull*, Indy is not only an older man but he also reminisces about the deaths of his father and Brody. Marshall College Dean Charles Stanworth reflects, "We seem to have reached the age where life stops giving us things and starts taking them away."

In the *Indiana Jones* films, even the casual viewer sees the obvious distinctions between the young, immature sidekick (Short Round, Mutt), the "old fool" (Henry, Marcus), and the ideal mean between these two, a person in the prime of life (Indiana). Aristotle provides an effective way to see the significance of these distinctions. It remains to be seen whether the fifth movie, with a much older Harrison Ford, will attempt to convey them again.

Heidegger on Time (and Being)

The way Indiana ages sheds light on his obsession with relics. These objects—from the Cross of Coronado to the Holy Grail—are not only timeless, but gain value with age, revealing an important difference between humans and the artifacts they seek. Indeed, the *Indiana Jones* franchise makes several useful observations about how a human approach to time and the presence of artifacts work in tandem to produce ideas of value and worth. In *Raiders*, for example, Indiana's charismatic yet selfish rival René Belloq illustrates the arbitrary link between time and value, motioning to a cheap pocket watch he bought: "It's worthless—$10 from a vendor in the street. But I take it, I bury it in the sand for 1,000 years, it becomes priceless!" With the mere passage of time, objects that possess little to no value are automatically bestowed with new value, while the humans who hunt such relics are beholden to a different timescale entirely, and their worth, in a world obsessed with youth, is seen to diminish with age.

Belloq also makes an important distinction between himself and the Ark of the Covenant, claiming that he and Indiana are "merely passing through history," while the Ark "*is* history." His comment operates in contrast to Martin Heidegger's (1889–1976) claim that "human life does not happen in time but rather is time itself."[7] For Heidegger, we conceive of time in distinctly human ways, and cannot think outside of human time. To this end, time is essentially human, and is irretrievably linked to an awareness of one's mortality. Without mortality, without finitude, time becomes essentially meaningless. This is one of the reasons why the Ark draws so much attention; it represents an aspect of time that evades Indy's, Belloq's, and *our* understanding of eternity. As Sallah reminds us, the Ark is "not of this earth," while Brody points out: "No one knows its secrets. It's like nothing you've ever gone after before."

It is ironic to use Heidegger in analyzing the *Indiana Jones* films, considering Heidegger's affiliations with the Nazi Party, the "slime of humanity," as Henry rightly puts it. But the philosopher's views in *Being and Time* are particularly helpful when thinking about *Indiana Jones*. For Heidegger, the common terms "past," "present," and "future" constitute a "vulgar understanding of time," because time is *not* simple and linear, contrary to common conception.[8] The past does not merely disappear as time goes on, and the future does not simply "arrive" and replace the past. Heidegger writes: "The 'now' is not pregnant with the 'not-yet-now', but the present arises from the future." The vulgar experience of time "knows only 'world time.'"[9] In its reliance on clearly separating past, present, and future, archaeological time thus corresponds to Heidegger's "vulgar" conception of time.[10] But the Ark and the Holy Grail evade world time, existing beyond time.

Multiple timescales are evident in the films. Think of when Indy enters the chamber in *Raiders* to retrieve the Golden Idol and when he enters the Knight's chamber to retrieve the Grail in *Crusade*. On the one hand there is human time, the time to which Indy and his sidekicks belong. On the other hand, there is archaeological time, which takes place over thousands of years and for which old objects are (or become) valuable, like the Ark and, eventually, Belloq's pocket watch.

Crusade shows us how much we abide by a distinctly human dimension of time. Recall Indy's encounter with the Grail Knight. The Grail Knight introduces himself as "the last of three brothers who swore an oath to find the Grail and to guard it." Indy informs him: "That was 700 years ago." To which the knight solemnly replies, "A long time to wait." Of course, 700 years is a significantly long time, in itself as we try to contemplate it objectively, but also as we attempt to imagine it from the Knight's perspective. Similarly, recall earlier in the film when Indiana reveals to Brody that he has finally retrieved the Cross of Coronado. Indy asks Marcus, "You know how long I've been looking for that?" The question is almost rhetorical, as Brody answers mindlessly: "All your life." To which Indy echoes, "All my life." The *way* Indy replies suggests that how he experienced that passage of time is different from how Marcus understands the 26 years Indy spent searching for the Cross. Objectively, 700 years is much longer than 26, and neither compares to the broader epochs of archaeological time in this respect. Nevertheless, there is (also) an "inner reality" to the passage of time as one experiences it.[11]

Heidegger distinguishes between "things" and "objects." "Things" are good, and "objects" less so. Furthermore, Heidegger contends that a "thing *things*."[12] In other words, a thing *does something* that corresponds to what Heidegger calls "ready-to-hand." A hammer, a jug, and, arguably, the Holy Grail *do* things. The Ark and the Grail have supernatural functions, such as melting the faces of Nazis and healing bullet wounds, respectively. In contrast, a broken hammer corresponds more to an object that belongs to what Heidegger calls "present-to-hand." It is merely *there*, like the Golden Idol and the Cross of Coronado.

Another important object appears in *Crystal Skull* (besides the alien skull itself). While pursuing Indy and Mutt, two Soviet agents crash into and decapitate a bronze statue of the deceased Marcus Brody, erected on the Marshall College campus perhaps at Indy's insistence. By essentially turning Brody into an object following his death, the film offers a telling commentary on the nature of objects and the value we give them. While objects certainly do gain greater symbolic and monetary value over time, we evidently place more value in the human; the bronze statue cannot fill the void left by Brody or act as a substitute for him. And while Heidegger would argue that the statue doesn't actually *do* anything, it nevertheless signifies Brody's absence, and is therefore an important object.

Heidegger's views on both time and things tell us much about the way we approach human value in human time. When Belloq says to Indiana: "Who knows? In 1,000 years, even you may be worth something," Heidegger's views on being and time converge, and we are left to ask what value we, as humans, have in contrast to the things we seek. While old objects gain value by the mere passage of time, our own relationship to time, by contrast, is defined by the struggle to make our own lives seem meaningful despite our fleetingness.

Adventure Time

Russian philosopher Mikhail Bakhtin's (1895–1975) concept of a chronotope suitably parallels the way time is experienced in *Indiana Jones*. A chronotope relates to the ways in which language and discourse are used to represent notions of time and space. Using Bakhtin's theory of a chronotope, Rosemary Joyce and Robert Preucel analyze the way archaeologists measure and narrate time. Joyce and Preucel write that archaeology exploits the chronotopes of evolution (or progress) and discovery. Discovery, they argue, "is part of the romance of archaeology" which "links past and present," and which "bears close comparison to *adventure time*, one of the chronotopes defined by Bakhtin, typified by popular culture (including *Raiders of the Lost Ark* and its stereotypic archaeologist Indiana Jones)."[13]

Indeed, Bakhtin's conception of "adventure time" (not to be confused with the television show of the same name), helps to explain the way in which *Indiana Jones* reconfigures conceptions of time (and space). Bakhtin's adventure time is a "highly intensified" one in which the heroes of a story experience "a most improbable number of adventures," encompassing "days, nights, hours, moments clocked in a technical sense within the limits of each separate adventure."[14] Adventure time, for Bakhtin, lacks any sense of cyclicity; it is unconcerned with maintaining commonly understood units of time and the regular passing of night into day and back into night. Adventure time both condenses and expands time for the benefit of the story, where hours can pass by in a matter of seconds, or where seconds are stretched into minutes.

As with many Hollywood movies removed from reality, the *Indiana Jones* films pack a significant number of events into condensed "cinematic" time. In *Raiders*, Indy spends the weekend in South America pursuing the Golden Idol only to lecture about the dangers of folklore in his undergraduate archaeology class on Monday. Such events, in turn, remind us of the importance of the moving "red line" that tracks Indy's whereabouts across the globe; it helps us conceptualize his many travels. For example, in *Temple of Doom* we see Indiana, Willie Scott, and Short Round hastily depart Shanghai by airplane. Indy's red line heads west. Soon, Indy, Willie, and Short Round need to jump from the plane—in an inflatable life raft no less—and they careen down a mountain side, over a waterfall, and eventually, but soon enough, into India—all in a matter of a few cinematic minutes.

The opening scenes of *Crusade* follow a similar pattern, not only in regard to time, but also in regard to space. Beginning in Arches National Park in Utah, Indy flees the pursuing grave robbers on horseback and manages to escape aboard a train on the Cumbres & Toltec Railroad, which heads through Antonito, Colorado (roughly 270 miles away) and Chama, New Mexico. In the *Indiana Jones* movies, real, lived time can be both accelerated and delayed according to the needs of the adventure's heroes.

Concerning adventure time, Bakhtin notes that "nothing changes: the world remains as it was, the biographical life of the heroes does not change, their feelings do not change, people do not even age."[15] Of course, this is not entirely the case for Indiana, who has noticeably aged in *Crystal Skull*, and who will undoubtedly look even older in the fifth installment (especially if *The Force Awakens* is anything to go by).

Bakhtin also holds that adventure time contains no element of historical time. The *Indiana Jones* films are less interested in maintaining historical accuracy and more invested in tailoring history for convenience and entertainment value. We're told, for example, that Hernán Cortés gave Francisco Vázquez de Coronado the infamous crucifix in 1521, yet Coronado—born in 1510—would only have been 11 years old at the time. Further, in *Crystal Skull*, we're told that Australian archaeologist Vere Gordon Childe "spent most of his life in the field," when in fact Childe spent most of his career working in museums. Justin Jacobs, moreover, argues that by 1936, when *Raiders* is set, Western arrogance in archaeological exploits had reached its endpoint, as he specifically states, "By 1936, the age of *Indiana Jones* was over."[16] Jacobs references the case of British archaeologist and Egyptologist Howard Carter, whose failed attempt to remove artifacts from the tomb of Tutankhamen—thanks to the Egyptians, who stopped him in his tracks—ushered in the "King Tut effect." This signaled the end of Western archaeological excavations in Egypt, as well as in Turkey, Iran, and Iraq by 1936.

Jacobs goes further. To him, Indy's oft-quoted line "it belongs in a museum," "conceals a far more contentious—and often racist—past than is alluded to in the films," and becomes an example of "cinematic bombast intended to redeem the less savory aspects of [Indiana's] profession."[17] Not only does the institution of the museum allude to the dubious acquisition of the artifacts, but Indiana's determination to put these "timeless" artifacts inside a stagnant repository of "Westernized" history is an attempt to reframe their status according to a human-based understanding of time. Outside of the museum, these artifacts are not easily reducible to human scales of time. Inside the museum, they are subject to the rigid dimensions of human time. Taken from their tombs, chambers, or other places of origin, these timeless relics are seen as objects to be gazed at, becoming, in turn, the very essence of spectacle.

Time Philosophy Convergence

In the *Indiana Jones* films, time is seamless, fast-paced, exciting, convenient, and all over the place. It epitomizes Bakhtin's conception of adventure time in its defiance of linearity, cyclicity, and historical accuracy. In this sense, *Indiana Jones* also resists Heidegger's conception of "vulgar" linear time; after all, the original trilogy begins with *Raiders*, followed by a "prequel" (*Temple of Doom*), and was meant to conclude with *Crusade*, as Indy, his father Henry Sr., Sallah, and Brody rode off into the sunset, unequivocally ending the beloved trilogy. A prequel television series followed in 1992—*The Young Indiana Jones Chronicles*—before *Crystal Skull* was released in 2008. Online, fans debate whether to watch *Indiana Jones* chronologically or in the order in which the installments were released, while also debating whether River Phoenix or Sean Patrick Flannery played a more "authentic" young Indiana Jones.

Negative fan reception of *Crystal Skull* shows that while Harrison Ford may be allowed to age as a flesh-and-blood actor, Indiana Jones as a character is frozen in time. Like the Ark and the Holy Grail, Indy is timeless. This helps to explain the disappointment that some fans felt when plans for a fifth film were announced, showing just how much fans share Aristotle's skepticism about the usefulness of "old men." We have a fondness for Indy in his prime, and more sequels will only serve to remind us of the unfair ravages of real time, in contrast to Bakhtin's notion of adventure time, where characters never age and time defies convention.

Notes

1 "The Confessions of Saint Augustine," by Saint Augustine Bishop of Hippo, 2002. Public domain.

2 Simon Reynolds, "George Lucas Explains 'Indy 5' Plans," *Digital Spy*, May 19, 2008, available at: https://www.digitalspy.com/movies/a96267/george-lucas-explains-indy-5-plans.

3 Keith Harris, "Is Harrison Ford Too Old to Play Indiana Jones Again?" *Forbes*, March 16, 2016, available at: https://www.forbes.com/sites/nextavenue/2016/03/16/is-harrison-ford-too-old-to-play-indiana-jones-again/#71fc5a9c46a5.

4 Michael Idato, "Is Harrison Ford Too Old to Play Big Screen Adventurer Indiana Jones?" *The Sydney Morning Herald*, March 16, 2016, available at: https://www.smh.com.au/entertainment/movies/is-harrison-ford-too-old-to-play-big-screen-adventurer-indiana-jones-20160316-gnk3zk.html.

5 Aristotle, *Rhetoric*, trans. W.D. Ross (New York: Cosimo Classics, 2010), 85–86.

6 Kirsty Fairclough-Isaacs, "Celebrity Culture and Ageing," in Julia Twigg and Wendy Martin eds., *Routledge Handbook of Cultural Gerontology* (New York: Routledge, 2015), 363.
7 Martin Heidegger, *Supplements: From the Earliest Essays to Being and Time and Beyond* (Albany: State University of New York Press, 2002), 169.
8 Martin Heidegger, *Being and Time*, trans. Joan Stambaugh (Albany: State University of New York Press, 2010), 312.
9 Heidegger, *Being and Time*, 406.
10 See Larry J. Zimmerman, "Usurping Native American Voice," in Tamara Bray ed., *The Future of the Past: Archaeologists, Native Americans, and Repatriation* (New York: Routledge, 2001), 30.
11 Augustine of Hippo offers a classic account of how time is related to our sense of its passing in his *Confessions*, Book XI.
12 Martin Heidegger, *Bremen and Freiburg Lectures: Insight into that Which Is and Basic Principles of Thinking* (Bloomington: Indiana University Press, 2012), 12.
13 Rosemary A. Joyce and Robert W. Preucel, "Writing the Field of Archaeology," in Rosemary A. Joyce ed., *The Languages of Archaeology: Dialogue, Narrative, and Writing* (Oxford: Blackwell, 2002), 35. Emphasis in original.
14 Mikhail Bakhtin, *The Dialogic Imagination: Four Essays* (Austin: University of Texas Press, 1981), 90.
15 Bakhtin, *Dialogic Imagination*, 90.
16 Justin M. Jacobs, "Indiana Jones and the Big Lie," *The Washington Post*, December 11, 2017, available at: https://www.washingtonpost.com/news/made-by-history/wp/2017/12/11/indiana-jones-and-the-big-lie.
17 Jacobs, "Indiana Jones and the Big Lie".

21

Listening to the Music of *Indiana Jones*: John Williams and Aesthetic Appreciation

Lance Belluomini

> The basis of music is sound; its aim is to please and to arouse various emotions in us.
>
> —Descartes, *Compendium Musicae* (1618)[1]

Raiders of the Lost Ark might have the most memorable "opening scene" of all time. Recall when Indy enters the idol cave antechamber. Satipo, his remaining guide, says, "Let us hurry. There is nothing to fear here." To which Indy memorably replies, "That's what scares me." Indy carefully avoids the elaborate system of pressure-sensitive stones that release deadly darts from the surrounding walls and makes his way to (what becomes known as) the Golden Idol. It sits atop a stone pedestal. Indy needs to remove it without triggering the weight-sensitive security mechanism. He pulls out a bag from his satchel and removes a handful of sand to create a weight that he thinks approximates the weight of the idol. Indy then quickly replaces the idol with the bag of sand. It turns out to be the wrong weight and the pedestal lowers. All hell breaks loose as the cave collapses around him!

The action continues when Indy reclaims the Golden Idol from greedy Satipo. As Indy flees, a loud rumbling is heard as a huge boulder comes rolling after him. Indy runs from it and leaps out of the cave's entrance only to find himself cornered by a group of Hovitos and Belloq, his rival. Indy manages to escape, but the Hovitos chase him through the Peruvian jungle back to his seaplane. He then swings from a tree vine, plunges into the river, swims toward the plane while avoiding poisonous darts and spears, and boards the moving plane only to discover his

Indiana Jones and Philosophy: Why Did It Have to Be Socrates?, First Edition. Edited by Dean A. Kowalski.

pilot's pet snake Reggie in his passenger seat. Indy shouts, "There's a big snake in the plane, Jock! ... I hate snakes, Jock! I hate 'em!" To which Jock replies, "Come on! Show a little backbone, will ya?"

The acting, action, cinematography, editing, set design, sound effects, and costume design—including Indy's iconic fedora, whip, and leather jacket, of course—all play a role in making this a beautiful and memorable cinematic sequence, but it's John Williams's musical score that makes the largest contribution to our aesthetic appreciation of this iconic opening scene. In fact, the music's swashbuckling symphonic language not only heightens the excitement and leads the narrative, it also dominates the visuals.

The atmosphere and tension that Williams creates with his musical cue in the antechamber (titled "In the Idol's Temple") is incredible. While Indy considers the weight of the Golden Idol, and gets into ready position to perform the switch, Williams uses atonal arpeggios coupled with unsettling harmonic progressions that build to a crescendo. In effect, the music gains momentum and builds our suspense. When Indy replaces the Golden Idol with the sandbag, the musical progression pauses with a rapid upward scale. The "musical pause" heightens this captivating moment to great dramatic effect. And it leaves us wondering: What will happen next? Later, we hear repeating high-pitched trumpets when the giant boulder chases Indy. The music outlines the action, makes the rolling boulder menacing, and emphasizes the pace of Indy's wild escape.

Williams's cue during the jungle chase (titled "Flight from Peru") opens with a sinister dark horn motif that plays as Belloq laughs wickedly—an indication that Belloq is the villain. The music then transitions into a series of pizzicato strings and trombone staccato accents along with the high-pitched sounds of a piccolo clarinet—adding an amusing overtone to the jungle chase. Williams's score also describes Indy's character and sets the tone for the movie: he's a brave adventurer but not the traditional infallible hero we were expecting. The thrilling action music exhilarates our emotions throughout the chase. And in the final moments, one of the most recognizable pieces of movie music played by trumpets—the heroic "Raiders March" theme, now synonymous with Indiana Jones himself—puts us in a cheerful mood as the plane flies into the sunset. Unquestionably, this opening segment of the film wouldn't be the same without the genius of John Williams. He's arguably the greatest film composer of all time, for he has crafted the most memorable, powerful, and timeless scores in movie history.[2]

Philosophers like Professor William Tyree (whom Indy references in *The Last Crusade*) pursue truth, and they concern themselves with abstract questions about the ultimate nature of things. In the philosophy of music, we ask questions such as: What is the connection between music and emotions? And are the emotional responses we have to music relevant to aesthetic appreciation? In this chapter, we'll examine our reactions to John Williams's *Indiana Jones* scores with the help of contemporary philosopher Jenefer Robinson, whose insights will enhance our aesthetic appreciation of the music and the films.

Love and "Marion's Theme"

Aesthetics is the branch of philosophy concerned with the nature of art and beauty. So, "aesthetic appreciation" involves studying aesthetics to more clearly understand and thus better admire a work of art, including our responses to a film. Because our attention is usually directed at the visuals (such as the whip, traps, and huge rolling boulder), we may not realize the impact that Williams's score has on our emotions. Consider our response to Indy and Marion. Regarding "Marion's Theme," Williams said, "I thought that if the music were lyrical, and emotional, and warm, and the orchestra could sing this love theme … that it might be permissible to interject that kind of musical emotion in their relationship."[3] Williams succeeds.

Listen to the rendition of "Marion's Theme" that's heard aboard Captain Katanga's ship. After having been buried alive in the "Well of Souls," practically beaten to death by a hulking Nazi airplane mechanic, and thrown through the front windshield of a speeding truck—Indy, covered in cuts, scrapes, and bruises—crawls into a bunk to rest. Marion says, "You're not the man I knew 10 years ago," to which Indy famously replies, "It's not the years, honey. It's the mileage." Marion carefully dresses Indy's wounds while "Marion's Theme" is played by solo flutes and strings, and then is warmly repeated with cellos. When Marion kisses Indy on the lips, we hear the theme again—this time violins play, and then the full orchestra kicks in, leading to a passionate crescendo only to suddenly flatten out into a delicate motif played by piano as Indy has fallen asleep. The score creates the appropriate romantic atmosphere, and it even evokes joy.

"Marion's Theme" manages to elicit sadness in an earlier scene when Indy believes that Marion has died from the overturned truck and explosion. The musical timbre—the stringed instruments playing in a minor key, the dramatic chords, and that piercing final note by the horns—makes this a powerful motif. Afterwards, we see Indy sitting alone at a bar table where he soothes his grief with alcohol while a charming soft rendition of "Marion's Theme" is mournfully played by the woodwind instruments. Harrison Ford aptly describes this scene's music: "You see, it's not just a theme for Marion. It's about the love that Indy has for her. It's about the loss he feels when he thinks she's gone. It invites the audience and the viewers to emotional involvement. It encourages us to feel. It's an example of entertainment elevated to art."[4]

It's no surprise that "Marion's Theme" also plays a key role in our aesthetic appreciation of *Kingdom of the Crystal Skull.* Twenty-seven years may have passed between *Raiders* and *Crystal Skull*, but the music hasn't aged a bit. Recall the beautiful version of "Marion's Theme" that plays throughout Indy and Marion's wedding. The slow and warm feel of this piece always moves us. The melodic interval, the musical keys, and the tempo of the cue elicit emotional responses whenever we hear it. Feelings of love, romance, and joy always emerge from this theme—even in just the first two notes (the melodic leap from the first note of the scale to the sixth). We experience these feelings as Indy and Marion face one another at the wedding altar. These emotions continue to emerge from the melody and alternating chord progressions as they hug and kiss, and head down to meet the crowd. Truly, the role of the theme in *Crystal Skull* mirrors its role in *Raiders*: it serves to capture the love that Indy and Marion have for one another.

Because this love theme invariably arouses emotions in us, it lends support to the notion that there's an essential connection between music and genuine emotion. After all, Williams's *Indiana Jones* scores invite us to "emotional involvement" generally. As further examples, Williams's music makes us anxious and tense when Indy and Mola Ram struggle for control of the Sankara Stones on the severed bridge in the *Temple of Doom;* and it excites us when the treasure-seeking bandits chase young Indy through a passing circus train in *Crusade.*

Music and Culture

According to contemporary philosopher Jenefer Robinson, "People respond emotionally to music because of the associations they have to it ... different sorts of music have associations that are widespread in the culture."[5] Consider that the "Raiders March" theme is associated not only with the heroism of Indiana Jones but also with march and military music—which we connect with loyalty, honor, glory, and patriotism. It's no surprise that when we hear the iconic marching melody and rhythm of the "Raiders March"—even in just those first four bars played by the trumpets—we feel proud and cheerful.

Other examples can be found in the *Temple* score. "Short Round's Theme" is a jolly melody that arouses emotions in us partly because of its cultural association. It's musical scale and melodic tension evoke the styles and characteristics of Oriental music. After Indy and Willie plummet down from the top floor of Club Obi Wan and land in the backseat of the convertible, they find Short Round at the wheel. Feelings of joy and delight emerge from the theme as Short Round exclaims, "Wow! Holy Smoke! Crash Landing!" Additionally, the "Slave Children's

Crusade" cue is not only a powerful driving march with clanging metallic percussion but also has Eastern sensibilities during the sections played by the woodwind instruments. In fact, Asian music is typically associated with pleasing, relaxing, calming, and peaceful sounds. Consequently, when we hear "Short Round's Theme" or the "Slave Children's Crusade" cue, we feel pleased, relaxed, calm, and at peace—and we appreciate that the music does this for us. Nowhere is this more apparent than in the beautiful rendition of "Short Round's Theme" during the elephant trek to Pankot Palace.

It's not just instrumental music that has cultural associations. Choral singing and chants are connected with reverence and piety and can evoke corresponding feelings. In *Raiders*, Williams uses an amazing choral element in the map room when Indy discovers the spot where the Ark is buried—we're filled with this pious, reverential, and ancient supernatural feeling when the full orchestra and female choir voices emerge from the Ark motif. And in *Temple*, the male choral chants performed with Sanskrit lyrics during the Thuggee sacrificial ritual are unforgettable: though it's a gloomy composition comprised of percussion, it evokes reverential and pious feelings or awe and mystery.

Emotions of Appreciation

Robinson rightly points out that music also arouses emotions "when we're moved by the sheer beauty of a melody or of a harmonic progression."[6] The type of emotions we experience are what philosophers refer to as "emotions of appreciation" (such as amazement or excitement). When we pay attention to Williams's *Indiana Jones* scores, we recognize that we're emotionally moved by the incomparable beauty, inventiveness, and craftsmanship of the melodies, rhythms, and harmonic progressions within these musical compositions. In other words, we evaluate the music as beautiful and well-crafted. This explains why Williams's scores grip us. We're filled with awe because of the beauty we recognize and appraise as belonging to the music itself. And this enriches our aesthetic appreciation of the movies.

Recall the unrelenting "Desert Chase" cue from the *Raiders* score that accompanies one of the greatest action sequences in the history of cinema. Sallah says, "Indy, we have no time. If you still want the Ark ... it has been loaded onto a truck for Cairo," to which Indy emphatically replies, "Truck? What truck?" An awesome musical balletic sequence follows, lasting 7 minutes and 44 seconds, as the score captures every visual nuance while also constantly directing our attention to where the bad guys are. We hear the Nazi march motif when we see the convoy escorting the Ark. We then hear the first part of the heroic "Raiders March" theme over the shots of Indy riding the horse. Next, we hear the second part of that theme when Indy takes possession of the truck and rams the Nazi car, and then once again when Indy takes control of the vehicle a second time (after having been thrown in front of the moving truck and dragged from behind it!). Williams masterfully changes the tempos, builds tension, and weaves familiar motifs. Notice that the music is full of pounding rhythms and loud brass instruments, all of which add to the intricate instrumental detail of this piece. The beauty of the music enhances the scene and arouses "emotions of appreciation"—particularly amazement and excitement.[7]

Clearly, Williams composed the musical themes and motifs in order to accompany the narrative and visuals of the *Indiana Jones* films—to capture the essence of the characters; to reveal the emotions the characters are experiencing; and to carry the energy, drive, and tempo of the unfolding drama and action sequences on screen. Because the music is meant to be heard in the context of these adventure stories, it's difficult for us to disassociate the musical themes and motifs from the stories and the scenes they're heard in. But does the merit, meaning, and emotional impact of the music depend on the stories and visuals? No, the music has its own legs and can stand on its own. For example, we don't need to see the scene where Spalko uses the crystal skull on Indy (to better understand Oxley and the route to Akator) in order to feel unsettled by the eerie crystal skull theme.

Appreciating Complexity

Another way in which music arouses emotions is through our appraisals of how the musical structure of complex pieces unfold. Indeed, we can actually understand a complex piece of musical structure through our emotional responses to its shifts and turns. That is, having our emotions aroused at the right times and in the right ways alerts us to understanding important features in the music.[8]

Undeniably, Williams's *Indiana Jones* scores are filled with dazzling, complex compositions that shift and turn as the music unfolds. For example, recall Indy and Henry's escape from the Nazis at Castle Brunwald in *Crusade*. The escape's final sequence is an epic motorcycle chase scene. Right before the chase, Henry hilariously says to Indy, "Would you say this has been just another typical day for you? Huh?" to which Indy replies, "No! It's better than most!" Indy moves back from the dock, pushes the boat away, and says, "Come on Dad! Come on!" When the camera pulls back, we see a large box that suddenly breaks apart as Indy is on a motorbike with his Dad in the sidecar. They roar past the dock, hitting two Nazi soldiers, knocking them in the river. Then, Nazi soldiers on motorcycles pursue them. After smashing through barricades, Indy grabs a flagpole, and then uses it like a medieval lance to knock one of the Nazi soldiers from his motorcycle. A remaining Nazi soldier rides alongside their motorbike and cocks his gun preparing to fire, but Indy jams the remaining portion of the flagpole through the spokes of the Nazi's front wheel causing the Nazi motorcycle to flip and tossing him high into the air—a spectacular shot!

The visuals of this scene are captivating, but the fast-paced scherzo tempo of the cue (titled "Scherzo for Motorcycle and Orchestra") heightens the excitement and adds emotional depth. The delightful music not only conveys peril and lighthearted silliness, but also captures the frenzy of the action—making us feel the impending danger from the Nazi goons, the refinement of Henry's movements, and Indy's spontaneous nature. The effervescent music shifts and turns causing moments where we're shaken up emotionally. We're surprised, relieved, and satisfied when the heroic "Raiders March" motif suddenly surfaces. We then feel unsettled and alarmed when we hear the sinister brass fanfare for the Nazis. Yet we also feel excited, amused, and content each time we hear the playful motif (consisting of dancing flutes, brass trills, glockenspiel percussion, and the bell-like tones of the celesta) that perfectly captures the strained relationship between Indy and his father.

Because the harmonic changes are extensive and unpredictable at times, we get lost in complexity. Notice that the emotions the cue elicits are the result of us appraising how the music is developing. Feeling how this scherzo cue harmonically shifts and turns as it unfolds is a way of understanding and grasping its musical structure and style—all of which augments our aesthetic appreciation of the music in *Crusade* and thus the film itself. Further, it draws us to the important expressive moments in the music—those that excite, amuse, surprise, unsettle, or satisfy us.

Moods of Music

Music can arouse moods as well as emotions. For instance, Williams creates an impressive mood in *Raiders* when the Ark is finally opened. The musical cue (titled "The Miracle of the Ark") provides a reverential and spiritual background mood. Regarding the scene, Williams said, "For the opening of the Ark, I wanted to try and evoke a biblical atmosphere."[9] As the electrical equipment suddenly malfunctions, we hear the Ark theme played by trumpets. We then see fog and spirits billowing out from the Ark. Indy senses the danger, instructing Marion to keep her eyes shut "no matter what happens." The score deftly represents a divine presence, allowing us to feel the wrath of God's power. We hear loud brass instruments playing while the spirits float and swirl around the Nazi troops. Suddenly, they turn from beautiful angels to agents of death as bolts of lightning shoot out from the Ark, striking the Nazi soldiers and melting the Nazi leaders. The scene culminates with Belloq exploding. The Nazis meet their fate because they treated the Ark with irreverence, viewing it only as a source of wealth and power. We then hear the ancient Ark motif again but this time with an angelic female choir as the remains of the Nazis and their equipment are sucked up through the parted clouds.

When Williams creates the right mood for a particular scene, the music accurately describes and reveals the essence and meaning of what we see on screen. Philosopher Arthur Schopenhauer (1788–1860) aptly writes, "When music suitable to any scene, action, event, or environment is played, it seems to disclose to us its most secret meaning and appears to be the most accurate and distinct commentary on it."[10] In *Raiders*, when Indy embarks on the plane to Nepal (to find Marion and retrieve the Staff of Ra medallion), the score directs our attention to the ruthless Nazi agent Toht who is spying on Indy from behind the *Life* magazine. We hear dramatic "villain" chords when Toht slightly lowers the magazine and peers at Indy. The music expresses and arouses emotions—surprise, anxiety, and uneasiness. Schopenhauer would rightly say these musical notes provide us with the most accurate commentary on this scene, enhancing our aesthetic appreciation of this sequence. The brief and sudden key changes to the dramatic chords disclose to us the true nature of Toht's character while foreshadowing the risky adventure Indy is embarking on.

Music can actually arouse emotions and moods in different ways simultaneously. First, we may respond emotionally to the cultural associations of a type of music—feeling proud and inspired when we listen to march music—like the "Raiders March," and feeling reverent when listening to religious music such as the "Ark Theme." At the very same time we can be emotionally moved and experience profound pleasure at the sheer beauty and craftsmanship we appraise as belonging to both themes. Our emotions are also aroused as we follow the complex structure of these musical cues, and we are moved by what's expressed in the music. It's also possible for the music to create background mood states, as in the "Raiders March" and "Ark Theme" motifs—cheerful and reverential ones, respectively.

The Music (and Philosophy) Plays On …

The powerful and enduring emotional effects of John Williams's *Indiana Jones* scores should continue to encourage us to explore the nature and value of music, and the emotional richness of our musical experiences. Make no mistake about it: the real "fortune and glory" of the *Indiana Jones* films is not the Sankara Stones as Indy once claimed—it's the music of John Williams! And just like Indy said to the Shaman at the end of *Temple*, we understand its power now.[11]

Notes

1 Descartes, *Compendium Musicae* (1618). Public domain.

2 With his latest score for *Star Wars: The Rise of Skywalker* in 2019, he's now received an impressive 52 Academy Award nominations, and he's won the Oscar for "Best Original Score" five times (for *Star Wars*, *Jaws*, *E.T.*, *Schindler's List*, and *Fiddler on the Roof*).

3 Quote is from "The Music of Indiana Jones" featurette from "Indiana Jones: The Complete Adventures" Blu-ray release from 2012.

4 Quote is from Ford's tribute speech to John Williams at the 44th AFI Lifetime Achievement Award Gala.

5 Jenefer Robinson, "Emotional Responses to Music: What Are They? How Do They Work? And Are They Relevant to Aesthetic Appreciation?" in Peter Goldie ed., *The Oxford Handbook of Philosophy of Emotion* (Oxford: Oxford University Press, 2010), 654–655.

6 Jenefer Robinson, "Music and Emotions," *Journal of Literary Theory* vol. 1 (2007), 411–412.

7 For more on "emotions of appreciation," see Peter Kivy's *Music Alone: Philosophical Reflections on the Purely Musical Experience* (Ithaca, NY: Cornell University Press, 1990).

8 See Jenefer Robinson, *Deeper than Reason: Emotion and Its Role in Literature, Music, and Art* (Oxford: Oxford University Press, 2005), 360–361.

9 Quote is from "Indiana Jones and Me: John Williams," *Empire Online*, October 2012, available at: http://www.empireonline.com/movies/features/indiana-jones-john-williams.

10 Arthur Schopenhauer, *The World as Will and Representation*, vol. 1, trans. Judith Norman and Alistair Welchman (Cambridge: Cambridge University Press, 2011), 262.

11 I'm very grateful to Dean Kowalski and David Kyle Johnson for helpful comments on an earlier draft of this chapter.

22

"Germany Has Declared War on the Jones Boys!": Asymmetric Strategy and Honor among Raiders

Nikolaj Kærslund Andersen

Indiana Jones and Marion are fleeing through the streets of Cairo. Outnumbered, our heroes do everything they can to outrun or hide from their pursuers. Indy turns a corner and finds himself confronted by a scimitar-wielding fighter dressed in black. The new adversary swings his saber in intimidating circles, clearly offering a challenge to the already exhausted Jones. A contest of skill. *Mano a mano*. How does our hero respond? (As if you don't already know.)

We might expect a true hero to accept the challenge and defeat his opponent on the proposed terms, demonstrating his superior fighting ability. Such behavior would fit our common conception of a hero as someone who defeats his enemies fairly and squarely. But instead of accepting the challenge and winning an honorable fight, he shoots his opponent.

The scene is iconic because it demonstrates the nonchalance of Indiana Jones and his ability to defy our expectations. At the same time, the scene may cause some unease. There's something profoundly dishonorable about Indy's behavior. Imagine the scene, only with the roles reversed: Indiana Jones turns a corner and finds himself faced with an elite enemy fighter. Jones cracks his neck, raises his fists, and shouts a challenge to his adversary. The fighter shrugs, pulls a gun, and shoots our hero. We would cry foul. The villain would be acting dishonorably. Why not say the same thing about Indy? Is our hero dishonorable?

As a rule, Indiana Jones avoids the strength of his enemies and strikes at their weaknesses. He fights asymmetrically. This chapter looks to the philosophy of war to shed some light on Indy's default fighting strategy.

Indiana Jones and Philosophy: Why Did It Have to Be Socrates?, First Edition. Edited by Dean A. Kowalski.

As we'll see, there are two aspects worthy of further discussion. One is practical: An asymmetric strategy is a way for Indiana Jones to fight a much stronger enemy, by avoiding their strength. But how does it work, and what are its limits? The second aspect relates to the ethical implications of asymmetric warfare: Why do we consider symmetric fighting more honorable than asymmetric, and what kind of "hero" is Indiana Jones really?

War as Wrestling

Let's begin by considering how we usually think about war and fighting. Prussian general Carl von Clausewitz (1780–1831) wrote the classic book on modern war after a life of military service at war with revolutionary and Napoleonic France. In *On War*, Clausewitz presents an idealized picture of "absolute war" as "nothing but a duel on an extensive scale."[1] He depicts war as a wrestling match—a contest of strength and will to render the opponent incapable of further resistance. The idea is fundamentally symmetric in its logic. Two opposing wrestlers seek the same purpose by the same means following the same rules—even if they may differ in their ability.

Wars are fought among nation-states, not wrestlers, but the purpose is still to disarm the enemy, rendering it incapable of resistance. Instead of a single body and mind, the means of war are the thousands of bodies and minds that make up the armies of nation-states. Two opposing armies will never be identical in size and ability, but they are of the same purpose.

In symmetric warfare, an enemy combatant is usually defeated by dealing a decisive blow—a "knockout punch"—that leaves the opponent unable to offer any further resistance. This usually means the obliteration of the opposing military force. With such a knockout, the enemy nation-state is forced to concede defeat. Both sides seek to deal such a decisive blow to their enemy.

Yet Clausewitz also realized that one combatant might be so overmatched that victory in symmetrical warfare is virtually impossible. In fact, Clausewitz is the first Western strategist to discuss guerilla warfare as "a particular indirect form of defense through which it is expected the enemy will be destroyed, not so much by the sword as by exhaustion from his own efforts."[2] This is an asymmetric approach to war: One combatant seeks to engage the other and land a decisive blow, but the other seeks to avoid direct engagement.

One of Clausewitz's lasting contributions to the philosophy of war and strategic thinking was the idea that war is a continuation of politics by other means.[3] War is a means to a political end, and it is that end that defines the relevant war strategy. When studying war and strategy, we must therefore understand the goals of the combatants. Sometimes the goal is to obliterate the enemy, but not always. The goals chosen will dictate the costs that combatants are willing to sustain to win.

Facing Overwhelming Odds

Let's investigate the idea of symmetry and asymmetry in the *Indiana Jones* movies. In *The Last Crusade*, antagonist Walter Donovan signals the fundamental asymmetry at play when he notes that "Germany has declared war on the Jones boys!" Nation-states traditionally declare war on other nation-states, not individual people. Indiana Jones (and his father) obviously don't have the military firepower to match the German nation, and this fact forces them to seek alternatives to head-on confrontation with their foe. They must fight asymmetrically.

Indeed, from opening scene of *Raiders of the Lost Ark*, where Indiana is deprived of his prize by René Belloq and his band of natives, to the fight and flight through the streets of Cairo, to the cultist forces in *Temple of Doom*, to the bandits in the prologue to *Crusade*, Indiana Jones is almost always outnumbered. Even when he's not at a numerical disadvantage, Jones often appears to be physically weaker than his opponent (recalling the fistfight under the plane in *Raiders*) or less skilled in a certain weapon (the aforementioned scimitar fighter). The odds are *always* stacked against Indiana Jones, leaving him with no other option than to engage his adversary asymmetrically. Fighting symmetrically and on his opponent's terms would surely mean defeat.

The only time Indy comes close to symmetrical warfare is in *Crusade*. Together with Sallah and a group of rebels, Jones ambushes a German convoy in the desert of Jordan, attempting to use the element of surprise to deliver a decisive blow. But the symmetric part of the battle is short-lived. Given the military superiority of the German forces and their Mark VIII tank, the dynamic quickly turns asymmetric. Horse mounted, Jones directs the firepower of the tank against its allies, before boarding it to save his father and Marcus Brody. Note again that the enemy isn't destroyed by Indy's direct application of force, but by his efforts to lead the tank and SS Colonel Ernst Vogel off a cliff.

Fighting the Power

The one example from *Crusade* aside, we never see Indy engage a numerically superior foe in a static way, that is, on a clearly defined battlefield. Instead, the fights are unfixed, moving battles in which the enemy is unable to use its entire force against Jones at once.

Indeed, recall Indy's ambush on the Nazi convoy in *Raiders*. In pursuit of the Ark and again on horseback, our bold archaeologist takes on a detachment of soldiers and officers spread across multiple motorized vehicles. During the confrontation, Jones tactically positions himself so that he's never exposed to more than one or two foes simultaneously. And he uses the element of surprise to gain the initial advantage. By forcing the enemy to fight him one or two at a time, he greatly reduces the usefulness of their numerical advantage.

Jones's secret to victory often involves fight-and-flight tactics. In *Temple*, Indy and his comrades never stop to engage their foes head on but force them into a moving battle. They flee the cave on a racing mine car, often careening off the tracks, and combat Mola Ram's soldiers one enemy cart at a time (only to narrowly escape the flooded tunnel). Similarly, in *Crusade*, Indy and his father flee from Nazi soldiers on a motorcycle. (Did you think you'd ever live to see the day where Sean Connery rides in a sidecar?) Nazi soldiers pursue them, each on separate motorcycles. Indiana and his father defeat each biker individually; memorably, Indy uses a flagpole as a medieval lance, much to his father's pleasant surprise (only to return to the "lion's den" to retrieve Henry's Grail diary much to Indy's *unpleasant* surprise).

Turning to single combat, Jones strives to avoid his opponents' strength. Recall Indy's airstrip encounter with the German strongman in *Raiders*. He initially agrees to a conventional fistfight, perhaps assuming that escape is impossible especially with Marion trapped inside the airplane cockpit. Indy makes his first move, essentially ambushing the strongman with a surprise blow, hoping to end the duel quickly (or at least allow for a quick escape). But it's clear that Jones is physically outmatched and unable to win symmetrically. Rather, and with a little luck, Jones manages to position his opponent in the path of the plane's propeller blades, letting them land the decisive blow and do the gruesome work for him.

This scene provides one of the clearest examples of an opponent who insists on approaching combat as a symmetric contest of strength. Notice how the German offers his challenge openly and even lets Jones throw the first dirty punch. In fact, the German exemplifies the perfect gentleman, refusing to hit Jones when he isn't on his feet (which is at least half the time), and limiting himself to punching—as we would expect from an honorable prize-fighter. In turn, our protagonist bites his opponent's arm, punches him below the belt, throws dust at his face, and persistently tries to get a hold of his revolver to finish the duel fast. The contrast between the two is striking!

With this, consider again the scimitar-wielder in *Raiders*. A symmetric approach to that foe would have involved some form of hand-to-hand duel, but instead of engaging his challenger's strength, Jones nonchalantly shoots him. And again, this sort of move is the rule and not the exception for Indy. He attempts the exact same trick on two similar saber-wielding combatants in *Temple*, only this time his holster is empty. He grins (grimaces?) uncomfortably. Although Jones defeats his two adversaries in a symmetric melee, the incident reveals his preference for asymmetric fighting. Even on the rare occasions where he *can* defeat his enemies on their terms, he prefers not to.

Changing the Stakes

Another way of making a fight asymmetric is by raising the stakes of the fight. In a conventional, symmetric duel, each combatant seeks to incapacitate the other while avoiding the same fate. Alternatively, one combatant may choose to accept defeat—or become incapacitated—in order to bring down the other. This renders a conflict asymmetric because one combatant is willing to make greater sacrifices than the other. The two combatants don't share the same goal. This is the asymmetry that provides suicide bombers and kamikaze fighters with an advantage against their foes. They're willing to impose greater risks to themselves than their adversaries are prepared to accept, which provides them an advantage.

Indiana Jones makes a move like this in the climactic bridge scene of *Temple*. Cultists of Kali converge on him from both sides. Once again facing overwhelming odds, Jones first threatens to throw the Sankara Stones into the river below to deter his enemies and allow his escape. This fails, as Mola Ram believes he and his followers will soon recover the stones. Jones then decides to cut the ropes of the bridge, slamming it into the side of the cliff at great risk to himself and his friends. This move isn't as risky as a suicide bomb; since Jones (correctly) bets that he will survive the impact. Still, by imposing greater risk to everyone involved, he nullifies the cultists' numerical advantage. They're again forced to fight Jones one at a time.

Indy's threat to sacrifice the Sankara Stones is similar to the scene in *Raiders* where he threatens to blow up the Ark of the Covenant. Jones ambushes the German procession and threatens to destroy their prized treasure if they don't free Marion. But Belloq calls Indy's bluff and invites him to "blow it back to God," surmising that this is too high a price even for Indiana Jones. Belloq is correct and Jones is captured.

Even Heroes Have Limits

It's telling that Indy's ultimatums to Belloq and Mola Ram fail. He is invariably unwilling to sacrifice everything for his cause and this leads him into trouble. Indiana's enemies identify what he isn't willing to sacrifice and use this knowledge against him. While Jones may seek to thwart the evil schemes of the Nazis, he also takes a professional interest in the Ark of the Covenant, which makes him unwilling to destroy it. He would rather let his enemy possess the Ark than see it destroyed. For this reason, his ultimatum—free Marion or lose the Ark—proves false. Belloq and his men can safely keep Marion *and* the Ark in their custody. Similarly, in *Crusade*, Donovan and his Nazi cohorts coerce Indiana Jones into helping them by shooting his father. This places Indiana in a position where he has to serve the German cause and retrieve the Holy Grail to achieve what turns out to be his most precious goal: to save his father.

At this point, the Germans clearly understand the asymmetric nature of Indy's strategy. They know they cannot goad him into a symmetric battle and deliver a decisive blow through physical force. Instead, they target the things he values more than his mission and his own safety: the integrity of the Ark and the lives of Marion and his father. While this may be evidence of Indy's heroism, Belloq, Donovan, and the Nazis use it to their advantage.

Indeed, Indiana's struggle against Germany does not culminate in a final, symmetric battle. Instead, Jones sticks to his asymmetric strategy. In *Raiders* and *Crusade*, the foes are ultimately destroyed by the divine power they sought to control. In *Temple*, British soldiers save the day by rescuing our heroes. In a way, Indiana Jones is never able to land the decisive blow. That job falls to God and Britain.

Strategic Advantage and Honor

Symmetric fighting always favors the strong. A schoolyard bully will prefer to settle a dispute through fisticuffs since that enables him or her to use his or her strength to the greatest effect. The same is true for wars. The nation-state with the strongest military will prefer a direct, pitched battle to settle a war quickly rather than a prolonged campaign because a decisive battle enables it to leverage its military to full effect against its weaker enemy.

There are important ethical implications of symmetrical and asymmetrical warfare. For example, symmetry is intimately tied to our shared cultural ideas of honor and valor in war. Thus, symmetrical warfare is generally considered more honorable than its counterpart. To defeat your opponent in a face-to-face swordfight is commendable, but doing so with a knife to the back seems cowardly by comparison. These norms are epitomized by common ideas of medieval chivalry and knighthood. Jousting knights represent honorable combatants. Confronting each other head on, equipped similarly with clearly visible weapons, they follow well-accepted rules. By contrast, stealth use of concealed weapons, killing someone in their sleep, and poisoning someone's drink are worthy of censure, if not simply the ways of the morally corrupt. This isn't fighting *fair*.

In a contemporary context, we associate asymmetric and dishonorable means with terrorism. Terrorists purposely avoid confronting the military power of their enemies, knowing they stand no chance against such superior forces. They target supply lines, command structures, or even the civilian population instead. The purpose of such strikes isn't to deliver a decisive blow to the enemy army but to hurt them indirectly. If sufficient harm is continually inflicted, the superior force is likely to withdraw.

Indiana Jones utilizes similar strategies when he disguises himself as the enemy (or a flamboyant Scottish tapestry aficionado) and hitches a ride on a German submarine to infiltrate a secret Nazi lair. These are not honorable ways of fighting. Nor are they permitted by international law. They're asymmetric and therefore associated with dishonorable and thus unheroic behavior. All of this places us in the awkward situation of rooting for someone—one of our most beloved characters—who clearly violates plausible intuitions about how heroes are supposed to behave. Simply put, Indy often acts unheroically. So, why do we continue to root for him?

Is It Okay to Fight Dirty for a Good Cause?

It might be argued that the moral condemnation of asymmetric warfare should be lifted when the protagonist faces sufficiently bad odds and a sufficiently evil foe. Thus, it might be that unheroic behavior is sometimes permissible. After all, Indiana Jones could never prevent Nazi Germany from obtaining the Ark of the Covenant or the Holy Grail via symmetrical warfare; there is no decisive blow he could land against the entire

Third Reich. Because thwarting the goals of the Nazis would be a good thing, Indy (or anyone) ought to be allowed asymmetrical strategies.

That is, when it comes to defeating powers like Nazi Germany, the ends justify the means, especially when someone like Indiana Jones has no real alternative. Thus, for the sake of the greater good we allow him some moral leeway to act in ways that otherwise would be dishonorable. Fair enough. However, and interestingly enough, it's also true that Hollywood heroes usually don't require this kind of moral flexibility.

Popular culture is often a helpful mirror for our cultural values and norms. Like Indiana Jones, many protagonists in movies and books find themselves facing terrible odds as they struggle against evil foes. But unlike Jones, they usually find a way to defeat their enemies without resorting to dishonorable means. Part of what makes them real heroes is that they remain honorable in their conduct—even when this puts them at a disadvantage.

To that end, consider another George Lucas production: *Star Wars*. Like Indiana Jones, the protagonists in the *Star Wars* films are fighting an evil empire. The asymmetric nature of the struggle is even clearer here as they call themselves rebels. They're clearly outnumbered and outgunned. Such a situation should justify asymmetric strategies. Nonetheless, all nine episodes of the *Star Wars* saga culminate in massive, symmetric battles.[4] While fleets and armies converge in battle, we also see individual Jedi and Sith fighting symmetrical saber duels during the movies' climaxes. In the *Star Wars* films, true victories are won through decisive blows and symmetric battles. Our view of Luke Skywalker would fundamentally change if he were to somehow strike down Darth Vader or blast the Emperor from behind. (Note how this issue connects to Harrison Ford and the debate as to whether Han shot first.)

Whether the Rebel Alliance would have been morally justified in defeating the Empire by asymmetric means isn't quite the point. Rather, the *Star Wars* saga shows that real heroes fight and win symmetrically, no matter the odds or the evil they face. The rebels of *Star Wars* (especially in Episode IV) are real heroes because they insist on fighting symmetrically no matter what.

So, is it morally acceptable to fight dirty for a good cause? Perhaps, as long as there is no honorable alternative, but real heroes don't stray from the path of honor. That is, we might accept the ethical basis for Indy's choice of an asymmetric strategy. He's facing the entire Nazi German nation after all. Still, if he was a *real* hero, he would find a way to maintain his honor while beating impossible odds. If Indiana Jones was like most other heroes on the big screen, he would have ultimately won through a fair fight. But he doesn't. In fact, he *regularly* doesn't, which—perhaps surprisingly—makes him unheroic. How can there be a hero who is unheroic?

The Way of the Raider

So, what should we say about Indy's hero status? It's clear that he is far from a textbook Hollywood hero. Perhaps the title of the first *Indiana Jones* movie provides additional clues. Recall the original title was *Raiders of the Lost Ark* and not *Indiana Jones and the Raiders of the Lost Ark*. Thus, it was (intentionally?) left unclear who the "raiders" of the film were: Belloq and the Nazi excavators or Indiana Jones and his crew. Let's say that a "raider" is someone who enters a place illegally and usually violently, and steals from it. Someone who acts illegally and violently, and takes what does not belong to him or her acts dishonorably and is clearly unheroic.

In military terms, a "raid" is a short sudden attack, usually by a small group of people. Raids are fundamentally asymmetric in nature, since the point is to strike quickly and get out before proper resistance can be mounted. Raids target the unprepared. A band of raiders is not an army and would quickly be crushed in a symmetric confrontation.

Interestingly, Indy infiltrates, regularly employs violence, and only associates with small groups. Furthermore, his immediate objectives in *Raiders* and *Crusade* don't include defeating Nazi Germany as a whole. In fact, in *Crusade*, he has the chance to kill Adolf Hitler, but settles for his autograph (albeit written in English). Rather, Jones is motivated by stealing valuable artifacts from his enemies. Though they may not be the rightful owners of these artifacts, neither is Jones. His motivation seems to combine the ambition to avoid having powerful artifacts fall into Nazi hands and pure professional archaeological interest (recalling his "It belongs in a museum!" mantra). Along the way, he sometimes acts heroically, as he does in *Temple* when he and his friends seek to free enslaved children. Still, retrieving the Sankara Stones is central and we assume the villagers are their rightful owners. Mola Ram and his cultists surely consider Jones a thief.

Can Raiders Ever Win?

Although Indiana Jones fights asymmetrically like a raider, he does not really win like one. At the end of the day (and the movies), evil is vanquished either through divine intervention or by the hand of another empire, the British. This leaves us with the question of whether it is at all possible to win using asymmetric warfare. As we saw in *Star Wars*, heroes may fight asymmetrically up until the final, climactic battle and then change to a more symmetric strategy. The rebels persistently score their final victories in symmetric battles. In Clausewitz's terminology, they deliver a decisive blow from which the enemy cannot recover. A knockout punch.

In one sense, Indiana uses the guerilla-approach by avoiding direct confrontation with his enemies. But the term "guerilla" is actually misleading since, in Clausewitz's description, it denotes a *defensive* strategy, wherein the defender fights a protracted conflict over a large territory, by gradually pulling back from the advancing enemy (a strategy that has frustrated the United States on several occasions). But Jones is on offense, not defense, and he does not have the luxury of a large territory throughout which to fight his enemies. "Raider" seems the more apt term, as it emphasizes the offensive, while maintaining the asymmetric logic.

Indiana Jones is notoriously unable to deliver a decisive blow since he remains committed to asymmetric fighting. Clausewitz argued that guerilla warfare might be pursued until the point where a decisive blow becomes feasible, but Jones never makes this switch to face his enemy head on. For this reason, he relies on the intervention of outside forces (or his surroundings).

Jones would surely be considered a terrorist by the German Reich (although we might prefer the term freedom fighter). Together with a small band of friends, he takes on a nation, and this makes for a fundamentally unequal struggle. Jones turns this asymmetry to his advantage, avoids the strength of his enemies, and strikes at their weaknesses again and again. For these reasons, Indiana Jones isn't a soldier or a heroic white knight, but a raider.

Watching the movies with this in mind illuminates his strategic choices in battle. At the same time, it poses fundamental questions about the ethical challenges of fighting for a good cause against a vastly superior enemy. Though it may be morally permissible to fight dirty for a greater good, most Hollywood heroes somehow manage to keep their white armor and moral scorecard clean and intact.

Perhaps, then, part of what makes the *Indiana Jones* movies great and Indy himself so memorable is that Jones isn't like most Hollywood heroes. He's imperfect and thus more human, which makes him more relatable. Even if he acts heroically in some ways, he remains decidedly unheroic in others. Perhaps it's Indy's being a less than perfect hero that makes him one of our favorite characters.

Notes

1 Carl von Clausewitz, *On War* (Hertfordshire: Wordsworth, 1997), Book I, I, 2.

2 Clausewitz, *On War*, Book VI, XXV.
3 Clausewitz, *On War*, Book I, I, 24.
4 Episode V, *The Empire Strikes Back*, is arguably the exception, as this movie begins rather than ends with the great battle of Hoth.

23

Indiana Jones in India, India in *Indiana Jones*

Pankaj Singh and Dean A. Kowalski

In *The Big Bang Theory* episode "The Space Probe Disintegration," Rajesh "Raj" Koothrappali is anxious about a high-profile deep space probe he helped launch. Seeking serenity, he wishes to visit a Hindu temple and invites his good friend Howard Wolowitz. Howard is both supportive and sarcastic: "Oh. Okay. It's not like *Indiana Jones and the Temple of Doom*, right? Some bald guy with horns isn't gonna rip my heart out." Raj swiftly replies, "Dude, that movie's an imperialist fantasy that makes the followers of a beautiful and peaceful religion look like a bunch of bloodthirsty barbarians." Howard calls Raj's bluff by reminding him, "You love that movie," and Raj admits, "Yeah, it's pretty great." Howard then presses Raj about visiting a Hindu temple at all: "So, as a scientist, you believe the way to understand the universe is through facts and evidence, and now you're counting on some blue chick with a hundred arms to help you?" Exasperated, Raj replies, "That is so offensive," and then takes his turn at sarcasm: "Does everything you know about Hinduism come from *Indiana Jones?*"

This terse exchange between fictional best friends represents a common view about *Temple*: Although cringy, and perhaps sometimes offensive, it's still a highly enjoyable action-adventure film. But the exchange also highlights how influential *Temple* has become in terms of what it conveys about India and Hinduism. Some Americans have scant familiarity with either India or Hinduism outside the film, and, for many of us, our very first images of both originated with the film. Raj, as a practicing Hindu originally from India, suggests there might be something amiss about this, which, in turn, places a spotlight on *Temple* itself. What responsibility, if any, do Steven Spielberg and George Lucas bear regarding the messages that *Temple* conveys about India and Hinduism? Do filmmakers—directors, producers, screenwriters—have a moral obligation to accurately portray historical or cultural facts in

Indiana Jones and Philosophy: Why Did It Have to Be Socrates?, First Edition. Edited by Dean A. Kowalski.

their fictional films? In this chapter, we'll explore that question by taking a careful look at how *Temple* portrays India and Hinduism.

The Responsibilities of Filmmakers

Contemporary philosopher Keith Dromm believes that the historical drama *Titanic* does a disservice to William Murdoch's memory.[1] The historical record shows that First Officer William Murdoch acted heroically, but the film depicts him taking a bribe, killing two passengers, and then committing suicide, when he did none of those things. In fact, he selflessly helped passengers to lifeboats before going down with the ship. Because the actual Murdoch did nothing reprehensible, the filmmakers did something morally wrong by distorting the historical record in the film. When Murdoch's descendants—and his hometown—complained about the inaccuracies attributed to the character, the production company made amends by donating money to a scholarship fund in Murdoch's name.

It's true that *Titanic* is a fictional story—it tells the tale of two young lovers, neither of whom actually existed—but the story also contains historical facts about the most famous ship to sink from hitting an iceberg. Dromm argues that the makers of historical fiction films have an obligation to not distort important historical facts when telling the story. Not everything in the story can be expected to be true, but if such films include historical inaccuracies, then filmmakers can be blamed for inaccuracies if harm results from them.[2] Not every historical inaccuracy will cause harm—perhaps some inaccuracies are simply expected or so minor that no harm is caused—and filmmakers are not always responsible, because sometimes, perhaps, the fault lies with the viewer. But sometimes, as with *Titanic*, the filmmaker is responsible for the harm caused by an inaccuracy.

The *Titanic* example conveys a vivid case of harm done to an individual, but Dromm believes other sorts of harm are possible. He explains: "The other kind of harm that can happen if a filmmaker is careless, so to speak, with the truth is to the filmviewers' understanding of history. They can come away from the film with incorrect beliefs about history."[3] The idea is that just as you should not speak about things you do not know, filmmakers should not film about things they do not know. If they do, and harm results—including propagating falsehoods about history—filmmakers can be held accountable.

Dromm acknowledges that for historical fictions, a filmmaker's "primary purpose is to entertain, not edify," and "it is a bad idea to try to learn history from the movies."[4] What's more, when a fictional film makes no pretense to historical accuracy—when it seems to be more fantasy than anything else—Dromm believes "it would be unreasonable of filmviewers to expect historical accuracy ... simply because its plot includes references to actual institutions or persons."[5]

Still, Dromm considers the possibility that his arguments pertain to nonhistorical fictions, and we believe that *Temple* provides an interesting case. Not only does *Temple* make specific references to important Indian historical events, for example, British colonization of India, the 1857 Rebellion against the rule of the British East India Company, and a passing reference to the British General Robert Clive, it (obviously) takes place in an actual country and portrays various religious and cultural elements of the people who live in it. What's more, although the main character is not making history, he is an archaeologist. It is not unreasonable for film viewers to expect that what Indy encounters is more historically and culturally accurate than not. At the very least, radically misleading filmviewers about India and its peoples ought to be avoided, especially if doing so does not disrupt the story being told. This is especially true of such highly popular and influential films as *Temple* (recalling Raj's droll rhetorical question to Howard about his knowledge of Hinduism).

Dining at Pankot Palace

In addition to exposition about Indian history, including the historically accurate British rule represented by Captain Blumburtt, and a tense discussion about the Thuggee cult (more on that later), the Pankot Palace dinner table scene also included, well, dinner. Willie was not the only one who was shocked by the cuisine being served that night. Many Indian viewers were also made uncomfortable by the menu.

An oversized local dignitary—complete with a comically oversized mustache—sighs with joy when the first course is served: "Ah, Snake surprise." Servants bring a large silver platter, uniquely fitted with a silver cone in its center. Wrapped around the cone and carefully laid out on the platter is a large boa constrictor. Wille whispers, "What is the surprise?" The servants must have heard her; one slits the snake open, and hundreds of live, baby eels slither out. (For some reason, Indy took *no* notice of all this!) Willie is simply aghast as the little creatures wriggle all over the table, but an Indian guest enthusiastically gulps two baby eels in one go using both of his hands.

Trumpets signal the second course: roasted black giant bugs. As the dinner guests pass the new platter, one—looking and sounding just a bit like James Earl Jones in Indian garb—asks Willie, "What, you're not eating?" Doing her best to smile and not wretch, she replies, "I had bugs for lunch." He chuckles and gobbles the insect (without utensils, by the way). As the guests greedily empty the insect platter, Willie asks a waiter, "Excuse me, sir, do you have anything simple, like soup?" He brings Willie a large, covered silver bowl. As she removes the lid and steam escapes, Shorty grabs his spoon and waits impatiently for Willie to share. Willie stirs the broth, only to bring eyeballs—that look a lot like *human* eyeballs—to the surface. She screams and then whines. Shorty, mouth agape, drops his spoon in disgust.

Next, the James Earl Jones looking Indian dignitary smiles and declares, "Ah desert!" Servants swiftly place in front of each dinner guest a silver and ivory chalice topped with a small monkey head. The same dignitary informs Willie, "Chilled monkey brains!" The man removes the top of the skull and enjoys a spoonful. As a servant removes the skull in Willie's chalice, her eyes roll back into her head and she passes out, falling backward from the low table. (Indy thoughtfully brings Willie a fruit plate later that evening.)

About this scene, popular culture researchers Lois Gresh and Robert Weinberg assert:

> The West has long presented Eastern customs as bizarre and fantastic, but the banquet scene in *Temple of Doom* is so over the top that it can only be a send up of this tendency. Of course, Indians do not eat anything remotely like what was served ... Had the Pankot Palace banquet been strictly accurate, we might have seen people eating from metal plates called thali, with bowls arranged on them. The bowls would contain various spicy vegetarian foods.[6]

James Luceno, the author of *Indiana Jones: The Ultimate Guide* concurs:

> The scene seems much like any other state occasion—until the food is brought out and the banquet begins. Dishes that no self-respecting Hindu would deign to touch ... are gorged on with such gusto that Indy feels something strange must be afoot.[7]

Luceno attempts to explain away the culinary inaccuracies of the scene (subtly suggesting, perhaps, that most of the guests are under the influence of the Black Sleep of the Kali Ma).

Food habits can be (and often are) a crucial aspect of one's culture. India is renowned for its vegetarianism and, indeed, has the highest percentage of vegetarians of any country.[8] So, it should come as no surprise that many Indians were offended by the inaccuracies of this scene. What's more, worries about the banquet scene are also found in the research of contemporary scholar Yvette Rosser. Surveying students of South Asian origin who were studying in American schools, Rosser aimed to explore the stereotypes about India and Hinduism, taught in American classrooms. She writes: "The wholly fictional depiction of

India in the Steven Spielberg film, *Indiana Jones and the Temple of Doom*, seems to have been taken as a valid portrayal of India by many teachers, since a large number of students surveyed complained that teachers referred to the eating of monkey brains."[9] Such stereotyping negatively impacted the South Asian students, many of whom were struggling to navigate their identity in a multicultural, predominantly Anglo-Christian environment; the banquet scene from Temple only made their attempts more difficult. Further, many nonresident Indians recall the stories of foreigners cancelling prior commitments to dinner, fearing there would be eel-stuffed snake, roasted bugs, and chilled monkey brains (which is not too far removed from Howard's callous quip about visiting Hindu temples).

Interviews reveal that Gresh and Weinberg's suspicions were correct about the comic intent of the scene. In *The Complete Making of Indiana Jones*, Lucas is quoted as saying:

> We wanted to infuse into *Temple of Doom* the humor you find in the old *Abbott and Costello* movies ... The dinner scene where outrageous dishes are served was something that I'd always wanted to put into a movie. Steven [Spielberg] has a sense of humor that fits right into that, so he went hog wild.[10]

Spielberg concurs: "This was a scene that really leaned toward gross-out comedy. But it was a lot of fun to shoot. It was a lot of laughs."[11] Interestingly, ethical worries about this scene could have been avoided (at least in part) if Lucas and Spielberg kept a bit of dialogue from the shooting script. In it, Indy shares a quiet after-dinner moment with Blumburtt and states, "Even if they were trying to scare us away, a devout Hindu would never touch meat. Makes you wonder what these people are ..."[12] That the desire to include "gross-out humor" won out at the expense of concerns about how Indians might react to the scene, especially when it could have been easily addressed by keeping a line of script dialogue, is troublesome. This suggests a disregard for Indian culture, which is morally objectionable.

The Thuggee and Kali

Set apart from Willie and Short Round, Indy engages Prime Minister Chattar Lal and Captain Blumburtt in dinner conversation. Lal not-so-subtly expresses displeasure about British colonization, but Indy wishes to broach a different topic. He states, "If memory serves me correctly, this area, this province, was the center of the Thuggee." A seemingly irritated Lal responds, "Dr. Jones, you know perfectly well the Thuggee cult has been dead for nearly a century." Captain Blumburrt agrees with Lal, "Yes, of course. The Thuggee was an obscenity that worshiped Kali with human sacrifice. The British Army nicely did away with them." Maharaja Zalim Singh abruptly adds: "I thought the stories were told to frighten children. Later I learned the Thuggee cult was once real, and did unspeakable things. I'm ashamed of what happened here so many years ago and I assure you this will never happen again in my kingdom." This discussion seems historical, punctuated by the young Maharaja's declaration.

Historical accounts about the Thuggee differ, but their existence is well-attested. The word "Thuggee" comes from the Hindi word "thug," which means "swindler" or "deceiver," especially one who robbed travelers. Gresh and Weinberg explain: "The Thuggees were a mob of sorts; its members lived throughout India in secret, networked groups ... They weren't merely highway robbers. Rather, they often befriended their wealthy victims, who just happened to be traveling. After gaining the confidence and trust of a wealthy victim, the Thuggee strangled, robbed, and buried him."[13] This only confirms that the dinner table conversation is more fact than fiction.

Temple cinematically conveys commonly held beliefs about Thuggee activity during the scene(s) when Indy is deliberating about whether to go back into Willie's bedroom to rekindle their amorous encounter. As Indy paces back and forth, if you look carefully, you'll see a life-sized mural of Indian-looking people in the background. Part of the mural is in shadow. If you look really carefully at that part of the mural, you'll see a man standing perfectly still in front of it. Because the man is dressed exactly like those in the mural, he conceals himself by "hiding" in plain sight. Indy is oblivious to this man's presence. At an opportune moment, the man sneaks up on Indy from behind, wraps a cord around Indy's neck, and begins choking the life out of him. This quick scene informatively conveys how the Thuggee utilized deception and stealth to kill their victims, typically at night in familiar places and without killing children (as Shorty's life is never threatened).

As the dinner table conversation reveals, it is also commonly believed that Thuggee activity had a cultish component connected to Kali worship. Gresh and Weinberg explain: "The Thuggee murderers did indeed kill according to ancient religious rituals related to Kali ... Every murder became a sacrifice to Kali, under her orders ... By strangling people, the Thuggees were performing an honorable, noble, religious duty." In the film, Mola Ram is a Thuggee high priest who conducts religious ceremonies dedicated to Kali, who, in turn, is represented by an imposing statue located in the caves beneath Pankot Palace.

Yet not everything portrayed in *Temple* is faithful to Hindu religion and Thuggee practice, beginning with its depictions of Kali. The film depicts Shiva and Kali as antagonists or competing supernatural forces, but in Hindu religion, the relationship is much closer. Along with Brahma and Vishnu, Shiva is a member of the supreme trinity (*trimurti*), which represents different aspects or manifestations—creation, preservation, and destruction—of one reality. Sometimes Shiva is seen as representing all three manifestations alone. When this happens, his consorts (*shakti*) stand in for the different manifestations of reality; Parvati and Kali are two such consorts. Hindu scholar David Kinsley (1939–2000) explains their relationship to Shiva this way:

> [Kali] appears to play the opposite role from that of Parvati. Parvati calms Shiva, counterbalancing his antisocial or destructive tendencies; she brings him within the sphere of domesticity and with her soft glances urges him to moderate the destructive aspects of his tandava dance. Kali is Shiva's "wife" as it were, provoking him and encouraging him in his mad, antisocial, disruptive habits.[14]

Kali is a personification of Shiva's destructive force, but is not different from Shiva. Kali's role is crucial for proper balance between preservation and creation.

Images of Kali typically show her with dark blue skin (recalling Howard's snide comment to Raj), possessing at least four arms (and rarely as many as 100, Howard), as gaunt with sunken eyes, wearing a tiger skin sari, and a garland of human heads around her neck. *Temple* accurately represents some of these features, especially the gaunt eyes and strands of human skulls. Kali is "goddess of destruction" but as the savior from all the evils, regardless of how powerful, that beset you. She is like a mother who will go to great lengths—including "devouring your demons"—so you can move forward on your path toward enlightenment.

To claim that Kali is an "evil god" who opposes Shiva misrepresents her important role in Hindu religious devotion. Not surprisingly, many Hindus took offense at this representation. Their worries were exacerbated by Mola Ram's fantastical plan to use Kali Ma (that is, "Kali the Mother") for global conquest: "The British in India will be slaughtered. Then we will overrun the Muslims. Then the Hebrew God will fall. And then Christian God will be cast down and forgotten. Soon Kali Ma will rule the world." Mola Ram's words contradict the reverence Hindus have for Kali. Kali *protects* Hindus from evil; she does not *promote* evil. So, when Indy exclaims, "Mola Ram, prepare to meet Kali, in hell!" his words only reinforce an incorrect message about Kali as an "evil god."

Despite depictions in *Temple*, nowhere in India (including among Thuggee) did priests sacrificially rip out the hearts of human beings, or drink blood or require their followers to do so. Voodoo—and zombies, for that matter—are much more at home in Haitian culture; neither makes much sense in Hindu culture. These historically inaccurate behaviors—in addition to misrepresentations of Kali—were added to the story, presumably for dramatic effect, and at the expense of cherished Indian cultural and religious sensibilities, about which the filmmakers seem insensitive. So Raj is right to object that *Temple* illicitly makes the followers of a peaceful religion appear to be "bloodthirsty barbarians."

The Responsibilities of Filmviewers

Temple is a fictional story meant to entertain, and nowhere is it expressed that what Indy encounters in India is "based on actual events." Further, no one plausibly expects films like *Temple* to carefully delve into the complexities of Indian history or Hindu culture. So, we believe that the *filmviewers* (also) bear some responsibility for any beliefs formed from the film. At the very least, viewers should be cautious before forming any beliefs based on the film alone. For example, the American teachers who proliferated the belief that Indians eat chilled monkey brains are blameworthy for not double-checking their sources before making this claim to their students.

By carefully viewing the film, one can discern that Thuggee activity seemed localized to the northern region of India. The Mayapore Shaman tells Indy that Pankot "again has the power of the dark light" and "it is that place that kill my people." The Shaman also claims that the Pankot Thuggee required the village to pray to "their evil god" (putting aside whether Kali is evil). Thus, *Temple* does not obviously portray Mola Ram's cultists as representing religious belief in India generally (even if Mola Ram's evil ways *could* spread like a monsoon across the country). Perhaps Raj should be a bit more careful when he suggests the film's message(s) pertain to all religious people in India.

Although Thuggee practice did not include the spilling or drinking of blood, it is noteworthy that Mola Ram resorted to the Black Sleep of the Kali Ma to ensure obedience among his followers. Recall one of the imprisoned children telling Indy, "You become like them. You are alive—but like a nightmare." Not even Indy can resist the mind-controlling effects of the Black Sleep once ingested. It seems that Mola Ram uses it to control the Maharaja, thereby making the young ruler his puppet. When Shorty releases the Maharaja from his "waking nightmare," he immediately aides Shorty and Indy's escape attempt.

This suggests that very few people would willingly follow Mola Ram, which mitigates any blame placed on the film for spurring the belief that India is full of blood thirsty barbarians.

Some scholars cast doubt on whether the Thuggee had religious ties to Kali. Indeed, numerous historians describe Thuggee as primarily an invention of the British colonial regime. For example, Martine Van Woerkens analyzed the evidence of Thuggee and dubbed it a product of "colonial imaginings." The imaginings arose from "British fear of the little-known interior of India, as well as limited understanding of the religious and social practices of its inhabitants."[15]

Dromm seems unsure about the extent to which filmmakers are responsible for addressing controversial or simply inaccurate source material, but he suggests that filmmakers ought to avoid historical inaccuracies if doing so doesn't hamper the telling of the story.[16] We agree, but it also seems implausible to expect filmmakers to do the sort of careful historical research that would allow them to settle disputes between competing scholarly accounts when crafting their fictional films. Furthermore, most of the works arguing against the standard account of Thuggee were published after *Temple*'s release. Spielberg and Lucas cannot be blamed for not consulting research that did not yet exist. So, while filmmakers should avoid radically misrepresenting historical events or cultural practices, it remains the case that learning history from Hollywood blockbusters is a bad idea. Viewers should be slow to form beliefs or judgments about a fictional film's historical or cultural accuracy. Recalling Raj's sarcastic retort to Howard, there is something amiss if our only understanding of India is from *Temple*.

A Warranted Apology?

While *Temple* remains beloved among fans, its flaws are more obvious than the other two films in the original trilogy. Many have objected to the implicit plot device of having Shiva preordain events so that an Anglo-American Indiana Jones crash lands in India, meets the brown-skinned and destitute Mayapore villagers who are desperate for a savior, and heroically restores the village to health, with some help from Captain Blumburrt's Eleventh Puma Rifle Brigade (and very little from any Indians). Little wonder Raj calls the film "an imperialist" fantasy. At the very least, putting Indy in this role makes many fans cringe.

Yet that concern was not the one that spurred Indian officials to request revisions to the script, and, when Lucas refused, led them to bar the film from shooting in India and then to ban the film in their country (at least temporarily).[17] The Indian officials were concerned about how *Temple* portrayed various elements of Indian history and Hindu religious culture. It seems that many of those concerns could have been alleviated by a more careful script. The filmmakers decided against this—preferring elements of realism for dramatic effect—and thereby risked offending Indian cultural sensibilities. In doing so, and although *Temple* is not a piece of historical fiction, the filmmakers were susceptible to condemnation for their implicit disregard for Indian history, culture, and religion. Just as *Titanic* showed disrespect for William Murdoch's memory, *Temple* runs the risk of disrespecting the people of India.

The extent to which Spielberg and Lucas are blameworthy is difficult to clearly discern. Their goal was to entertain, not construct a history lesson (unlike, say, the makers of *Gandhi*). Of course, sometimes, we can be faulted for not being attentive enough to others, not for what we directly intend to do, but also for what we fail to do because of our primary purpose. Unintentional harm is not always excusable. This might be the case here. If so, then Spielberg and Lucas might do well to follow the lead of Indy himself. When Jones fears that his well-meaning conversation with Lal and Blumburtt managed to offend his host Zalim Singh, he bows his head and says, "If I have offended you, I am sorry."

Notes

1 Keith Dromm, "'Based on True Events': Filmmakers' Obligations to History," *International Journal of Applied Philosophy* vol. 20 (2006), 263–276.
2 Dromm, "'Based on True Events'," 265.
3 Dromm, "'Based on True Events'," 265.
4 Dromm, "'Based on True Events'," 264.
5 Dromm, "'Based on True Events'," 273.
6 Lois H. Gresh and Robert Weinberg, *Why Did It Have to Be Snakes?: From Science to the Supernatural, The Many Mysteries of Indiana Jones* (Hoboken, NJ: Wiley & Sons, 2008), 99–100, 102.
7 James Luceno, *Indiana Jones: The Ultimate Guide* (New York: DK Books, 2008), 44.
8 See https://www.hinduamerican.org/blog/4-things-about-hinduism-and-vegetarianism.
9 Yvette Rosser, "Stereotypes in Schooling: Negative Pressures in the American Educational System on Hindu Identity Formation," *Teaching South Asia* vol. 1 (2001), para. 29.
10 J.W. Rinzler, *The Complete Making of Indiana Jones: The Definitive Story Behind All Four Films* (New York: Del Ray Books, 2008), 148.
11 Rinzler, *Complete Making of Indiana Jones*, 148.

12 Rinzler, *Complete Making of Indiana Jones*, 140. The date on the shooting script is April 10, 1983; principle photography began five days later. This bit of dialogue might account for Luceno's retcon of the scene, assuming he had access to the shoot script.
13 Gresh and Weinberg, *Why Did It Have to Be Snakes?*, 105.
14 David Kinsley, *Tantric Visions of the Divine Feminine: The Ten Mahāvidyās* (Berkeley: University of California Press, 1997), 70.
15 Martine Van Woerkens, *The Strangled Traveler : Colonial Imaginings and the Thugs of India*, trans. Catherine Tihanyi (Chicago: University of Chicago Press, 2002), 20. See also Mike Dash, *Thug: The True Story Of India's Murderous Cult* (London: Granta Books, 2011).
16 He discusses the example of *The Da Vinci Code*. See pages 273–274.
17 See Rinzler, *Complete Making of Indiana Jones*, 130–131. For concerns about stereotypes associated with the Willie Scott character, see Chapter 5 by Schmidt in this volume.

24

"Some of the Passageways in Here Can Run for Miles": An Aristotelian Exploration of Fact and Truth in *The Last Crusade*

Timothy Brown

In *The Last Crusade*, Henry "Indiana" Jones, Jr. learns that his father is missing! He is told his father—Henry "Attila the Professor" Jones, Sr.—had been persuaded to serve as the project leader for Walter Donovan's search for the Grail, but that he had vanished along with all his research. Donovan opines that if Indy searches for the Grail, he will also find his missing father. So, Indy picks up where his father had left off, traveling to where his father had last been seen: Venice, Italy.

Once in Venice, Indy quickly meets Dr. Elsa Schneider, and after stealing a rose and giving it to her, he and Marcus Brody accompany her to a Venetian library. Indy is able to identify three Roman numerals—III (three), VII (seven), and X (ten)—in the library window, and then he finds the corresponding Roman numerals III and VII in the library itself. However, Indy is unable to locate a corresponding Roman numeral X, until he moves around the room and gains a broader perspective; he then discovers that the floor of the library actually contains the corresponding Roman numeral X! Seemingly surprised, and perhaps a little embarrassed—given that he had previously taught his students that, "'X' never, ever, marks the spot"—Indiana is forced to admit that "X" really does mark the spot!

Indiana's admission in the Venetian library is telling, and serves to transport our minds back to a lecture he had given earlier at Barnett College, before he knew his father was missing. While lecturing about archeology Indiana told his students, "Forget any ideas you've got

Indiana Jones and Philosophy: Why Did It Have to Be Socrates?, First Edition. Edited by Dean A. Kowalski.

about lost cities, exotic travel, and digging up the world." However, it turned out that during his search Indy discovered the identity of a lost city with an "oasis due east" (Alexandretta), traveled to several exotic locations, and dug through the floor of a library in Venice. Indy had also taught his students, "We do not follow maps to buried treasure." However, during his search Indy followed a map his father had drawn in his "research." And, of course, it turned out that during his search Indy admitted there were times when "X" does mark the spot.

All these teachings follow what is certainly the most philosophical thing Indy said that day: "Archeology is the search for fact, not truth. If it's truth you're interested in Dr. Tyree's philosophy class is right down the hall." What, though, does Indy mean by the words, "fact" and "truth?" How does his statement relate to the other things he taught his students? Can philosophy say anything about the science of archeology, and if so, what? In this chapter we will rely on Aristotle (384–322 BCE) to help us philosophically examine Indy's fact-not-truth statement. But because philosophy can be rather extensive and deep, we all would be well advised to heed the counsel of Scout Master Mr. Havelock: "No one wander off. Some of the passageways in here can run for miles."

"The Pen Is Mightier Than the Sword"

In *Crusade*, Henry, Sr. is being held captive, and in an effort to resist his captivity he begins to struggle with one of his captors. Ultimately, he squirts ink from a pen into the eye of his captor, which—at least partially—leads to his escape. In response to Henry's having literally used a pen to defend himself against his captors, Marcus reminds Henry of the well-known adage, asserting that the pen is mightier than the sword after all. We too can say words are mighty, whether they are written with a pen or spoken in a lecture, and so a proper understanding of them is important. The best place for us to begin our examination is with Indy's two words "fact" and "truth," as understanding these words is integral to understanding Indy's fact-not-truth statement. Because an understanding of "fact" is closely related to an understanding of "truth," it is best for us to begin by examining "truth," and then move on to examining "fact."

Aristotle affirmed the correspondence theory of truth.[1] Simply put, Aristotle's correspondence theory of truth holds that a statement is true if it "corresponds" to reality (corresponds to what "is"), and a statement is false if it does not "correspond" to reality (does not correspond to what "is"). In Aristotle's words: "To say that what is, is not, or that what is not is, is false; but to say that what is, is, and what is not is not, is true; and therefore also he who says that a thing is or is not will say either what is true or what is false."[2] Aristotle's theory thus looks to reality itself (what really "is") for an objective standard of whether a statement is true or false, and so the truthfulness or falsity of a statement is determined by whether it does or does not correspond to reality.

Accordingly, we can say that the statement "*Crusade* is the third Indiana Jones film," is a true statement, because what it expresses actually corresponds to what "is"; *Crusade* actually is the third Indiana Jones film. Likewise, the statement "*Crusade* is the first Indiana Jones film," is a false statement, because what it expresses does not correspond to what actually "is." Reality itself is the objective standard of whether these statements are true or false, and while the first statement is true because it corresponds to reality, the second statement is false because it does not correspond to reality.

As mentioned earlier, an understanding of "fact" is closely related to an understanding of "truth." The word "fact" simply means a true statement, so an easier way to say, "a true statement about reality" is to say "a fact." And, clearly, a false statement about reality is not a "fact."[3]

Accordingly, the statement "*Crusade* is the third Indiana Jones film," is a "fact" simply because it is a true statement, and the statement "*Crusade* is the first Indiana Jones film," is not a "fact" simply because it is a false statement. By this understanding we can say that a book contains facts, and when we say this we mean that a book contains true statements. We also can say that a particular book contains no facts, and when we say this we mean that a particular book contains no true statements.

With this understanding of "fact" and "truth," how might we understand Indy's statement? Indiana would seem to be claiming archeology is concerned with true statements, but archeology is not concerned with whether those statements correspond to reality itself. This does not seem right, though, because this would be a self-defeating position to take. After all, to be concerned with true statements requires one to also be concerned with truth itself. It seems then, that unless we are willing to concede that Indy has taught something self-defeating, it is unlikely that this is what Indiana actually meant by his fact-not-truth lecture statement. Perhaps Indiana might not understand the words "fact" or "truth" as we have described, meaning as a philosopher might understand them. How then might Indy understand these words?

Indy does seem to understand "facts" as we have described them, understanding them to be true statements; he does, after all, claim in his fact-not-truth lecture that "70% of all archeology is done in the library. Reading. Research." By this Indy seems to indicate he understands that the overwhelming majority of the search for "fact" is researching various topics in a library, by reading library books. As we noted previously, books contain facts—at least to the degree that they contain true statements—and so one can search for facts by reading library books, as Indy suggests. So it seems Indy may understand facts as we have described them after all.

Yet Indy does not seem to understand truth in the way we described it. As Indy lectures about searching for "truth," he does not seem to be talking about searching for a relationship of correspondence to reality, but instead seems to understand truth as a kind of noble wisdom, that is perhaps not a concern of archeology, or is perhaps not accessible by archeology; a wisdom that requires much reflection or contemplation to find. Indy seems to be referring to a category of understanding, one perhaps that is a concern of philosophy, and is accessible by philosophy; a thing Indy might describe as, "Truth," not as, "truth."

How might we then understand Indy's fact-not-truth statement, with these particular understandings of "fact" and "Truth" in mind? Perhaps Indiana was trying to communicate to his students that archeology searches for facts—70% of the time by reading books in the library—about people from long ago, the places in which they lived, and the artifacts they produced. Archeology perhaps too—no more than 30% of the time—visits these places, and finds these artifacts, to learn more about these people from long ago. Perhaps, additionally, Indiana was trying to communicate that philosophy searches for what he would call "Truth" instead, which perhaps he understood to be a category representing things like Goodness, Beauty, Courage, and Justice.

Indy would seem then to be directing aspiring archeologists to the library to search for facts, and directing aspiring philosophers to Dr. Tyree's philosophy class to search for Truth. But can this understanding be substantiated? Let's continue our examination and find out.

"He's Got Witnesses—Five or Six of Them"

In *Crusade*, the young Indiana Jones takes the Cross of Coronado from men he believes are looting in the Utah caves, outrunning them to his home, while his friend Herman alerts the local sheriff. Thinking he was giving the sheriff a description of the perpetrators, he claims "there were five or six of them"; the sheriff, though, tells Indy that the "rightful owner" of the Cross of Coronado won't press charges against Indy if he gives it back, and tells Indy that this alleged rightful owner has witnesses to Indy's having taken the item, five or six witnesses. Indy had thought his identifying these five or six men to the sheriff was significant for one reason, and it turned out they were significant to the sheriff for another reason. Something similar is the case with Indy's fact-not-truth lecture, which we are able to see once we examine his lecture by using logic.[4]

Logic organizes our thinking, and one of the ways it does this is by codifying argumentation. When we make arguments, we reason through different statements called premises to produce a final statement called a conclusion. We do this every day, likely without noticing it. There are of course rules that logic expects to be followed when deductive arguments are put forth, and even if we can't name these rules we usually can tell when one has been broken. As long as these rules are followed, and as long as the premises of an argument are all true, then the conclusion of a deductive argument is also true.

Sometimes the premises and conclusion of an argument are all stated, but often one of them is omitted. For example, in the Utah cave, the young Indiana said to Herman—his friend who had been horse-sick—"That cross is an important artifact, it belongs in a museum," and as Indy said this, he made an argument, omitting a premise. The premise he omitted was his first premise: "An important artifact belongs in a museum." Young Indy stated his second premise, "That cross is an important artifact," and finally stated his conclusion, "it [that cross] belongs in a museum." When we understand that Indy is making an argument, and then supply Indy's missing premise, we can see how Indy was reasoning through his premises to come to his conclusion.

Once we examine Indy's fact-not-truth lecture by using deductive logic, we are able to identify that Indy was making an argument. Words like "thus," "therefore," and "so" often serve to indicate that the conclusion of an argument has been reached, and Indiana's lecture at Barnett College contained a statement that began with "So ..." We can identify the argument Indy seems to make in his fact-not-truth lecture, and we can even supply Indy's missing premise. His lecture argument looks like this:

PREMISE 1: (Stated) Archeology is the search for fact.

PREMISE 2: (Unstated) The search for fact is that which does not concern lost cities, exotic travel, digging up the world, following maps to buried treasure, and "X" marking the spot.

CONCLUSION: (Stated) Archeology is that which does not concern lost cities, exotic travel, digging up the world, following maps to buried treasure, and "X" marking the spot.

Such an argument is called a syllogism, and Aristotle was instrumental in the development and use of syllogisms by philosophers.[5]

As noted earlier, while giving his lecture about archeology, Indiana taught his students that there were five or six things with which archeology did not concern itself. Indy seemed to think that his stating each of these was significant because it described things with which archeology did not concern itself; however, each of these things was instead significant for another reason: during his search, Indy went on to do five of these five or six things. Thus, in a way, the five or six things Indy had claimed archeology did not concern actually became "witnesses" against Indy's lecture argument!

Let's discuss one of these "witnesses" further, to be clear. Recall that in his lecture argument Indy claimed that in archeology "'X' never, ever marks the spot," but in the Venetian library, Indy himself admitted that there apparently are times when "X" does mark the spot. When these two claims are compared, we see a contradiction. Logic tells us a contradiction is when something is both said to "be" and "not be" in the same respect at the same time. Indiana's father could not "be" and "not be" missing, in the same respect at the same time; further, his students' papers could not "be" and "not be" graded, in the same respect at the same time. Likewise, "X" cannot both "mark the spot," and "never, ever mark the spot," in the same respect at the same time. When Indy admitted that there were times that "X" did mark the spot, his admission contradicted his earlier lecture. What's more, Indy's admission that it did falsifies his lecture conclusion. The same can also be said for the other things Indy did in his search, which further disproves his lecture conclusion.

Because Indy's conclusion is false, then either one of deductive logic's rules was broken in the argument, or one of Indy's premises was false. Since there is no obvious violation of logic's rules in the argument, it seems there is at least one false premise in Indy's lecture argument, and it seems it is his unstated second premise.

It seems that Indy's claim about what the search for "fact" regards is false, but what about his claim about archeology being the search for fact, and not truth? Let's continue our examination and find out.

"I Suddenly Remembered My Charlemagne"

In *Crusade*, Indiana and his father were on foot and being pursued by an airplane, with no apparent way to defend themselves. Henry, Sr., being a professor of Medieval Literature—"the one the students hope they don't get"—suddenly grabbed his umbrella, and by opening and closing it erratically, caused nearby birds to take flight. This caused the plane to lose control and crash, and both men were able to escape. In explanation of his actions, Henry, Sr. said he had suddenly remembered a particular Carolingian writing, which had conveyed to him the course of action he needed to take. We too might remember particular philosophical writings, which can help us examine Indy's statement: "Archeology is the search for fact, not truth."

While archeology is a science, obviously there are many other sciences as well. What then is common to all sciences? Medieval philosopher and theologian Thomas Aquinas (1225–1274), who was heavily influenced by Aristotle's philosophy, said that what is common to all the sciences is that they are able to demonstrate their conclusions from principles.[6] Peter Kreeft simplifies this somewhat, describing science as being that which provides rational explanations through causes.[7] But obviously too, for there to be distinct sciences there must be something distinct about each of them. So then how might they be divided from each other? For Aristotle, one way to divide the sciences from one another was to base their division on the goal of their intellectual activity, meaning what they were trying to accomplish. He noted the goal of a science could be practical, productive, or speculative, and these different goals could be used to divide the sciences from one another.[8] The many sciences do not simply divide themselves; rather, they are divided by a superior science, and Aquinas claims this is a philosophical science.[9] While this doesn't tell us whether Indy's claim that archeology is the search for fact and not truth is correct, it does tell us that Indy's claim is not an archeological claim and that Indy did not come to formulate his claim by practicing archeology. Because his claim seeks to delineate the science of archeology from other sciences, it is a philosophical claim.

So, is the science of archeology actually the search for fact, and not the search for truth? Recall Aristotle's contention that one way to divide the sciences is by what they try to accomplish: practical goals, productive goals, or speculative goals. But what do these goals mean? Kreeft indicates, "Aristotle pointed out, twenty-four centuries ago, that there are three reasons for pursuing truth and three corresponding kinds of 'sciences'…"[10] Kreeft contends that the distinction between different sciences is not whether they do or do not pursue truth, but the different goals they try to accomplish by their pursuit of truth. The practical sciences—like ethics and politics—pursue truth for the purpose of acting on truth. The productive sciences—like engineering and medicine—pursue truth for the purpose of using truth to produce or improve things. And the speculative or theoretical sciences—like mathematics or philosophy—pursue truth simply as its own goal, with no further goal than knowing truth. All sciences pursue truth, then, even though they act on the truth they obtain in different ways. This means that regardless of what kind of science archeology is, it is a science, and as a science it searches for truth. Whether archeology searches for "fact" as a means to pursue "truth" is another matter, but it seems false to claim that of any science—including archeology—that it does not search for truth, at least as Aristotle described "truth."

As pointed out earlier, in his fact-not-truth lecture, Indy may not have meant "truth" as Aristotle described it, but rather something he would call, "Truth," which perhaps he understood to be a category representing things like Goodness, Beauty, Courage, and Justice. Even so, Indy claims he obtains artifacts like the Cross of Coronado because they *belong* in a museum. But this is not an archeological statement; it is a philosophical statement. Indy indicates it is "good" to obtain artifacts because, as they belong there, it is "good" for them to be in a museum. Further, Aristotle claimed that every action undertaken by humans is done in the pursuit of some good.[11] "The Philosopher" makes this claim in a philosophical work on ethics. Even if by "Truth" Indy understood a category representing things like the Good, it still seems Indy practices archeology in the pursuit of Goodness, which—even according to his understanding—means he practices archeology because of "Truth."

"Follow Me! I Know the Way!"

Near the conclusion of *Crusade*, Marcus shouts "Follow Me! I know the Way!" Both Indy and Henry have doubts that Marcus ought to be followed, especially as he is seen almost falling off his horse as it wildly gallops down a canyon corridor. Many people similarly have doubts that philosophy is able to help with anything in the real world and thus have doubts that philosophy should ever be "followed." However, is it really possible to disregard philosophy as the Joneses dismiss Marcus's sense of direction? Put another way, can philosophy be relegated to the classroom down the hall, and confined there, as Indy seems to be claiming in his fact-not-truth lecture? Not really.

Whether we are aware of it or not, we all use philosophy every day. We don't need to pretend that philosophy can answer *every* question a person can ask, and we shouldn't think that *every* philosopher throughout history has come to equally correct conclusions about *every* matter they considered. However, if someone presented reasons for being *completely* dismissive of philosophy, that person would have to use philosophy to make his or her case, which seems paradoxical, if not self-defeating. Further, as Edward Feser claims, "There is no one as dogmatically beholden to a metaphysic as the man who denies that he has one."[12] So the question isn't really whether or not one uses philosophy in their life, but whether one uses philosophy well.

Notes

1 Peter Kreeft, *Socratic Logic 3.1: A Logic Text Using Socratic Method, Platonic Questions, and Aristotelian Principles* (South Bend: St. Augustine's Press, 2010), 143–145. Kreeft notes that some additional technical

clarifications and qualifiers about truth as correspondence might be in order, but the subsequent discussion suffices for our purposes.

2 Aristotle, *Metaphysics*, trans. W.D. Ross (Oxford: Oxford University Press, 1925), 1011b.

3 On pages 134–145, Kreeft distinguishes between "propositional truth" and "ontological truth," such that the former regards statements and the latter things; this distinction might be important to those philosophers who contend facts refer to reality and not statements about it.

4 Logic itself may not be philosophy, but philosophers utilize it to find the truth. Further, systems of logic do have philosophical assumptions; see Kreeft, *Socratic Logic*, 13. Much of the discussion of logic in this section is indebted to Kreeft; see (for example) pages 191–199 and 264–271.

5 See, for example, Aristotle, *Prior Analytics*, 24b18–26.

6 Aquinas, *Summa Theologiae*: I–II, 57, 2, ad. vs. 1.

7 Kreeft, *Socratic Logic*, 7.

8 Aristotle, *Metaphysics*, 1025b.

9 Aquinas, *Commentary on the Metaphysics of Aristotle*, Prologue.

10 Kreeft, *Socratic Logic*, 7–8.

11 Aristotle, *Nicomachean Ethics*, I, 1.

12 Edward Feser, "The Metaphysics of Conservatism," *TCS Daily*, January 12, 2006.

Index: "If I Walk It through Mayan First..."

Indiana Jones and Philosophy: Why Did It Have to Be Socrates?, First Edition. Edited by Dean A. Kowalski.